Ernestine Hill was born in 1899 in Rockhampton, Queensland. She worked as a journalist, but when her husband died in 1933 she embarked on a life of almost continual travel and writing. Her first book, *The Great Australian Loneliness*, was published in 1937, and met with great success. A strongly visual account of outback travel, it had the added interest of being from a woman's perspective at a time when such publications were rare. It was followed by *Water into Gold*. Hill also wrote a novel based on the story of Matthew Flinders, *My Love Must Wait*, published in 1941. Apart from *Flying Doctor Calling* (1947), based on the work of the Inland Mission, her best-known book is *The Territory* (1951), a vivid and accurate chronicle of travelling in the Northern Territory. Ernestine Hill died in 1972.

Also available in IMPRINT by Ernestine Hill
The Territory

IMPRINT

THE GREAT
Australian
Loneliness

ERNESTINE HILL

Sydney New York Amsterdam

An IMPRINT book
Imprint is a division of ETT
83 Victoria St, Potts Point, NSW 2011, Australia

First published in Australia in 1940
First published in Imprint Travel edition in 1991 by HarperCollins
This edition published by ETT IMPRINT in 1995

Distributed by
HarperCollins *Publishers*
25 Ryde Rd, Pymble, NSW 2073, Australia
31 View Rd, Glenfield, Auckland 10, NZ
HarperCollins *International*
10 East 53rd Street, New York, NY 10022, USA
In de Knipscheer *Uitgeverij*
Singel 450, 1017 Av Amsterdam

ISBN 1 875892 06 0

Cover design by Julie Allbutt, Whizzbang Art, Canberra
Printed in Australia by Griffin Paperbacks, Netley, Adelaide

For the co-operation and most kindly consideration that have helped me through the long pilgrimage, my thanks are due to *The Advertiser*, Adelaide; *Sun Newspapers*, Sydney; *West Australian*, Perth; *Herald*, Melbourne; *Courier-Mail*, Brisbane; *Sydney Morning Herald*; *Sydney Mail*; Melbourne *Argus*; and the Australian National Travel Magazine, *Walkabout*, in which my writings have appeared.

ERNESTINE HILL.

FOREWORD

THIS is the story of a journalist's journey round and across Australia, far from the rhythm of 'the big machine' and the sameness of cities.

A magnificent empty land; of six and a half millions of its children, six millions set their lives and their watches to the clanging of the tram-bells and the train-whistles. The odd half-million share three-quarters of the Continent between them, and tell the time in months and years.

It was in July, 1930, that I first set out, a wandering 'copy-boy' with swag and typewriter, to find what lay beyond the railway lines. Across the painted deserts and the pearling seas, by aeroplane and camel and coastal-ship, by truck and lugger and packhorse team and private yacht, the trail has led me on across five years and 50,000 miles, a trail of infinite surprises.

Many a time have I unrolled the little swag by creek and sandhill, alone in the silence and starlight with a white man and a black. I have interviewed men living in wurlies of paper-bark who read Gibbon and wrote Greek and danced in corroboree; witch-doctors of the Warramunga and the Kulukularagudu in their own national costume, which was minus, and pidgin; lepers and the dying, deep-sea divers and prospectors for gold, and white women fighting the splendid battle of the pioneers, rearing their children in bough shades in the wilderness.

With never a step outside the three-mile limit in a purely British country, I have attended Japanese Feasts of Lanterns, Chinese banquets, blackfellow burials and Greek weddings, and turned to the west with the Mussulmans when they knelt on their prayer-mats to Allah at the call of the *muezzin*. Many of the notes have been taken by the flickering of a camp-fire; many of the pictures developed by the port light of a lugger, or with a bit of blackfellow's turkey red wrapped round a hurricane lamp in the bush, the films washed in a billabong or hung to dry on a tree.

The typewriter has always been with me, dangling from a camel-saddle, jingling on a truck, covered with a camp-sheet in the rains. On anything that came along, I followed 'the story.' It was all in a journalist's job, and it was all good hunting.

Australia is like its own unique and glorious jewel, the opal. A great jagged square of colourless crystal, you must hold it up to the light to catch the flashing fires of romance.

Dreaming in a little ship down the crocodile-infested reaches of tropic rivers; out on the stark sandhills of the Centre, where the bones of the diprotodon and notatherium lie white in the sun; by miners' tents of the infinite mineral hills; or sitting on a petrol tin in the din and dust of corroboree, so have I learned a little of the amazing private life of this Australia, still a stranger to the world and to its own people. To quote the oath, as administered to native witnesses in courts of the North:

> ' No more gammon, no more lie,
> I been see him, longa my eye.'

Leaning out of an aeroplane, I have looked upon the limitless wastes of the spinifex stretched out like a snakeskin 8,000 feet below me. From the ruby headlands of the North-west, I have watched a fleet of eighty luggers set forth for the pearling-grounds, their sails like opening lilies in the dawn-light. I have lived for a week in a cave, with the opal-mining troglodytes of central deserts, followed breathless in the wake of a gold rush, and battled on a 26-ton ketch in the south-east trades, 1,500 miles across the empty wind-swept waters of Carpentaria, sleeping on deck with a goat for company.

The adventure is over. But my heart is out there for good. Always, across the city lights, I shall be seeing the glitter of blacks' fires in the ranges, hearing through the roar of the traffic the ghostly echo of pack-bells, and telling over in memory the names of that lost legion, to whom I was but a swiftly-passing pilgrim, but to whom they gave of their best.

It is their unfailing chivalry and kindliness that have made these journeyings of a lone woman not only possible, but one of the happiest memories of life. Therefore, to the men and women of the Australian outback, and to all who take up the white man's burden in the lonely places, I dedicate this book.

ERNESTINE HILL.

CONTENTS

BOOK I

PORTS OF SUNSET

BOOK II

ROYAL MANTLE OF THE TROPICS

BOOK III

THE LIVING HEART

CONTENTS

BOOK I
PORTS OF SUNSET

CHAPTER I

A MORNING SPIN

'OF course you'll take a gun,' they said to me when I left Melbourne, 'even if it's only one of those little mother-of-pearl things the vamps used to carry in their evening-bags. Apart from wild blacks there will be crocodiles, and Malays running amok, and men that haven't seen a white woman in thirty years. There might be three hundred miles of desolation on a truck with a drunken Afghan, and you'll be alone in the night-time, in those pearling-towns of sand and sin, with a half-caste woman keeping the shanty—'

'Yes,' I reflected, 'I had better take a gun.'

One morning in a Perth hardware store they showed me a whole armoury, from double-barrelled Savages and ·303's down to a baby automatic guaranteed not to go off in the pocket. My particular fancy, which was something in the nature of a fountain-pen, nail-file, pen-knife and revolver, swivelled together in a little nickel case, they had not yet in stock.

'Do you shoot to kill?' the shopman asked me casually.

'I only want something to brandish in moments of peril,' I laughed.

'Then don't take it,' he advised. 'Nobody that hasn't a definite target in mind should ever buy a gun.'

At the last moment, apprehensive still, I consulted a leader and organizer of the Australian Inland Medical Mission, a man who had travelled the continent for ten years, perpendicularly, diagonally and in circumference, by air and car and donkey team.

'Believe me,' he said earnestly, 'a nursemaid could wheel a baby in a perambulator across Australia with far less danger of being molested than in any city park. It would be a ridiculous insult to the finest people in the world, and you would be the joke.'

So it was without any more desperate precaution than a badly sharpened lead-pencil that I booked my ticket with Western Australian Airways and set out, unknown into the unknown, to meet the people of the real Australia, and to find that, black and white, they were all friends. Many a time, making one among them in the wilderness, I have looked back to the gun episode, and have scarcely known whether to laugh or to cry. All that I can plead is that, with the other six million post-office clock Australians, I knew nothing whatever about them.

The pilots and planes of West Australian Airways fly 100,000 miles a year in the North-west, week in, week out, to a clock-work time-table, across its five great zones of wheat and gold and sheep and cattle and pearls, from the vine-clad banks of the Swan River to the squdgy crocodile flats where the Ord runs into the sea. Towns of the 2,000-mile upward run are as familiar to them as suburban sign-posts. Geraldton, Carnarvon, Onslow, Roebourne, Hedland, Broome, Derby, the Fitzroy Crossing, Hall's Creek, Wyndham, Ord River, and Katherine—and there they snatch a sandwich and start back.

No spotlight of bright publicity follows their flight through hurricanes and blinding heat. On the contrary, when they do not arrive on time, the local postmaster whets his nib and puts a black mark against them, leaving them to tell the story, which they never do, except in a memo. to head office. But carrying crayfish and prize Pomeranian dogs to the Never-Never, bringing down the dying and sometimes the dead, and scattering a small snow-storm of weekly letters over a country that was once out of the world for five months at a time, they have brought the Great Australian Loneliness well on to the map.

The first bright feathers of the sunrise were drifting slowly down as we rose above the river and the flooded fields. Over our shoulder stared last night's moon, pale and inconsequent. It was winter and flood-time in Perth. Long chains of trees and their reflections seemed to join in a phantasmal dance. Houses, up to the lips in water, each marking a little rhomboid of garden or orchard, sent up spirals of breakfast smoke into the shining air. The outer suburbs and the hamlets of the Darling Ranges were as neat riders in geometry, worked by a diligent pupil; the hills a relief map, with cotton wool of mist in the hollows. Lawn-smooth and curly with scrub, the landscape on the other side looked laughably like a clipped poodle.

Clear into the face of morning we flew, the great half-circle of Australia ahead of us. To Perth we were a dot in the growing blue. To us, Perth was a child's exercise book. Away across the marshes a surly sea bared its white teeth, and just beyond the wing a fragment of rainbow hung vivid as a chevron. The air-screw sang high in the head-wind.

Salt lakes came into evidence, round as pudding-basins, increasing in size as we hurried northward. A ground-mist rolled away from them as though they were cauldrons boiling. Dazzling in their beauty are these salt lakes and rivers of the West, bright with reflections and sweet with pools, swept with rosy colours, bordered with towering alps of sand-hills and the fresh green of trees, and the mirage creeping in, blue as the incoming tide. A dream and a bitter reality—translucent as alabaster, they are bitter as brine and solid as marble.

Into the heart of a grey shower we went, and out of it with wet, silver wings. Far down, the Geraldton road, a pencil-line, disappeared in a cluster of roofs built together like a child's blocks. There was sudden silence as the engine shut off, and 'taking half a mile of sunlight in one sweep,' we dropped a clear 8,000 feet to a field in the hollow of the rain-dusky hills, where little birds were fluttering in the red berries of a boxthorn.

Above the harbour and the crescent town again, bound for a threatening dark blue cloud, we looked down upon a curve of breakwater and ships that lay at anchor, and then upon acres and acres of tomato frames, like departmental pigeon-holes. Cosy farms stretched for many an earthy mile, from the sea-shore to the softly bosomed high land, then on to barrenness. Now the earth was brown and stony, smeared with queer volcanic markings of creamy white, as though Ganymede, flying heavenward, had spilled his brimming cup. Gaily we skirted the showers, the right wing deep in mist, the left in sunlight. Seven thousand feet below it was an empty land, the beginning of the great wide spaces, tawny and savage—'Land of the Lioness,' the shrewd old Dutchmen called it long ago.

Just off the coast between Perth and Carnarvon lie the islands where the Great South Land first loomed out of the night of oblivion. 'Shadows of clouds' they were to the old Portuguese mariners, 'shadows of clouds' they are to us to-day, uninhabited save by the sea-birds. Many a Dutch ship, blown up by prevailing winds on the voyage round the Cape, left her bones and her treasure upon these reefs. Guns and coins of the seventeenth century, little cheese-bottles neatly arranged in rows and swept under the sand, and rusted shoe-buckles and clay pipes have been unearthed there in a fisherman's idle hour, telling stories of shipwreck and habitation when the South Pacific was a mighty blank on the map.

Through an hour of tedium the wings moved forward an inch at a time, an inch that left behind three miles of earth. The open country became mottled as a lizard, green, grey, sand-colour and black, cut by lines of road and telegraph mercilessly straight, studded with salt lakes like a chain of cats' eyes. At last Hamelin Pool gleamed on the left, an oyster shell 100 miles wide of pearl-green, with matrix drifts of colour. Ethereal blue misted the sea, and the wastes of the saltbush only less infinite.

Fauré Island showed as a dark gold blur. Tiny roofs of station homesteads 90 miles apart could not break the treeless monotony. Here and there whitish rain was let down on the plains like a curtain.

A little spell of steady sunshine. We crossed the bed of a great dry river that writhed like a brown snake, and glimpsed a jetty big as a girl's hockey stick. Then the jig-saw roofs of Carnarvon swung upward, settled, and resolved themselves, as we taxied in, to the familiar perspective of the world we knew.

A single coco-nut palm was tilted against the sky. Three camels smiled at us over a nearby fence as we alighted. Seagulls, feeding with the fowls in a nearby yard, reminded us that it was lunch-time, and we were frankly hungry, having come from the temperates to the tropics, from the rain to the sun, in the space of one short morning. For such is the new progression of man, that mocks at time and distance, and closes the zones of earth together like the sticks of a Japanese fan.

I write only of the unusual, leaving statistics to the year-books. As Dampier once said in his quaint and delightful

Voyages: 'The Porcupine being a Creature well known,
I pass it in silence.'

Carnarvon is a well-behaved and prosperous little town
of 2,000 people, at the mouth of the Gascoyne River. Port
of the great wool country of the West, in a good season it is
girt for a thousand miles round with

> ' The saltbush green and gentle from the blessing of the rains,
> And the everlasting daisies of the everlasting plains.'

Right on the rim of the tropics, colours of dawn and
sunset linger lovingly there, until even the road glows in
ochre and amethyst.

To its jetty, a mile and a quarter in length, five or six
ships in the month call in, to carry away the loading of the
six-ton wool trucks, and sandalwood from the desert that
is shipped to the East from Fremantle. Apart from its one
cherished coco-nut tree and the fact that you can catch
eighteen-pounder kingfish from a fascine in the main street,
there are three things that redeem Carnarvon from the
commonplace.

The first is the weirdest vehicle imaginable, a railway
trolley with a mast and sail, tangible evidence of a fantastic
faux pas of long ago. When the Singapore ships are in, this
sober little truck heaves up her square of canvas and, to the
amazement of onlookers, goes sailing along the jetty, gay
as a pearling-lugger in the south-easter, to scatter the seagulls and come to her moorings in the railway yards beside
the respectable freight engine.

The second are the suburbs, all within two miles of each
other; Yankee Town, with the glittering sails of two or
three hundred windmills; Silver City, a village of tin at the
foot of the jetty; Rainbow Town, with a few Cadbury
complexions left over from pre-Aliens Restriction days and
Morgan Town, where the old hands foregather in the little
shacks that are home to them Australia over.

The third is the Gascoyne River, a sand-bed 200 miles
long and two miles wide at its mouth. The Gascoyne
materialises, as a river, once in two years or so. As it
approaches, the news comes in from the far stations by
telephone. 'Look out! The Gascoyne's coming!' they
shout to each other across ninety miles of wire, and then

Carnarvon calls up its camels out of the river-bed, and sees its hen-roosts swept to perdition. By a remarkable system of centrifugal pumping that raises the sunken river through its sands to the tune of 50,000 gallons an hour to each pump, a series of plantations has been established along the banks, which supply Perth with heavy-weight tomatoes and bananas the whole winter through, a semi-tropical agriculture that shows promise of increasing prosperity.

For the rest, there is an ocean filled to the brim with fish; great seas of the saltbush, an excellent fodder for hundreds of thousands of sheep, but so treeless that the baffled crows build their nests in the telegraph posts, and last, but not least, Grannie Glasgow, the white-haired 'Sairey' of Carnarvon, who in fifty years has brought 700 of its babies into the world, and mothers them all still. There is an up-to-date maternity wing in the hospital in these days, and all its chickens incubated according to the best modern methods, but, at seventy-five, Grannie Glasgow still finds a job of work occasionally, and it is her proud boast that she has never lost mother nor child.

In the deserts for many hundreds of miles north, east and south wander the sandalwood-getters, nomads of the mulga, mates or alone, lost to civilization sometimes for a year at a time. Flogging along with a camel or truck, they seek in the sparse bush country the slight white fragrant wood, saw it in lengths, strip it, and when they have gathered enough, bring it in for shipment and replenish their stores. The price of sandalwood in the Eastern markets is high. To those who find it, it brings £13/10/- a ton from Fremantle agents, but the precious wood is rapidly thinning out, and sometimes it takes six months to cut a ton.

The life is a hard one. Out in the blazing sun and the dust-storms, a few of the sandalwood-getters have their families with them, wife and children and dog and goat and gramophone, home sweet home by a nightly camp-fire. Babies are frequently ushered into the world by a lubra. Nourished, in the worst seasons, on rabbits and young salt-bush, and water from the clay-pans boiled and strained, they soon grow into strapping brown youngsters, healthy and happy as any.

At Carnarvon I was in time to see the monthly mail set

out for Madman's Corner, which is, in its saner moments, North-west Cape. Across 300 miles of ribbed sand-hills, the mailman, Mr. Desmond ('Joe') Stokes, set off in a prairie schooner to find the road that the wind blows away just after he makes it. His passengers, according to their importance to the North-west, were three rams and a honeymoon couple.

Past the lighthouses and the old Norwegian whaling station at Point Cloates, he would make up through Exmouth Gulf station to the three families tending the big light at Vlaming Head. This is one of the most important beacons of the coast, signalling down the ships from Singapore, throwing its beam on a dark night 50 miles across the Indian Ocean. At the feet of the cliffs, the ribs of wrecks tell a fairly exciting history. Madman's Corner derives its name from the fact that the first three pioneers of a neighbouring solitary station were ultimately found and 'taken south,' and to the curious sandstone effigy of a man, standing out in a range of low hills.

'You want to see him when the sun's setting,' the mailman told me. 'You could swear he was shouting and beckoning, that he'd found gold or something, and wanted a trip in. I'm as hard in the head as the next man, but I reckon if I was out there on me Pat Malone for too long—well, I reckon I'd be like them other poor blighters, and follow that old bloke out.'

CHAPTER II

A HUNDRED miles west of Carnarvon, and only two days' boat journey north of Perth, yet so remote from the world that sometimes neither a stranger nor a daily paper is seen here in a period of years, lies the extraordinary little settlement of Shark Bay, whose streets, like the nigger heaven of old revivalist hymns, are literally paved with pearl.

A fishing village of 250 people, white and coloured, Shark Bay, in its quaintness and isolation—and happily in its aura of dead shell-fish—is unique on the Continent. Away from the tracks of steamers and the main roads to the North-west, other than the telegraph, there is no link with civilisation beyond the passing of the West Australian Government coastal ship *Koolinda*, that once in the month anchors seven miles off-shore, a wisp of smoke in the day-time, a spangle of lights at night. An old-fashioned lighter with grey sails, manned by seven burly young half-castes, lumbers out to meet her, exchanging bags of pearl-shell, frozen fish and shell-grit for the necessities of life, and news of the world.

To visit the port I was swung overboard from the *Koolinda's* decks in a cargo-basket—the only human cargo at three in the morning, to shelter behind bags and cases of stores for a two-hours' journey of bitter wind and whipping spray. The waters of the bay are so shallow that two miles out we trans-shipped to a dinghy, and finished up by wading the last couple of hundred yards to the beach with our luggage on our backs. Then I found myself marooned for a month, awaiting the steamer's return.

This is why there are so few travellers. A politician before election time, a clergyman or a pearl-buyer once in two years, and one visiting governor in half a century—that is all Shark Bay knows of the world, and all it needs to know. They told me that the first newcomer in eight years walked overland 500 miles from Perth—and they put him in gaol when he got there.

Those tawny, scrawny sand-hills look back to the dawn of Australian history. Dampier named the shallow inlet when he searched its shores for water in 1692. Freycinet and Baudin followed him a century later. Twenty-two miles away lies the mauve and blue patchwork of Dirk Hartog Island, where the unknown South Land showed up under the arched white sails of the *Eendraght* in 1616. Dirk Hartog is a sheep station to-day, its musterers cooking their lobsters and turtle-steaks of the evening camp on the beaches where Dirk Hartog and Vlaming, a century between them, set up the famous tin plates that were the title deeds of a continent, and, luckily for Britain, lost them both.

The town is a half-circle of modest little homes, one street wide, built on the beach, with huts of Darktown huddled at both ends. Below the line of indentured labour this coloured community is descended from the Arabs, Malays, Chinese and Manilamen, who found it a profitable fishing-ground before the passing of the Aliens' Restrictions Act, and of aboriginal tribes now practically extinct there. In fifty years of seclusion there has been such interbreeding among the coloured races and intermarriage of the whites that to-day the population is variegated indeed, and mostly related—a Pitcairn in Australia.

Toilers of the sea to the third and fourth generations, the people live by gathering shell-grit, found in countless millions of tons on the shores of Hamelin Pool, chilling fish in a little tin refrigerating works, of which the engineer is a South Sea Islander, and, principally, by pearling. Here they fish, not the magnificent *margaritifera meleagrina* of Broome seas, 10 inches across and pounds in lustrous weight, but *margaritifera radiata*, the golden-lip, not more than three inches in diameter, that produces the little honey-coloured pearls beloved of Hindu and Chinese women.

I watched them securing their pearls and pearl shell by a method curious and very primitive. Pegging the shallow bay into leases from 500 to 1,000 acres, fenced off like poultry-yards, the pearlers travel across it a week at a time in tiny cutters, dragging the ocean bed with hand-dredges of wire, sails set to some three miles an hour. At the week-end they return with the haul, each ship bringing from ten to twelve bags, and carry it up on shoulders bent double beneath the weight, for half a mile and more through the shallows.

In tumble-down tin shacks known as pearling-pits it is opened, trimmed, packed and graded, mainly by women of the settlement. Only the first quality is eligible for auction in London. The residue is piled high in heaps, or splintered along the beaches, where in fifty years it has become a mosaic of sparkling beauty, paving the road with living moonlight, and turning the world to dark blue before the eyes.

To obtain the pearls, the oysters are placed in 'pogey-pots,' boilers and barrels that line the seashore, forever steeping the town in the odour of long-dead shell-fish. There they are left to putrefy into a vile and liqueous mass, and when putrefaction can go no further, are boiled to a seething and even more evil-smelling scum, in which the sediment of pearls sinks to the bottom.

Gold and buff-colour and deep green, these tiny stones have now an increasing value in Eastern markets, but where the white and roseate beauties of Broome have realised as much as £8,000 for a single stone in the good days, the jewels of Shark Bay, 26 grains at most, rarely touch the £100 level. Its pearl-shell brings from £14 to £35 a ton, as opposed to £180.

In the very heart of the town, with its wool-sheds and yards, is the station homestead of Peron, with 15,000 sheep in the shearing season running in the main street, frolicking along the hotel verandah, and rollicking round the bay in barges.

Pursuing its sleepy destiny for half a century unbroken in a world of cataclysmic change, Shark Bay still slumbers on. Never has it heard the ringing of a church bell. No picture show has disturbed its solemnity to laughter. The only aeroplane that ever passed over came seeking the lost *Köbenhavn* some years ago. At first its whirring was mistaken for a whale blowing off, then for the menace of a coming hurricane. When at last it dipped and roared above the clustered roofs with a horrifying swoop, the inhabitants of Shark Bay looked at each other with a wild surmise. They had read of such things.

Tongues were wagging with a local—a very local— scandal in the tiny township, which consisted of a broken-down store, a hotel and a beacon on the sand-hills for the fishermen at night. The half-caste, Helen, who earned her living cooking at the station, shampooed her pretty curly hair twice a day, and lent a dash of colour to her dusky charms with lip-stick, was suing her equally half-caste husband in divorce. A half-caste divorce is very rare—in affairs of the heart the coloured people do not bother with formalities—but the lady had prospects of becoming the wife of a white man, or imagined she had. When her husband retaliated with a counter-suit, naming three of the most respectable residents as co-respondents, the fishing-village was pleasantly electrified.

'Why don't you let her go, Oscar? Then you don't have to keep her,' one of the casual nor'-westers asked him.

'I'm paying a solicitor over in Carnarvon £25 to fix all this,' said Oscar, 'because he says, if she wins it, I have to give her the aluminium.'

South of Shark Bay, on the shores of Hamelin Pool, are eight or nine prosperous sheep stations set in a sandy waste. Several of the homesteads are built of the shell-grit that has silted up the beaches in a solid white speedway for 100 miles and more, a lagoon-drift deposit of millions of tiny molluscs of some prehistoric time, that below the level of the sands have set into a cement block, easily cut. White and cool and clean and comfortable, these shell-grit houses withstand the years in that stoneless, timberless sand country, and are probably unique. Bores that run a million gallons a day provide the water for this excellent, if apparently barren, sheep country, and stores are frequently carried across the mud-flats by a camel-string, to and from the lighters at anchor, where the ships of the desert meet the ships of the sea.

At the little settlement of Hamelin Pool at the head of the bay—three roofs in blankness—Mr. Paddy Knight, one of the loneliest postmasters in Australia, has been in residence for thirty years, each morning punctiliously taking his weather and calling head office at Perth to keep this quaint corner in touch, while at Fauré Island lives Mr. Tom Simpson, an exile from the Lakes District in England, with never a passer-by from year's end to year's end to bear him company.

For Tom Simpson, the Crusoe of Fauré, the world holds nothing but memories. Sitting on an upturned boat, he told me his life-story. In 'God's Own Corner' he was one of the idle rich, with a country home, a yacht on Windermere, the systematic pleasures of an assured life. An unlucky gamble on the Liverpool cotton market—and a rude waking up in middle age, with nothing in the ledger but a happy youth of lost opportunities. From £2,000 a year his income fell to 13s. 6d. a week, and that earned gipsying round the North Country as a mole-catcher, with moleskin pelts at a farthing apiece.

Then came a period as ferryman on one of the lakes, the Boer War, and nine years in Africa. Twenty years ago he crossed to Australia, and on outcamps of the Gascoyne stations, and pearling in a little dinghy in Shark Bay, 'knocked about for colonial experience.' Fauré Island is a sheep-run of 11,000 acres and 3,000 sheep. It belongs to a Shark Bay pearler, who has given the management to Simpson as the only white man who will live there in isolation. His predecessor on the island, an old Malay, left him a legacy of forty-eight cats. He shot all but seventeen, because they killed the natural history specimens.

For the hermit of Fauré is a nature-lover. Turtles build their nests in the sands there unafraid, and every shell that is washed up, every bird that alights, is noted. Two or three times a year he heaves up the sail of his cutter and, with a fair wind, makes the mainland 15 miles away, cheerfully walking the next 15 miles in to Shark Bay for stores. Until he goes to look for them, he sees none of his own human kind, but there is no trace of taciturnity about him.

'Lonely? Me! Never!' he laughed. 'I have some books, and I have my dog Bubble. There were three of us when we came over, Bubble and Squeak and I. Squeak died, leaving us two together. It's a good place for an old fellow, and why should I be lonely? Long ago I learned the lesson that a man can have too many friends.'

A smile in which there was no trace of bitterness, a whistle to Bubble, growing a little deaf with age, and the shepherd of Fauré tipped his hat to me and took the trail of the sand-hills to Monkeymia, where his little skiff waited to take him back to the silence.

CHAPTER III

TOWNS THAT BLOW AWAY

FROM a clay-pan at Carnarvon we swung up into the dawn. The Great Australian Loneliness—now we were for it in dead earnest. Rounding the hip of the Continent, we made due east along the coast of hurricanes, the coast of pearls.

We carried a bouquet of roses on the 'plane for the Resident's wife at Roebourne, 800 miles from a florist's shop in Perth, because she had not seen a rose for three years, and there was also a crate of fluffy, yellow, day-old chicks travelling double the distance to crow in the dawn on a cattle-run in Kimberley.

The station roofs of Minilya and Yanrey were little white dots far beneath. The saltbush gave way to snake-rings of the spinifex. Now and again we sighted a mob of sheep —they might have been white ants—or the dark moving blur of fifty or sixty emus, the bird that flies on its great horned feet, making 30 miles an hour over the flats. The shadow of the 'plane was a little scudding crucifix.

Down below it was a trail of tragedy, the coast of lost opportunities. After a splendid pioneering history, the war and the centralisation in Australia's cities that followed it have written a terrible story in the North-west. From this remote corner of the world, practically every available man answered the call in 1915. For those who returned, the world had changed. They never came back. There are 450,000 people in West Australia below the 15th parallel, and less than 5,000 above it.

To travel the West to-day in an aeroplane is to look down upon a graveyard of industry. Here are literally millions of pounds' worth of valuable machinery left for the blacks to play with, towns and settlements without number, faded, and still fading, off the trade-routes and into the spinifex, with the furniture left in the houses and kangaroos hopping in the streets. There are lobster-canneries and shark-skin tanneries, salt mines and whaling stations, factories for the distillation of dugong oils and turtle soup, cotton plantations and peanut plantations, meat works and mica mines, tantalite mines, and mines of silver, and copper, and lead, and tin, and the finest asbestos in the world—gold mines two a penny, and a town and a railway given away with them. The buried treasure of the West is no legend. If the Dutchman and the Don left no iron chests of doubloons and pieces of eight hidden in the sands, the English Stock Exchange has planted it there in millions.

From North-west Cape eastward and northward, one follows the trail of the ghost towns. Onslow, Beadon, Cossack, Roebourne, Balla-balla, all of these were on the Singapore trade route some years ago, but now few ships call in. Many of the houses, unoccupied and uncared for, have been blown down by hurricanes.

From the coast southward for a thousand miles, across the famous old goldfields of the Pilbara, stretches the great desert of spinifex and gold, with scores of towns forsaken, some of them with an ancient mariner of a prospector alone to tell the story of the mad, glad days of yore. Warrawoona and Cue and Nullagine, Bamboo Creek and Menzies and Lawlers and Nannine, to-day they stand for poppetheads stark in the wilderness, sixty-head batteries buried in the sand, and a couple of hundred empty houses and stores and hotels and halls, the haunts of owls and bandicoots.

Next to the war in its record of destruction comes the great sea-anger that the blacks call 'willie-willie.'

When the moon turns blue. . . .

When the divers, groping about down under, strike alternate currents of warm and cold. . . .

When the barometer drops an inch in an hour, or preserves an uncanny steadiness for days at a time, as though it were broken . . . they watch for the willie-willie.

Surely there is no coast on earth more cruelly scourged by Nature as the thousand miles of sand-dunes between Northwest Cape and Wyndham? There is the home of the harpies, the summer cyclones, and the 'cock-eye' storms that rise out of the wreckage of the gorgeous tropic sunsets of the wet season, and descend in a shrieking Valkyrie chorus of wind and wave upon land and sea.

For the greater part of the year silver-calm as a millpool, or rollicking blue in the swing of the trades, it is only during the north-west monsoon that these seas are perilous, and the record of the summer hurricanes, during the past seventy years of colonisation, is appalling. Many times has the pearling fleet been swept to destruction, with scores of ships and hundreds of men engulfed in a night, the last visitation being in April of this year, when 140 coloured men and 20 luggers were lost at the Lacepede Islands.

Sweeping down from the north in a great clock-circle of death and disaster, with a wind force of 120 miles per hour, deluge and sandstorms and electrical discharge, the willie-willie when it comes, is unanswerable. Sometimes it leaves the coastline completely changed. To track back the history of these cyclones is to stand aghast at the concentrated malevolence of Nature and the magnificent defiance of men. For the pioneers of the North-west have hearts of iron. Patiently, year by year, they rebuild on the slopes of Vesuvius, because there is wealth to be won. Last year the town of Onslow disappeared for the ninth time, and the shocking record of this small and inoffensive seaport runs only third to that of Cossack and Roebourne, which have blown away eleven and fifteen times respectively. The most notorious danger zone lies between Exmouth Gulf and the Eighty-mile Beach. Onslow, Roebourne, Cossack, Port Hedland, Broome, Derby and the now defunct settlements of Condon and Fortescue, each in its turn has blown away, some of them twice in one year or three years in succession. In 1912 the coastal ship, *Koombana*, with 135 passengers and all hands, was lost to human ken an hour's run from Port Hedland. 'Drowned in willie-willie,' run countless pages of old fatality records, while the stumps of costly jetties, the twisted lines and bridges of many a railway, and hundreds of wrecked schooners and luggers, rotting in the mangroves, tell tales of unimaginable horror in the stormy past.

From November to April the willie-willie can be expected at any moment. It is then that small ships huddle close inshore for safety, and that coastal captains watch the barometer with an anxious eye. Originating far out to sea, or swinging down from Darwin for 1,500 miles, they suddenly turn inland, strike the coast, circle the compass in a mad fury for twenty-four hours, then make off across another couple of thousand miles of desert, east of the goldfields of the Southern Ocean. Clinging to the spinifex through hours of darkness, watching his home and his wind-mills and livestock, and perhaps his family, blown away before his eyes, the nor'-wester learned to build his house of stone and his jetties of concrete, and triumphed for a time. Then came the war and the depression, and the little tin and cement shacks of hard times have no hope in the hurricanes.

A weird weed is the spinifex, an armed grass that sweeps across a third of the Continent, thriving on sun and sand where there is nothing else to thrive on. A tussock of spikes, inhospitable to a degree, in fact, frankly hostile, it is but one of Australia's many curses that might be made a blessing. Richly resinous, inflammable as motor spirit, it will burn brightly for hours, particularly when wet. The natives make waxes and gums from its secretions, weave the sinuous spikes into fishing-nets and baskets and mia-shelters, while for matting a car through sand and mud and water, mingled with ant-bed, there is nothing to touch it. They are building their roads of reinforced spinifex in this country now.

Of the three varieties, buck, ringed and crested, the crested, when in bloom, as it is for most of the year, pro-vides a golden harvest of thousands of square miles of wheat-ear tassels from two to five feet high, an excellent fodder for cattle and sheep and horses; in fact, the only fodder of an infinite station country. It has, moreover, an amazing natural history of its own—lizards and beetles and snakes and insects and iguanas and mottled and blue-crested pigeons peculiar to itself. Rabbits and bandicoots burrow beneath it in millions, grateful in those dazzled sands for a spear-blade of shade. So that even the maligned spinifex, the white man's curse, has its virtues, and it belongs to the country of gold.

Two hundred million pounds' worth of solid gold have these deserts already yielded to the West. Out there, in 1887, a boy picked up a stone to throw at a crow—it was shot through with living gold. At the same time, one Rory McPhee, putting up his tent in the flinty hills of Pilbara, kicked his toe on 400 ounces in one shining lump, the 'Bobby Dazzler' nugget of Marble Bar. In 1889, Tom the Rager, battling down from Kimberley with his dog Paddy, a thousand miles through wild nigger country, found the fortunes of the Murchison. Bayley and Ford, farther south, chipped off 500 ounces in one day, and Coolgardie was the cry. Hannan lost his horses, and found Kalgoorlie, a city that has kept its promise for over forty years.

Still they pick up a record nugget occasionally, and there are secrets of the spinifex yet to be unearthed. With a valiant past and a magnificent future to be unfolded, by the grace of God and government, in the next twenty years, the North-west is the land of opportunity for the individual. Here men have come in as bar-tenders and finished up as world-famous financiers. Here men have won fortunes upon fortunes from the golden dust and the golden fleece. With its sands and seas teeming with wealth, and hills and deserts that hold the secret of every known mineral and metal, some day soon, perhaps, this country will begin to realise its destiny. What is needed in the initial stages is the faith and work of the Australians who have forgotten it, with men who know its vagaries at the head of affairs, but, above all, people, people, people.

We romped about in the air-pockets over the dimpled hills, and I was on the point of being ignominiously air-sick into the brown paper bags provided for the purpose—I could never have bought anything in a paper bag again—when we put down at Roebourne, a quaint little village of old stone houses nestling beside the pretty Harding River, with some of the highest mountains and the finest scenery in the West behind it. From the air it seemed a town of considerable size, but when I alighted I roamed mostly ruins, and a few occupied houses ludicrously chained to the ground with cables. Thirty years ago, Roebourne had a population of 4,000, with 40 or 50 teams in the main street on boat day, a jeweller's shop, a bank that cost £8,000, and 20 miles of railway running down to the Port Sampson jetty. They all blew away. The war and the motor-truck have written Roebourne's doom. Nothing stirs there to-day save the heat-waves on the hills, the white cockatoos flying in clouds up and down the green river, and the whiskers of the grey-beards wagging on the store verandah as they tell of the great days gone.

Now and again a donkey-team comes in from one of the

B

stations, loaded with wool, the fine light wool that is produced, incredibly enough, from a couple of thousand miles of spiky spinifex. Now and again an old prospector turns up with a little nugget, and there is great excitement, but not for long. The time, it seems, is not yet. Gold is such an old story to these people, yet always, for one brief moment, breathlessly, deathlessly new.

I was the only boarder at the old Jubilee Hotel there, with a dusty punkah hanging in disuse above me in the big, empty dining-room floored with Singapore pume as a protection against white ants, and the bar-room walls and door covered with Old Masters of North-west outback life. They had been painted by a 'blow-in,' an Englishman named Malcolmsen, said to have been a crack steeplechase rider in his day. However that may be, Malcolmsen had a flair for form and colour and action, and he knew his North-west history. The masterpiece, discreetly displayed on the back of the billiard-room door, was a bearded pioneer galloping across the landscape and whirling his lassoo above the curly head of a lubra streaking before him, on her pathetically thin legs, for dear life.

Warm gold are the hills of Roebourne, dreaming away to the sunset, and warm the hearts of its people, with the ruined stone church of Mount Welcome looking down on them all. They find their happiness in simple things, a scrap of garden stockaded from the goats, the swimming-pool in the river, a Sunday trip to Cossack, gathering wild-flowers on the clay-pans, or meeting the weekly aeroplane that might bring a cheery stranger.

A few of the homesteads farther out are prosperous and pretty, with lawns and refrigerators to temper the heat of day. Station people are the aristocrats of the outback, and Roebourne envies them the price of wool.

Zoni, an old-time Cossack pearl-diver, brought me morning tea, carried down my washing to the river in the only rickshaw in Australia, and hung a hurricane lamp above me in the evenings, while I sat writing history. The hurricanes and the white ants have left nothing else to write. On the Saturday night I was disturbed by a loud spluttering, as of a motor-launch in distress, and learned that there was a picture show and dance in progress in the hotel, to which some had driven in sixty and eighty miles. By cordial invitation I attended, and found the big dining-room full of enthusiastic stockmen clumping round in their 'elastic sides' with the belles of the village and a few 'creamies,' as the half-castes and *multum in parvo* are affectionately called. I sat down on a form near the door to watch the fun, but was promptly removed for my own sake. 'That seat's reserved for drunks and Afghans,' they told me without a smile.

Newspaper stories were few, because nothing happens except a wedding once in twelve years, so patiently I listened to tales of old pioneering and the toll of the hurricanes, and explored the majestic old stone gaol where hundreds of natives once worked in chain gangs for murder of the white man and spearing his cattle and sheep. Very few natives are left in this country now. At the coming of civilisation, the aboriginal tribes dwindle like chaff before the wind. The cells that have seen a good deal of mute misery are store-rooms for police gear. In one of them, the sergeant showed me a few tins of beef and jam, some bottles of tomato sauce, a swag and a camp-oven. 'A dead man's estate,' he explained. 'Poor old Tim Hegarty. We found him out on the plain. Nobody knows if he has any heirs.'

The railway, with its ruined carriages being visibly eaten away by the white ants, disappears in the sand within half a mile, and it was a wool-truck that carried me down across nine miles of clay-pan, through the ironstone hills that hold many a vault of native skeletons, to Cossack, once the head-quarters of the pearling ships, now a few scattered ruins of the adventurous past. Two or three government buildings of architectural grace had fallen into a sad decay. A Greek fisherman's family was installed in the court-house with its impressive Corinthian columns, dirty coats hung up by the neck in the court-room and a big white enamel teapot on the bench. I met a quaint little old woman with a brown eye and a blue eye, pottering about in a garden walled in with tin from the goats. I admired her fowls.

'I did have a decent lot,' she told me, 'but they always blow away. The cow blew over to the island. You can't keep anything in this country. My husband blew away. He had a good contract for building the road to Roebourne, and had it close on finished when a blow came, and him and the road and the contract, they all blew away together. He's down in Kalgoorlie now.'

There was a leper island across the creek. Through water striped yellow and black with sea snakes, I rowed across with the doctor, who was also Government Resident in his spare time, to watch him inject chaulmugral oils into leonine eyebrows and grisly nodules that mark the ravages of the disease—only one of the menaces to the aboriginal race in the North-west. There were forty-four cases isolated on the island, all blacks, save for an Afghan teamster. The doctor was doing good work, and had several cures to his credit, including a white man. The afflicted seemed resigned enough. There were only two incurables, an emaciated woman who whimpered over a fire in the blazing heat, and Charlie, the cheeriest soul on the station, dying in a bough shade.

As I peered beneath the leaves, a white smile in a black face flashed back at me from the darkness. Charlie had tamed every lizard that played in the boughs above him, taught them to sit up and beg for crumbs, and to come at his whistle—the leper and the lizard, a good alternative heading, and a lesson in life's logics I have not forgotten.

A little while later the station at Cossack was abandoned. Its unhappy people were freighted north in a pearling lugger to yet another island leprosarium near Darwin, to live and die among strangers accursed as themselves. Wending her way for 1,500 miles north, white sails threading through seas and islands lovely as a dream, with her ghastly human cargo unable to stand upright in the hold where they carry the pearl-shell, the leper ship was a nightmare—and a streamer special for the southern Press. Such is a journalist's philosophy. The worse it is, the better it is, transcribing life in printer's ink.

For your true journalist is a little more, or a little less, than human, a child taking notes. He knows no partialities, no class-distinction, no creed distinction, nor colour-line, nor bias, nor loyalty, save to the story. He probes the depths of humiliation and misery with his stylo pencil, and paints the picture for 1½d. He prefers a murder to a suicide, and both to a wedding. He skims the cream of science and the practical experience of years in a few comprehensive phrases, and gives it a snappy title. He is all things to all men, and to him all men, living and dying, are copy.

CHAPTER IV

BLACK IVORY

BLACK ivory! Nubian slaves, sweating at the oars in the galleys of Imperial Rome! Hell-ships, from Bully Hawkins to Bully Hayes, dipping down through the tropics in the ghastly trade of flesh and blood!

It is a far cry from the Gold Coast to the twentieth century, yet a woman's life bridges the gulf. It was Mrs. Henry Francis Hilliard, one of the few still living who remember, who could tell me the story of Australia's own black ivory days of wicked memory, not so long ago. It is rarely that romance touches one woman's experience in such glowing colours as it has that of Mrs. Hilliard. Her husband, an English naval captain, and a descendant of Robin of Reddesdale, by the way, was one of the first to bring Malay crews across to Australia from Timor. For nine years she lived offshore, in schooner, barque and brigantine, on 10,000 miles of lawless coast. The eldest of her eleven children was born in the swing of the 1887 willie-willie, one of the worst cyclones ever known in this zone of hurricanes, with 37 ships and 300 men gone in a night.

An active, white-haired old lady of seventy-five, Mrs. Hilliard rarely speaks of the old times—sufficient for the day is the evil thereof—but mention a name or two, Chippindall, who came down in the 'eighties to fish pearls for the Prince of Wales, and died on the *Sree pas Sair* in Carnot Bay—powdered bamboo in the porridge, old rumour tells; Captain Claude Ker, knifed through the heart by the Malay serang on the schooner *Dawn* in Cossack Roads; Captain Riddell, who with his mate and young son was done to death by the coloured crew of the *Ethel* off Gantheaume Point—and the story-book opens, for Mrs. Hilliard knew them all. Before her eyes has been unfolded the whole pageant of pearling in Western Australian waters.

Joseph Conrad and Robert Louis Stevenson, with sails set far eastward by the tilt of a coco-nut palm, looked upon these flat, sandy coasts with uninterested eyes. So they missed Broome, missed Cossack, and the sweep of aqua-

marine seas between them that in the last years of the last
century were a highway of undreamed romance.

It was in 1881 that Mrs. Hilliard came to Cossack,
Tientsin they called it in those days—'Tea and Sin.' It
consisted of the coloured rabble of the ends of the earth,
and two pubs. One of them was the barque *Perseverance*,
high and dry in the sand where she had been shipwrecked.
They sold rum aboard her to white men in sarongs and
pyjamas, and black men with gold rings in their ears, and
men of all shades of the rainbow, who paid for it in rupees
and pesetas and lira and Chinese and Mexican dollars and
gold-dust and pearls—anything but real money. In the
bar of the other one, Mrs. Hilliard was married, and as
one of the first two white women of the great North-west,
they toasted her in mugs that were jam-tins whitened up
by the blacks each morning. Her first home was the brigantine *Annie Taylor*, of which her husband was in command,
and there, on the night of the great hurricane, the first child
was born.

'Five miles off Lagrange Bay at five in the evening,
ninety-five miles away at dawn, and back almost to our
anchorage at dusk,' said Mrs. Hilliard. 'We were battened
down, with the waters swirling up to our knees in the cabin,
the ship's masts cut away, and a rug and hammock in the
rigging to keep her head to wind.' In the midst of death
we are in life. With the seas littered with wreckage and
the beaches littered with dead, the new-born baby lived.
I met her later as Mrs. Maguire of Derby, one of the most
pacific and silent of women.

Pearling was then in its infancy, and promised a fortune.
Two or three gems worth thousands had been discovered,
or bought from the blacks for a stick of tobacco or a broken
pocket-knife. It was only a few years since Tommy Clark,
a boy of twelve, dry-shelling on the reefs with an old lubra
at low tide, had picked up the Southern Cross, jewel of a
century. Adventurers were many and various, and Cossack
was the home-port of a hundred ships. Thirty or forty
big windjammers were scouring the reefs. Bought for a
song in the Seven Seas, many of them bore famous names.
There was the *Sree pas Sair*, a merry little yacht, sky-blue,
built for the pleasure of Brooke Pasha, Rajah of Sarawak,

and brought to Australia by Lord Delaware on a cruise of the North. From her decks, with naked divers, Chippendall, R.N., fished the first pearl-shell from Darwin Harbour in 1885. She was later sold to Streeter, son of the well-known jeweller of Hatton Garden, and still later to a Spanish captain, Roderiguez. There was the *Agnes Donald*, that had seen red mutiny in the South Seas, and figures in one of Louis Becke's tales; the *Muriel*, whose serang had been a powder-monkey on the *Alabama* in the American Civil War. Her captain, Hemsworth of the *Costa Rica Packet*, was alleged to have done in a shipload of Malays for their arrack, and, tried and gaoled in Java, was ordered to be released by the British Government. There were the *Lord Loftus* and the *Dayspring*, the *Alto*, the *Ivy*, the *Florence*, that brought down a prohibited immigrant woman from Singapore, sitting above the water on a bird-perch in a tank; the *Harriet*, that belonged to old John Chi, the Chinaman who saved the whole personnel of a Northwest station from death by a mad dash to tell them that the Malay cook had poisoned the soup; and the *Duralia*, built of driftwood by a beachcomber of King Sound, who was once a silk hat manufacturer in London, and manned by his seven half-caste sons.

'Lost in hurricane,' 'sank at her moorings,' 'wrecked up east'—the sea has taken most of them, but there is a story to tell of every one.

In the lee of misty islands that bear the names of the old French navigators, De Puch and Bedout and Delambre, the schooners lay for months at a time, fishing pearls. The treasure was kept in pickle-bottles on the galley shelves. Now and again a Singapore buyer rowed in among them, bought up a few of the big stones, drank their luck in square-face, and made back to the wool-clipper waiting in the roads, with gems for a coronet in his little bag.

Nearly all of the pearlers employed aboriginal divers, for whereas those that engaged Malays were responsible for wages, baksheesh to an Island Sultan, and repatriation, native labour was free, too free. A bag of flour and a stick of tobacco bought a human life. The recruiters were paid £5 a head by the pearlers, and they made a good profit.

In little ketches they travelled the coast, following the

camp-smokes for a thousand miles, there on the beaches in the firelight, buying the young men from the old. From hundreds of miles inland the blacks were brought, men who had never seen the sea and now were to live and die in it. A dark sentence of history tells that when they refused to come voluntarily they were lassoed from horse-back, and dragged.

Once secured, they were taken over to the Lacepedes, those shallow islands of blown sand and sea-grass where the turtles nest in summer. There Shiner Kelly kept house, guarding the natives while the blackbirder went further along. It is on record that three of them escaped on one occasion, and swam twelve miles through shark-infested waters and appalling tide-rips to regain their tribe.

There was a form of agreement to be signed in Cossack, but one nigger was as black as another. With a clumsy cross the natives signed their death-warrants. Few of them lived longer than two years. Of those that did, maimed and paralysed, many were put ashore to find their way, hundreds of miles through hostile tribes, to home. 'Most of the pearlers were kindly to the blacks,' said Mrs. Hilliard, 'but there were some who were not. We were very isolated. The blacks were bad, too. It was never safe to dally too long in the mangroves.' Desperate men and desperate days, and justice prompt and primitive.

The farce of an agreement signed, the natives were taken off to the ships. At dawn the dinghies pulled out from the schooner's side, each with a white man and eight or ten naked divers. A good patch was selected, and one by one they slipped into the sea, to turn over a few feet below surface and swim to the bottom. Six and a half fathoms was regulation depth, but sometimes they went to ten, groping along the reefs, blurred eyes wide open, for a treasure they could neither appreciate nor share. A minute was the record time limit. One by one the wet black heads would appear. A few shells thrown into the boat, a few minutes' breathing-space, and the rap of an oar on the knuckles would send them down again.

All day in the dazzle of sun and sea they worked, slaves to the eternal vanity of woman. Fatalities were many. Swept along by the swift tide underneath, quite frequently a diver would be caught on the coral cups and disembowelled, or bitten in halves by a shark as he swam for the dinghy, or tangled in the weeds, or blotted out of existence by a huge blanket ray below there. Sometimes he would miscalculate the power of his lungs, his straining, bursting lungs, and, within a foot of the surface, a horrible gush of bubbles, a rolling of white eyes, and the black shadow of his body would go drifting gently down. . . . There were plenty of others to take his place.

In the late afternoon, a flag on the mast of the schooner called the dinghies home to the big meal of the day, the opening of shell, and a well-earned rest. A tot of rum and a dose of pain-killer were panacea for the weak and the ailing, and salt water cured all wounds—a cruel life, but the white man's rum and whisky were sweet enough, and damper and fish-curry on the hatch at dusk.

Women lived out on the schooners, babies were born in the little crowded cabins, and children played in the shadow of the sails. Weird tales of love and lust and vengeance were written then in living characters, many a bottle of squareface raised to a lustrous beauty, and in the mad season of hurricanes, many a tall ship swirled like a cardboard toy to her doom.

It was in the late 'eighties that the blackbirding of the Australian native was forbidden, and all pearling-crews brought over, unrestricted, from Manila, Timor and Japan. The rich beds farther north were discovered. Broome, a lonely cable station in the sand-hills, became an Eldorado in mother-of-pearl. A Japanese town sprang up there, with a population of 4,000, a kaleidoscope of silk kimonos, with Cingalese jewellers, Malay sail-makers and Manila carpenters, adventurers from all parts of the globe. The diving suit was introduced. The schooners lay forgotten in the mangroves while fleets of luggers put out to sea. The price of pearl-shell rose to £250 and £300 a ton, single stones touched the £8,000 mark, until, just before the war, with 400 ships off-shore fishing fortunes, Broome drank only champagne, and lit its cigars with the proverbial pound notes.

Mrs. Hilliard has seen it all, the zenith and downfall of ships and towns and men. Handling rare gems all her life, and never wearing them, nor wanting to, as a historian of the West Coast her memories are invaluable—memories of the white-winged schooners and the strange life she shared, 'the old swimmin' days' of black ivory that to the younger generation of Australians are now but a highly-coloured chapter of the past.

Cossack still has its adventurers that 'blow in' occasionally, and two of them Cossacks, the first that the little port in all its varied history has seen. Both are Australians with a war service record, Captain Turner and Colin Gregson, running a turtle soup factory for an English company there by the creek. Both have ridden with Russian regiments, one in Wrangel's army under Locker-Lampson, the other with the Canadian Siberian Forces.

'First catch your turtle,' runs the recipe for turtle soup, and Colin Gregson is the man who does it. Bare as a nigger and nearly as black, Gregson has lived magazine-cover adventure since childhood, when he ran away from a merchant service training ship to become whistle-boy in a Californian lumber-camp, bell-hop in New York, an Anzac twice wounded at Gallipoli, a salmon-fisher in Alaska and a shark-fisher round Rarotonga, small-part actor with a travelling troupe in America and then Australia, one of the Prince of Wales' chauffeurs during his overseas tour, and then a bird-catcher and gold-digger in Kimberley. Nearing forty, he is still a boy at heart. The world is his oyster.

His latest job is diving after turtle from the deck of a fast launch in a costume that consists of Japanese boots. Most people prefer to wait until the mother comes up on the beaches to lay her eggs in the sand in summer, and then turn her over. Gregson is the first white man to emulate the black in an unfailing all-the-year-round method. To him, riding a turtle down into five fathoms is every bit as exhilarating as picking up your handkerchief in your teeth in a flying gallop across the Steppes.

'Quite easy,' he told me modestly. 'My young cousin Joe and I go out in the lugger. When we see a greenback, we get into the launch and drive it into the shallows. As it comes up for a breather, I dive. I land on its back, grip it with the left hand by the back of the neck, then shoot both hands under the fore-flippers. Both the turtle and I go to the bottom, where I can easily heave it over on its back, at the same time giving a push upward with my feet. That is where the Japanese boots come in. The coral cups are pretty sharp. I am never down more than a minute.

'As I come to the top, Joe throws me a sling, which I swing under the fore-flap, and tighten up. With a block and tackle we heave it aboard. There is no danger. Sometimes the turtle gets a good bite in, and, like a donkey, it won't let go, but it can't bite hard. The factory will not take anything under 200 lbs. We get 30 or 40 a week, and could make it 100 if they wanted them. There's no adventure about it, it's just straight out plugging. Anyone could do it. You only have to know the banks where the turtle feeds, and its playful ways. Now and again you sight a "tiger," but the sharks round here are nearly all hammer-heads.'

In the hold and on the deck of the lugger, with hourly waterings to keep them alive, the turtle are brought in to the factory each week, butchered of their calipash and calipee, and boiled, shell and all, in steam-jacket boilers with distilled water, a few secrets from London chefs, and a liberal allowance of sherry—three days from the sea to the soup-plate. One turtle makes 600 lbs. of soup.

Showing their equestrian prowess on turtle-back down under, and battling hard against difficulties of water-shortage and isolation, the Cossacks of Cossack are so far winning through, and with an encouraging success beginning to realise the wealth of these tropic seas, and to introduce Australia's epicurean delicacies to the dinner-tables of the world.

CHAPTER V

OLD HANDS

HE was sitting among the pots and pans in orderly array outside his little camp, skewering a startling blue patch to a pair of trousers.

'Can I do it for you?' I asked with a smile.

He regarded me solemnly over his spectacles, then, 'Thank ye kindly,' he said, and handed over the patch, a needle nearly four inches long, and a linen thread well licked at both ends. He found another petrol tin for me to sit on, and lit a cigarette that looked as though it were manufactured of wet tea-leaves.

'Never was no good at sewing,' he volunteered. 'With a hammer and gad there's no man on any field can run me second, but these instruments has got me beat. I remember once Davy Shaw and me was mates outside Broad Arrow. Struck it rich. Pickin' up the stuff in lumps as big as potatoes while we was puttin' up our tents. Six hundred ounces in the first week, and then Davy couldn't stand it no longer. He went in to Coolgardie, bought the d.ts. and came back and cut his throat on me. I heard him groanin' in the night-time, and there was only one thing to do. I put a hundred of flour on his feet, chained him down with a camel-hobble, and sewed him up again. That was a ticklish job. Dave was so bad he didn't know whether it was happenin', or whether he was dreamin' it was. Anyhow, I got the edges all tucked in and seen that it was holdin' good. Then I gave him a feed of condensed milk and roped him down for four days. By that time he'd come to himself, and knitted a bit. Dave never had another drink in his life, but wasn't he mad? Reckoned he had to grow a beard to hide them dorg-leg stitches of mine.

'No good at sewing,' he finished up mournfully. 'It lorst me the best mate I ever had.'

Who will tell stories like that when the old hands are gone? Not the neat bank-clerks and motor-salesmen of to-day, I fancy.

To take the sun-down trails is to find them still, all that

are left of them, the men whose roughened hands have made history, who have circled the Continent again and again on the far-flung lonely stock-routes or the fever-trails of gold. Thirty years ago they were friends of the old Australia. The new one has left them behind. Little they grieve. Mates together, in little white tents of the mulga and the dry creeks, they share a pipe in the evenings, dollying over the dross of the years for a speck of romance. Let the younger generation have its talkies and its flying machines. Theirs were the days.

By a sunny little river at Roebourne I came upon a trio of them camped together, Maguire McPherson, Galloping Paddy and Wheelbarrow Bill. Paddy Benson had ridden his bicycle 12,000 miles round Australia, north from Ballarat, and, through thirty years of golden history, Bill Schmald, a gentle old German, had followed him, pushing his worldly goods in a wheel-barrow. Four fortunes and three trips round the world had Bill accumulated in that barrow one time and another, but it all dwindled away again. Mates on every goldfield, these two had shared wild triumphs and disillusionment, and had lived in many a canvas city that came to light in a night and faded in a day. They knew the secret history of every gold find in Western Australia, and had seen a chain of towns spring up in the spinifex and disappear from ken in a few months or years, as the case may be, abandoned and tenantless, with wallabies making their warrens in the mines.

'A will o' the wisp,' said Paddy sadly. 'Men lived for it and died for it. We went through hell to get it, and when it came our way, we let it go again. On we'd follow like madmen, with our eyes always on a bigger find farther out —and it leaves a man nothing in the end. Gold fever! Yet, if it were all to live again, if a real rush broke out to-morrow, we'd be there.'

Swung in a hammock between a camp-fire and a bough shade, Maguire McPherson, impervious to gold fever, was reading *The Black Bloodhound*. 'A good yarn, too,' he told me. 'Just what you want up here to break the monotony.' A crack stockman of the North in the old days, Maguire McPherson had made a hobby of breaking the monotony by drinking pots of beer on the backs of the most vicious buckjumpers they could find him in West Kimberley.

Dry-blowing and fossicking along the hills and gullies of Marble Bar and Hall's Creek, and camped in bough shades by water-holes of the Ord and the Fitzroy and the Katherine, scouring the thousand-mile deserts of Central Australia, I was to meet many more of them, chivalrous and kindly old characters known to the outback of five States, men from the Darling and the Murray who had come over by way of the Overland Telegraph when it was in course of construction, sixty years ago.

There was Dobson of Australia, who said: 'Come up wid me to the Eighty-mile Beach, and I'll make ye an omelette of turtle eggs will rise up like an ant-hill'; the Musical Tramp, singing along through the great wide spaces with a frying-pan tied to his bicycle; the Tropical Frog, turning up at the stations when it rains; Deep Down Paddy, who got so low that he stole the cook's boots; old Ned Home, who discovered a new star in Aquila, named by an American observatory in his honour, and left a diary in Greek and code that has not been deciphered yet, and Lord Bent, who in fifty years' crossing and re-crossing Australia, told me that he had been lost only once in his life, and that was in a bargain basement in Melbourne. One never asks their real names. For the first half-century the ports of the North-west were the ports of missing men.

In Derby country one meets those that have casually sauntered across from Queensland. While I was there, Oodnadatta Joe walked in from his home-town, 3000 miles steering by the sun across the desert, only a little the worse for wear, but noticeably thirsty. He had left Oodnadatta eighteen months before with a gallon of beer, and proudly informed me that he had done six miles to the gallon. There, too, was Billy Dixon, who had sailed round the globe five times, as anything from second mate to stowaway, and never yet paid his fare; the Torn Pocket, the Last of the Ryans, Ripsy Boo, Mickey the Priest, and Snowy the Poet, writing bush verses under a fly-veil as he thrashed along behind a mob of bullocks.

With a rare sense of the dramatic, leaning over the horse-paddock gate, great yarns they could tell me of the days 'before the yeast bread.' Old hands—a call at the tent flap, a knock on the mulga post, would bring them out, a little perturbed at first at the apparition of a white woman. A hurried retreat, the sounds of a frantic tidying up, and they would appear, trim and proper, to proffer the bushman's unfailing hospitality of a cup of tea and a yarn, the very soul of gallantry and helpfulness.

It was in True Blue Gully, near Marble Bar, that one old miner metamorphosed himself out of all recognition in a brand-new shirt of brightest blue and a pair of trousers that still bore a reassuring cardboard label: 'Ironbark Brand. Guaranteed not to rip or tear.' But a word of old days, and, no longer self-conscious, they were launched into epic memories, these true bush gentlemen who have lived all their lives outside the orbit of convention, yet are almost childishly reverent in the presence of a woman.

For white women are rare as roses in the great North-west. Of all the prospectors still out on the hills of Pilbara, not one is a family man. Home ties seem to have passed them by. Big Paddy and Tarpot down at the camp have their ever-laughing lubras. Piccaninnies play about the camp all day, Adam and Hardcase and Lucy and Windbag, dressed in their shiny little selves. But the old men, opening their tins of beef and stewing their tea, never feel that something is missing. Gold was their only love, betraying and robbing them many a time, and leaving them for dead, but even now, in the twilight of the day, they know no other fidelity.

At Port Hedland one day I thought I had discovered the exception to the rule. I was in the little dark sitting-room of the hotel, talking to old Jim Robinson, the man who found diamonds at Nullagine, and I bought him a pot of beer to 'oil him up.' Many a stirring tale could Jim tell me of Warrawoona and the man who died to find it, of a mate of his who rammed his spade into the wall of his three-feet shaft out beyond Bamboo Creek, and went away under a tree to boil his billy, and came back and hauled out a shovelful of gold. 'He said nothing to nobody—a good digger won't tell you his name—but he walked 380 miles in to Roebourne to register it, and that was Robber's Gully.'

'And did it pay?' I asked ignorantly.

Jim spat. 'Pay!' he said scornfully. 'Did Robber's Gully

pay?' His voice rose to a dreamy ecclesiastical sing-song. 'A hundred and fifty ounces to the *bloody* ton!' One evening, hearing a faint new rattle in the sluice-box—diggers can hear gold, y'know—he himself had discovered the white-blue gleam of two or three Australian diamonds. One of them he sold in Melbourne for £73.

To all his dolly-pot romances he lent the emphasis of blood-curdling blasphemies and rolling labials. I appreciated the swears, they heightened the drama, but grieved for the ideal.

'Drink up your beer,' I told him sadly. 'The dog will have his nose in it.'

'That's all right,' he said. 'They don't like beer. Ah, well, they're out there yet, most of them, faithful to the finish, fossicking for a few weights a week till they're too blind to see it. Better than the pension.'

'Then why have you deserted?'

He scowled at me darkly. 'There's a woman keeping the pub at Nullagine now,' he said bitterly. 'Once you see a parson or a clothes-line come in to the place, it's done. The best thing a woman can do for a man in this country is to leave him alone, and one way or another they never will.'

I allowed myself a smile at his candour and said good-bye to Jim. Then, with a sudden swing, he righted himself, and the old miners were vindicated. Straggling back to the bar, he parked his pot, sucked his whiskers, and announced in a roar of laughter: 'I been having a yarn to the little bloke that's writing a book.' In that dim shanty sitting-room, unaccustomed to the ways of the new woman and deceived by my outback shirt and trousers, Jim had mistaken my sex. For, as one of the old cavaliers remarked to me: 'There never was a real digger who would swear in front of a woman Not a strange woman, anyway.'

Between Roebourne and Hedland the 'plane swings low to the deserted mines and township of Whim Creek. Hundreds of thousands of pounds' worth of mining gear and machinery, including 13 miles of railway, three or four streets of houses, and a hotel of steel and asbestos specially bought from England to withstand the heat, are lying there useless. From 1907 to 1914 Whim Creek, with hundreds of employees, shipped 50,000 tons of oxidised copper ores to London, in the Singapore ships and its own fleet of three-masted barques. The ores yielded, and still yield, an average of 15 per cent. of high-grade copper, but the shipping difficulties of war-time, the fallen price of the metal, and finally a willie-willie which blew three of its barques to perdition on De Puch Island opposite, were the end of the chapter. A solitary mines manager, Mr. H. R. Sleeman, and his wife, keep vigil in the little lost town to-day, with one well-furnished room of their domicile away down in the bowels of the earth. They are waiting for the rise in copper that will put Whim Creek back on the map.

There is a little more of Port Hedland than most towns of the North-west, it being the outlet of a vast area of fair sheep and cattle country that extends south across the rim of the sand deserts. Although there is nothing scenic about the blistered little town, its sea life is amazing. Port Hedland is the place where a fisherman's wildest dreams come true.

Looking down from the jetty on a clear morning, the water is literally black with fish, liquid, moving black, with now and then a silver flash as, feeding, they turn over. Myriads of sardines, delicious eating; garfish two feet long, diaphanous greeny-blue; black bream, silver bream, red bream, skipjack weighing up to thirty pounds, schools of mullet and shoals of whiting, while the bottom is a moving blur of acres and acres of flathead, and among them all the goggle-eyed cuttles, dreamily wavering. In a flash they are gone, as through the translucent water cuts the silver fin of an eighteen-footer shark, incredibly swift.

Men with a forty-pounder kingfish slung over their shoulders are everyday at Hedland. One bonita provides the coloured men with steaks for a week, and every now and then a giant rock cod that tips the scales at four hundred pounds is hauled ashore to have his picture taken. But the best sport is when the salmon come in, in schools of about a thousand, a swift fish and fierce biters. In habit, form and edibility, these North-west salmon are close cousins to those of the Atlantic. They leap as they run, and at the turn of the tide are frequently caught in a foot of water.

But all these are child's play from the jetty. Hedland people tell you that if you want real fishing you must pull out a mile to the Beacon. There, in 25 fathoms, are the fish that even a fisherman cannot exaggerate, many of them as yet unclassified in the encyclopædia of Australia's fishes.

A sharp angle of the Indian Ocean, hedged in by the great pearling reefs and the Dampier Islands, Hedland is one of earth's chosen corners for the marine naturalist. With a tide rise and fall of 24 feet, the live reefs that surround the seaport at low-water springs are teeming with the mysterious, half-sentient life of the sea.

As I wandered along the mud-flats in the early morning or the trade wind sunsets, an astounding pageant of sea-wonder unfolded itself. Things that I believed inanimate showed a startling suspicion of me. Barnacles and chitons clung closer with a little sucking sound. Daintily coloured shells scuttled about in the shallows, and horrible smaller octopi were there in thousands, watching with sunken eyes, squirting inky liquids, and then writhing into the mud with a movement like that of the incoming tide. Star-fish, sea-urchins and the usual small rabble of the tide-flats were there in multitudes, and a wealth of anemone and jelloid life, the flowers and half-fish that recoil, grip or change colour at a touch. Sea-snakes wriggled in the water, striped and mottled; mangrove fish climbed their trees, and in the deep rock-pools, among wine-jellies gently undulating, the rainbow parrot swam along the coral cups. Here is the lung-fish, queer little amphibian, link between the lizards and the fish; the stone-fish, with its sardonic devil-grin, viciously poisonous; green mangrove crabs, big as a dinner-plate, with nippers that can amputate fingers in one grip.

A deep-sea stranger often caught at the jetty has black and white feathers, long as a fowl's, and claws like a cat. Other weirdities are the knight-fish, with black eyes that shine like glass; the sergeant, with his three stripes, a rooster-fish with red comb and brilliant tail-feathers, and the 'Spanish flag,' green and yellow stripes on a dark back. Some of the sea-curios are 12 feet long, with scales as big as pennies, covered with oysters and barnacles. Others are neither fish, fowl, nor good red herring.

Sometimes the divers bring in from the pearling-grounds west of Cossack little gnarled branches of black coral, known as deep-sea ebony, from a submarine forest uncommercialised. Great rays haunt the coast, lifting the luggers on their flat backs, blanketing their prey. Bays and beaches are thick with turtle, and here, any day, you may gather a necklace of the blue, shining operculum that the children love, or see the mother-of-pearl sail of the chambered nautilus as he goes sailing by.

The seas are full of dugong. With a face like a pair of boxing gloves and an internal organism like a fireman's hose, a lumbering and unbeautiful creature, with the whale and the seal the dugong is the only mammal of the sea, and said to be the origin of the mermaid legend. Its mournful, muffled call, its half-human body ending in a finny tail, and the slow grace of its movements under water may well have fired the imagination of Ulysses with the fantastic vision of a woman half-fish.

But the song of the sirens is long forgotten. The Ulysses of the north of Australia, white and black, grills the mermaid and finds her good. Dugong is the tastiest and most nourishing meat that ever came from the waves. Rich and appetising, its flavour is the combination of steak and bacon, a delicacy for an epicure, a feed for a hungry tribe. Coloured men of the pearling luggers prefer the pork to the cured variety or the expensive tinned meats they carry, while the inhabitants of island missions and tiny settlements often procure no other meat save goat and dugong for months at a time. I first tasted it in Broome, from the hotel menu. 'My word, Felix, this is good,' I remarked to the old Manila waiter. Felix shrugged his shoulders and registered disgust. 'I don't eatim,' he said. 'Too much like peeples!' I refrained from asking how he knew.

A dugong hunt out among the islands where they abound is a thrilling affair. One method is the simple expedient of diving on to the creature as it comes up to breathe, and holding it down to drown. This is very popular with the Torres Straits Islanders, amphibians themselves, who can swim as swiftly as the animal and tire it out in its own element. The second is with dinghy, or native canoe, and harpoon, whaling on a small scale, in the manner of the blacks. Cruising about in bays where its favourite weed attracts it, as soon as a dugong is sighted the natives paddle towards it, and within a few yards launch the spear or harpoon. Away goes the dugong and the canoe with it, speeding across the water in flying spray like a hydroplane, the blacks paddling for dear life to keep it from upturning.

Twenty minutes at breakneck speed, and, as the beast floats puffing with exhaustion on the surface, a blackfellow leaps in and splits it up with a knife. The booty is quickly hauled ashore and butchered, the smoke of the funeral pyre bringing all the tribes in the neighbourhood quickly to the feast, which any passing white man will be glad to share.

As the whale its bone and blubber and ambergris, the dugong has commercial possibilities that might well be exploited and never are. The yellow oil obtained from it, clear amber and far more palatable than cod-liver, possesses untold virtues in the treatment of chest complaints and the nourishing of the anæmic or delicate, and also as the foundation for cosmetics and perfumes. The hide provides a leather that tans excellently, much more pliable and handsome and durable than pig-skin. Quite recently a request was received from London for salted hides for use in the manufacture of football covers, and as a substitute for porpoise hide in making the uppers of shoes.

So tough is this leather in its crude state that mariners of the North use it for rowlocks, finding it more satisfactory than iron. The ivory of the bones, clear white and without a grain, of which a small consignment was sent to London some time ago, was used in the manufacture of tooth-brush handles. The agent wrote that it had been found more suitable than ox-shin bone, and demanded a further supply. I met a wife of a beachcomber up in the Buccaneers who told me that, being anxious to make household soap and having run out of tallow, she obtained some dugong oil from a catch of the blacks, and included it in the recipe as an experiment. Not only was the soap a distinct success, but on his return from an island trip her husband reported that it lathered surprisingly in salt water—a quality that should make it worthy of a universal market. In an age where nothing is sacrosanct, perhaps the mermaid of mythology may be 'floated' into a company.

Coastal boats stay twelve hours in Hedland, waiting for the turn of the tide. There are yawning travellers who feel that even that is far too long. They do not know that, beyond the white tin roofs and the mesquite trees and the Chinese laundries, there is a secret that a few lifetimes are all too short to unravel.

CHAPTER VI

A FENCE ACROSS AUSTRALIA

ONCE a week from Hedland, if they remember to send it, a small engine with half a mile of train behind makes laboriously out to Marble Bar, a little white town in the ochre hills famous for three things—74 rich metals plentiful in 500 square miles of country; a brilliant bar of jasper, like a gigantic flitch of bacon, in the Coongan River; and one of the highest mean temperatures in the world. Mean is the word. One hundred and twenty-five degrees all the week and 128 on Sundays is Marble Bar's proud boast.

It takes the train from 8 a.m. till dusk to travel 114 miles, and it is welcomed all along the way by camel-teams in from the stations, blacks in clean shirts, and teams of thirty or forty gentle grey donkeys harnessed to enormous wool wagons. Trucks are left at the sidings to be loaded for the return. There is no sign of a refreshment stop, but under the big tanks at the Shaw River at noon the engine-driver boils up a billy of tea for all aboard, and hands it round in red-hot pannikins, plenty of sugar and condensed milk whether or not.

Next morning the train comes back, to pick up the bales and the mails, but I preferred to stay a while, to roam the gold and malachite hills, to listen to the tales of the old fossickers dry-blowing in the gullies, and the whistling of the butcher-birds by moonlight in the little waterless creeks, and to return on the following Saturday by the Kalamazoo.

There were 45 shearers from Warrawagine in the pub dining-room at Marble Bar when I arrived, Knights of the Shining Blade, in from their yearly pilgrimage of the stations. They rushed audibly through the menu, which consisted of tomato sauce and bully beef, and faded away into the night, singing. Next morning, Marble Bar, with about 35 people all told, took me to its warm and flinty heart, showed me the gold it could still pick up everywhere, brought me shining little bottles of silver lead ore and tantalite and sticks of silken asbestos eight inches long as 'speciments,' and wafted me away twelve miles or so on a battered old wool-truck to Moolyella, the ghost of a great tin-field, with a population of 3,000 twenty years ago, and two old men to-day.

All along the river-bed the blacks are yandying tin, flutter and rhythm, flutter and rhythm, of sand in the dishes, filling their dilly-bags with a dead weight of metal, and trailing across to trade it at the broken-down store for playing-cards, gina-ginas, tinned fruits, hot bread, coloured corroboree wool, sweets and other trifles dear to their childish hearts. The old storekeeper—'Coupla Bob' the blacks call him—stirs the tin with a big magnet to free it from iron, and gives them so much a bag. Time was when tin was well worth a white man's energy, and when one white man made £30,000 in a few years at Moolyella.

A remarkable sleight of hand peculiar to the Australian blacks is this yandying. Filling her coolamon or old tin dish with gravel, the black woman can winnow it with an upward toss repeated in a swift rhythm, until the tin is all at one end and the gravel at the other. She can yandy infinitesimal grass-seeds from their husks for the camp breakfast, or ants' eggs from dust. I have seen a lubra, with just this quick flutter of dish and hands, manipulate a quantity of tea, sugar and sand that a station-owner had deliberately mixed together. She handed it back miraculously divided into three distinct heaps in less than five minutes. They installed a mechanical yandy at a cost of thousands in the good days of Moolyella, and left it to wilt in the sun. The hands of the lubras were infinitely more efficient than the machine.

There are numbers of blacks—and generally blacks only —under a white overseer—employed on the stations about Marble Bar, quite civilised, as all of the lower North-west blacks are to-day. There are numbers more, uncivilised, in the desert that runs for 1,000 miles due south of it. Badly fed in a poor and waterless country, they are sad physical specimens, emaciated and diseased, their eyes swarming with flies, and afflicted with a purely native disease known as granuloma, that gives to the shin-bone the perfect outward curve of a boomerang. One of them was brought in to the A.I.M. Hostel on the hill for medical attention.

They had found him dying in the desert, victim of a tribal feud, his femoral artery pierced in five places by stone-headed spears, and the wound stuffed with human hair, dead grass and other rubbish, swollen and gangrened. A call was sent to the doctor at Hedland, who made an urgent journey through the night and operated in the morning, with one of the pretty A.I.M. sister's prettiest nighties as his overall, and a pudding-cloth wrapped round his head. the patient was frightened to death at the sight of instruments and anæsthetics, and instructions were given to him in lurid swears—the only English he knew. Abdul, the Afghan yardman, stood at the door to see that he did not give trouble and bolt. For further attention, he was wrapped in an old table-cloth and carried back to Hedland, with the doctor, on the Kalamazoo.

The Kalamazoo is a motor-trolley, some six feet by three. Merrily it pops along the line at about thirty miles an hour, and upon it I reclined, being the only passenger, in the manner of Cleopatra on her Nile galley. If there are others, they sit sideways and dangle their legs. It is the proud special charge of Roberto Parola, a good Australo-Italian.

'At what time will we get to Hedland, Bob?' I asked.

'Sposa I tella you, maybe I tella you lie,' smiled Bob in reply. Judgment Day itself will be held up in the Australian outback.

A push off, and away we spurted into the fresh morning, through far bright deserts of the spinifex, through the harlequin hills of Pilbara, an Eldorado of yesterday and, some day, to-morrow. The blacks' camp, full of philosophers, was not yet astir. Pretty little brown spiked and crested pigeons skipped away from our mad onslaught, Java sparrows in millions scattered out of the bushes like shot from a gun. An old man lizard scurried frantically along the track before us, like a bird that could not fly, and mobs of big brown and blue kangaroos stood in amazement, graceful heads and velvet paws folded, then bounced away with thudding tail.

In quick time we made the Eginbah railway camp with its 10,000 gallon tanks, and skimmed along a dazzling stretch of scarlet desert pea, here and there reflected in the shadowed pool of an otherwise dry river-bed. At Coongan, we passed a white tin shanty with a wall of bottles five feet high—relics of a long, long thirst—and many a lonely grave was by the track. Alas for man's mortality, the only one remembered was the post-and-horse-shoe monument of the engine-driver's dog, killed on the line.

A wild donkey careered across in front of us, and we had the inevitable breakdown. Stationary for a couple of hours, we watched the hills dancing with heat in winter, and tried not to imagine summer-time. Right at last, another couple of hours brought us to a deserted railway camp, the tidy shacks chained down against the hurricanes, the trunks of the gum-trees about it so blindingly white that you would swear they had been painted. Through spinifex and raspberry jam bush, and past a series of table-top hills, patchwork of black diorite and brilliant green of scrub, then over the flat tide-levels gleaming mirage, lay the last empty forty miles to Hedland. Twenty miles away we could see a tombstone shining in the cemetery there and the masts and funnel of a ship at the wharf.

Bob has his more adventurous moments. A dead kangaroo on the line over a 15-foot bridge made him think quickly one day. He stood in the centre of the Kalamazoo, watched which side it was falling, then jumped the other way. One night, with the doctor on board and no light, they hit something softly resistant, and all shot off into the prickly spinifex. They went back to find it was a camel sitting down, and still chewing. Three or four kangaroos and a bullock are considered a fair night's bag.

Old prospectors come down from the Pilbara; sometimes never to return. Blacks in their best board the train anywhere between stations, and pay no fare. Mothers bring new babies home, men who have struck it rich start southward, and the doctor comes popping through the night to tragedy in the wilderness, all on the Kalamazoo. Sometimes the shadow of death hangs above it, when the dying are brought down to hospital at Hedland.

It is just part of the life of the outback, a joke, perhaps, but an unfailing friend in emergency, and after you have travelled on it, through the clear wide spaces with the clear wide sky above you, you will give up your seat in the observation car at any moment for a bushman's ticket to infinity, with Bob on the Kalamazoo.

In the ultimate deserts beyond Marble Bar and Nullagine, beyond the last outposts of human settlement, beyond the abandoned gold towns that are skeletons in the plain, and beyond the farthest out of all the prospectors, there's a man riding.

Through the slow torture of a summer's day, his camels seem to be the only living things in that pale circle of earth and sky. Swiftly he shades his eyes. Did something move out there?—something that now stands stock still, watching? Or was it just the eternal dancing of the heat. At night, when he lights his camp-fire, he will know. The camel strides on, and his head sinks again upon his breast. He dare not look up for long, this glare means blindness. He dare not think, for that way madness lies.

He is a rider of the Big Fence, the only fence in the world that cuts a continent into two mighty paddocks—the Number One Rabbit Proof.

Clear across Australia runs the Number One Rabbit Proof, from the Southern Ocean to the Indian, from Starvation Boat Harbour in the south to Condon Inlet in the north, cutting through the big timber forests, the wheat belt, the gold country, the cattle and sheep stations, and out into the pearling seas—and there are millions of rabbits on both sides of it! Western Australia is parochial in the matter of its rabbit-pests. It objects to their inter-breeding with those of other states—hence the Fence. When the furry hordes arrive in their millions each spring, in a great western drive across central deserts, it is to find the road closed, closed with a wire netting 1,139 miles long, 42 inches high, 17 gauge and $1\frac{1}{4}$-inch mesh, costing £40 a mile a year upkeep. The only alternative is to go north or south, and swim.

There are five permanent riders to keep that fence in order. They travel north and south for 150 miles each way. To those of the south it is the ordinary routine of a vermin inspector, but only a tested bushman can ride the north, a man who can find water and food where there is none, a man with the tact and courage to deal with wild blacks when he meets them, and one who is not afraid to

face himself and never another living soul for two and three
months on end.

Until the retrenchment of the recent depression, these
northern riders travelled in pairs for their protection.
To-day they ride alone, 12 or 15 miles a day over the ribbed
sand-hills, with a string of three camels. To the west, for
500 miles, there is the spinifex, the saltbush and the sea.
To the east and south for two thousand miles there is
nothing, nothing but the country of the Rudall tribes, that
have never yet let a white man through unmolested.

At the crude soakage wells provided, he camps in the
evenings, and the camels come in, to sit with their heads
in the smoke as a protection from sandflies, and to listen to
bedtime stories. It is not until you have ridden the desert
alone that you learn what good companionship a camel can
give.

Never a rabbit they find on the fence up that way—even
rabbits won't tackle buck spinifex—but there is a lot of
trouble for all that. Sometimes the wire is down for miles
in the floods of the tropic wet. Dingoes and kangaroos do
a good deal of damage, and even the friendliest blacks have
an annoying little habit of using it as a snaring net, hooshing
the wallabies into it. Sometimes a flock of 50 or 60 emus
will playfully charge right through. Stores must never be
left unattended, or the ever-watching bush natives will raid
the camps, scattering battered tins behind them on a 50-mile
foot-trail in the day. They know that the contents of those
tins are worth having, but they overlook the little matter
of the tin-opener.

Adventure comes along once in a way. Camped at a
soak one night on the rim of wild country, a lone rider
looked out to a torchlight procession coming towards him
through the empty desert. Ten or twelve naked blacks
were making direct for his camp. He hid behind a sand-
hill and murmured the first prayer in years. On came the
savages, on to his very campfire, and then he saw it was a
white man they were bringing to him. An old prospector
far out of his reckoning had been speared through the chest
by wild tribes at a waterhole. The man had plucked the
spear from his breast, and crawled for miles delirious. He
died that night, his name and story unspoken. They buried

him on the Fence, and by the light of the spinifex torches
the boundary-rider fashioned a crude cross of wire that still
stands upon the grave.

The head camp is at Jiggalong, 623 miles north of the
Peak Hill railhead. You will not find Jiggalong on any
map. It is a couple of bough shades and a tin shack, not
even a store. But there are great doings there when the boys
ride in, and even Jiggalong has its notables. One of the
best known died a few years ago, Inspector Dick Walsh,
who rode the Fence for a lifetime, and had the queerest
hobby in the world. It was Walsh's leisure hour delight
to catch a 'peedong,' a writhing human shadow with not a
shred of spinifex to cover his nakedness, dress it up in a shirt
and trousers, teach it to understand English and ride a horse,
find it a job on a station, and then catch another one. Walsh
was accredited the best hand with blacks in the whole of
the North-west, but that does not prevent their telling a
good story of 'Dick.'

For some years he had promised a prominent musical
firm in Sydney the gramophone record of a corroboree. It
was a difficult undertaking. Wax goods in that country
melt out of sight long before they arrived. The gear was
smashed at railway sidings and on camel-back, the natives
went 'pink-hi,' which is 'walk-about,' at the wrong time,
and, worst of all, the accoustics of the great wide spaces
were against him. At last he conceived the idea of a
sounding-board, as featured by the jazz orchestras. He
gathered the leading tenors and bassos within three hundred
miles, called a rehearsal, then packed them willy-nilly into
the largest tin tank in the district, with promises of unlimited
baccy. Then he set the corroboree and the record going
together.

It was hot in that tank, and the singing grew more and
more breathless. Walsh put his mouth to a crack in the
tin. 'Sing up, you b——s!' he roared. They sang up, and
finished a first-class record. It is treasured yet in Sydney,
with the swear intact.

Out there you will meet Joe George, who wears his hair
in a Marina bob to keep the flies off the back of his neck,
and breaks in his new hats by burning holes in the crown.
Joe won £2,000 in a sweepstake twenty-two years ago, put

it in the bank at Nannine, and went bush. When the bank at Nannine closed down, not being able to locate him, they sent it down to Cue, and there it is waiting for him yet, with the interest accumulated. Joe says he 'haint got no use for it.'

There is Kitty the Capitalist. Kitty tucks the camp cat under her arm every morning, and takes it to the waterhole. As it catches the little spinifex doves, she filches them from it, wrings their necks, and tosses them, feathers and all, into her stew-pot. The cat gets the skinniest as wages.

There, too, are Maudie and Nellie, the two little half-caste girls that, having been taken south by boat to the Moore River Settlement near Perth, never having seen a map in their lives, ran away the first night and found their way back across 1,500 miles of unknown desert. These children travelled by instinct, licking the dew from the tussocks when there was no water, living upon the strange creatures of the spinifex, lizards, snakes, goannas, and beetles, stings and wings and all.

But they all come back to Jiggalong. Steve Paul came back, a rider of the rabbit-proof for eleven years, who had developed 'a heart.' They found him on the Fence, to all intents dead, and he was sent south to the angina specialists. A long time in hospital, and the Agricultural Department found Steve a sinecure in head office at a good salary. He was settled in the city for life. He stayed five months, and applied for his old job on the fence. When that was refused, as a case of plain murder, he resigned, and went north.

Steve has a rendezvous with death, out there where he has lived with it.

CHAPTER VII

PORT OF PEARLS

IN Broome I learned that most of the tales I had read of pearls are true.

Squat brown men, with expressionless faces, who spend their lives in a deep-sea twilight, tiptoeing grotesquely in the 40-pounder boots of the diver's dress . . . slant-eyed Asiatics, forever smoking on the bird-cage balconies of the coloured quarter, reading the perpendicular brush-drawing of the Japanese, and watching . . . white men sprawled in siesta upon shuttered balconies, in the red shadow of the poinciana trees, dreaming of the luggers that may bring them a fortune—such are the men of Broome, a patch of the Orient in Australia, and its only port of pearls.

Though pearls are found everywhere along the west and north coasts, from Shark Bay right round to the Barrier Reef, the prospectors of the deep are designated 'pearl-shellers,' the gems, in most instances, the perquisites of the divers. At Broome alone, where the reefs are rich and the regulations many, are they 'pearlers,' and the history of the world-famous stones that have come from these waters the life-breath of romance.

Misrepresented to the world by sundry novelists as an A-grade Hades of sand and squalor and sin, the town is actually one of the friendliest and most fascinating of the Continent, itself a pearl of ever-changing beauty in the pearling seas. By all who travel the desolate sand-wastes of the West, it is looked upon as a little haven.

To come in by air is one of the memories of life. We left Hedland at 'piccaninny daylight,' taking off from the clay-pan race-course, where the station hacks and their black-boy riders were galloping round us in the dawn in their early-morning trials for the annual bush race-meeting. Across the station-country of the de Grey River and along the Eighty-mile Beach we flew—eighty miles with never a pebble, here and there a flotilla of clouds resting on the sea, white as guano islands, here and there the glimpse of a fleet, pencil-sketches of small ships. By noon Broome glittered beneath us, a scattering of baroque in one corner of the great silver-lipped pearl-shell of Roebuck Bay.

From the ordinary human perspective, the town is a few squares of white-roofed bungalows among poinciana trees and palms, nestling behind the sand-hills on the rim of Dampier Creek. A league to westward, 'the Injin Ocean sets an' smiles,' and below a sandy headland an elbow of jetty a mile long swings out into the peacock-blue of its waters. Here come the luggers, from the pearling-grounds between Lagrange and Leveque, to unload their gleaming cargoes of 'No. 1 Silver-lip m.o.p. Broome,' big as a soup-plate and the finest quality in the world, and to slip back into the channel with furled sails, their riding lights like street-lamps in an Oriental village of the sea.

A mile up the creek, past the foreshore camps of a curving beach, where Malay sail-makers bend to the big white canvases, and the caulking-mallets of ships' carpenters ring from morning till midnight, is the Japanese quarter—Sheba Lane. There you may see sleek little Yum-Yums and Suzukis that, having come in before the passing of the Aliens' Restrictions Act, are elderly now, but with their high-piled hair still raven, and a solemn, smiling politeness, always charming. Here are the Chinese stores that provide biting curries, turmeric and blachan for the Malay crews; Chinese tailors bending above their sewing-machines, innocent as Smee the pirate in *Peter Pan*; the Tokyo Club and the Jap boarding-houses, headquarters of the divers ashore; the shell-packing shed and the old Roebuck Hotel, that looks out on the Buccaneer Rocks, where Dampier beached his crazy sloop two hundred and fifty years ago, and just missed the big news of a new continent. Still she comes, they say, when the south-easter sings in the shrouds before the season of mists, the ghostly *Roebuck* into Roebuck Bay, a mysterious frigate of other days, with sails milky-vague as the moonlight, and that should she pass you close enough you may even see upon her poop-deck, cloaked and high-hatted, the shade of Black Bill Dampier, who feared neither the devil nor the deep sea, buccaneer and cut-throat, figure-head of a new world. Dampier's ghost is one of the best-known characters of Broome.

'The soft pedal on romance,' said my better journalistic self, and I found romance, wearing size tens, walking the shell-grit footpaths all day and every day, for the little white town is a novelist's paradise, where truth is far stranger than fiction. I slept with a 'Dutch wife,' under a mosquito-net big as a room, with musky, dusky oleanders trailing their vivid blossoms along the balcony lattices. I woke to the sound of bells in the trade wind and fell asleep to the music of corroboree and the steady sol-fa of the sea.

I rambled the beaches, littered with old luggers and the wrecks of old luggers, and broken Japanese teapots, and turtle-backs, and fragments of pearl shell, and coils of chain that, in the alchemy of sea-salt, had become solid ironstone rocks, here and there a link visible like a fossil. I followed the tracks of Eastern clogs to the foreshore camps, and talked pidgin to the divers while their women squatted behind them on the matting-beds jabbering over the hana-flower game, and black-banged Jappy babies played about them in the laneways. I followed the flat simian footprints of the 'Binghi-pads' to the turtle-feasts and sing-abouts of the good Australian blackfellow, who works round the houses in the daytime and dreams his own dreams at night. After three generations of civilisation, he knows what a bottle of rum is, and the ace of spades, but a pearl is still 'little egg longa shell,' and he will give it away for either.

Out on the sand-hills, with the bush and sea whipped to white gold in sun and wind, I gathered armfuls of the North-west bird-flower, which grows there in profusion— the miniature replica of a sitting bird, beak, tail and delicate wings in a wonder of folded leaves, and one of the three green flowers in the world. I watched the luggers coming in on the tide, sails inlaid in mother-of-pearl on kingfisher seas, and the dinghies bringing in piles of shell, a Koepanger paddling in the stern. I listened to the click of pearl shell in the packing sheds and the bubble of Malay tongues out on the ships, and watched the colours of the south-east sunset creep over sea and sky and town in a glory of roseate light, covering white roofs and the white sails and even the white suits of the pearlers and the white habits of the nuns in the convent garden with the luminous wonder of pearls; and the moon rose, her light spreading out in a great

golden fan across the mud-flats and the mangroves, her
sweet serenity growing smaller and smaller, until she was
nothing but a 'double-button' in the clutching fingers of the
old black lubra night. And I gathered heaps of stories.

Broome boasts one of the finest bungalow hotels in the
Australian tropics—in fact, the only one adapted to tropic
conditions, and there, and in their own pretty homes, I met
the pearlers, the men who live adventure and talk politics.
A softgoods salesman will talk ties and socks any hour of the
day, but it is hard to nail a pearler down to pearls. Out on
the luggers—if he does go out on the luggers—with nothing
to see but ocean, nothing to smell but bad oysters, nothing
to read but old newspapers, and nothing to talk but pidgin,
he grows weary of 'shop.' Besides, pearling, even to-day,
is the most covert of all industries. Many a rare stone has
lost its value in the eyes of the Jewish buyers by being
handed round and haggled over. Among them was the
most glorious ever discovered in Broome, a perfect double-
button of 1916, weighing 160 grains, for which the bidding
began at £7,000, and, after a pilgrimage of the world, ended
up two years later at £4,000. It was known. To be invited
to open the pearl-box that the luggers have brought in from
sea is one of the greatest compliments that can be paid to
the visitor at Broome, to breathe a word of new-found
treasure the crime unforgivable. In quiet corners behind
the lattices, I was taken into the secrets, generally carried
on the person in a tin match-box, or perhaps the nucleus of
a necklace, graded seedlings of nacre wrapped in tissue-
paper blue as the seas from which they have come. Yet I
dared not urgent the news to the newspapers. Even
journalists learn to keep other people's pearls, as skeletons
in their cupboards, when it is a matter of friendly confidence.

At the end of the tepid day, fresh from a shower of
naturally hot bore water that smells bad but feels good,
Broome dines in gaiety and evening dress. A glance round
the Continental dining-room, with shell-fish soup on the
menu, and Etam, the Malay waiter, in spotless white, barefooted, is like the run-off of a picture caste. You hear the
drama later.

Nearly all pearlers are tall men, lazy men, men with
musical voices, attuned to speaking Malay, and, as all

callings produce their type, it seems that the lustre of the shell they handle sheds its light in their lives in humour and a nacre-coated kindliness.

The one with the pirate's laugh is Gregory, 'King of the Coast' from Fremantle to Darwin. Gregory hails from Devonshire, fought in the Boxer Rebellion, landed on the north-west coast as the second mate of the *Charon*, and shipped on the schooner *Kelender Bux*, owned by Mark Rubin, a Jewish gem-buyer who came to Broome as a 'blow-in' and ended up a world-famous financier in London. The *Kelender Bux* was swept away in the second willie-willie of 1910. Of a crew of seventeen, only Gregory and the Goanese bosun were saved. After sixteen hours' swimming half-conscious in towering seas, Gregory was tossed up on the beach at Lagrange, where he wandered for two days, stark naked and blinded with sea-water, until rescued by a search-party from Fraser Downs. They found the Goanese bosun twenty-two miles away. 'The Skipper' is a great conversationalist and a gracious host, but he will not tell the story of the *Kelender Bux*. It bores him.

The Viking of 6 feet 5, and the other Viking of 6 feet 5, are Mackenzie and 'Jimmie' James, both unending histories. Bringing down a fleet of thirty-six ships from the Aru Islands in 1915, Mackenzie was wrecked on the schooner *Alice* at Brué Reef, which the man at the wheel believed to be a low mist on the sea. With eleven coloured men, he clung to the masts of that schooner for three days. They descended to the decks in the low tides, and climbed like monkeys on a stick in the high, while the other two white men rowed in 100 miles to the Beagle Bay Mission for help. A few months later, Mackenzie's luggers brought in the 'Star of the West,' a 105-grain drop that sold for £6500 in London—menace of death one year, and a fortune the next, the average pearler's lot.

The quiet little man with the King Edward beard, who looks like a Presbyterian church elder, and is, has been pearling here among the rabble of world's end since 1887. The rack and ruin of romance, as such, have strangely passed him by, but his name will be written in historic records, and on three of H. D. Norman's schooners, the *Mist*, the *Mina* and the *Ena*, a Jew, a Norwegian, and a

o

Hindu from Allahabad were done to death in three of the goriest pearl murders of the coast. The brothers are the Bardwells, Bernard and Beresford. They shared £4,500 for a 60-grain gem a few years ago, and are two of the best-known conchologists in Australia, scouring the reefs before dawn for every other kind of shell but oyster; the other six-footer is Claude Hawkes, nephew of old Captain Riddell, one of the victims of the massacre on the *Ethel*. Hawkes is an artist in pearl shell carving. He has covered the dash-light of his car with a 'blister,' but the magnified light is so brilliant that he has had to temper it with three thicknesses of yellow gauze. He believes that there is a new fortune in pearl shell as a medium of powerfully diffused light, but he will not bother to make it. The pearlers have splendid ideas, but like their incomes and their pearls, they all dissolve in *dolce far niente*. Most of them are as placid and philosophic as their native oyster.

On a headland overlooking Dampier Creek and near the big stone gaol, Colonel Mansbridge had lived for years the Government Resident and magistrate, an erect military figure, disciplinarian and humorist, with a pet turtle, a Hindustani servant, and a horde of native cattle-stealers, harnessed to a cart and guarded by a warder with a rifle, to do his bidding and his gardening. He 'belonged' to Broome and Broome to him. He administered it well, and told its stories with a fine light humour. The most outlandish aspect of them was that they were true. There were gay parties at the Residency and in the pleasant bungalows, but, even so, the life is a lonely one. A solitary light shining through the oleanders in the evening tells of wives who will not stay in the tropics and men who spend their lives reading, reading on land and sea.

Each of them owns a fleet of half a dozen ships, but the Japanese divers are in control 'outside,' for six months of the year. A restricted alien, brought down through the agencies in Singapore and Australia, the Jap is allowed a residence of three years, guaranteed every national protection, and an encouraging remuneration, based on production. Until recently, a good diver could make £500 a year in Broome, and from £700 to £1,000 a year in Darwin and Thursday Island. This was in depression years, while

White Australians were on the dole in thousands in the southern cities.

With a crew of six Koepangers and a Japanese tender, the diver controls the lugger. There were eighty white shell-openers and many schooners with the fleets of Broome five or ten years ago, but to-day there is scarcely one. The selection of the pearling-grounds, the daily direction of the course of the ship by under-sea signals, the rendering unto Caesar of treasure found, are all in the hands of the Japanese, because, as a deep-sea diver, he is unrivalled. In 1916, in the advancement of a White Australia labour policy, six British naval divers were introduced as an experiment, an experiment that failed utterly. Not one of them showed the physical or mental endurance for the long hours under sea, the strain of the pressure, the isolation of the life.

Down in 20 fathoms from daylight till dark, with an occasional brief respite for a cigarette or a cup of coffee, the little brown man works with a grim tenacity of purpose while he is making money. His Buddhist fatalism knows no fear. His small physique, depth of chest, and remarkable muscular development of the heart enable him to withstand terrific and prolonged pressure. His courage and endurance are admirable, his habits cleanly, his conformance to the laws of a strange land beyond reproach— and if it is a fact that the pearl-buyers making their annual visits to Broome obtain as many pearls in the Japanese boarding-houses as they do in the offices of the master-pearlers—well, the pearlers find that the Jap is as honest, on the average, as the white man.

Each month on the full tide, 'top springs,' three ships call in with mails and stores, bound northward and southward, carrying away the pearl shell to Singapore. At the ebb they are left high and dry on the mud beside the wharf. A weird circumstance are these tremendous tides of the North-west, with a rise and fall of 28 feet at Broome, 34 feet at Derby, one of the highest in the world, rivalling the Bay of Fundy and the English Channel. Receding two or three miles, then sweeping in across the mud-flats, they rise six feet in an hour. Ships tilted over on the sand right themselves to an anchor fathoms deep while you are watching them. Jetties that were ribbed skeletons thirty feet high are awash, and a few hours later you can take a walk round your ship and autograph her keel.

From November to April, when the luggers come in for haven from the hurricanes, and the labour of 'lay-up,' Broome is filled with polyglot, divers with big money to spend, blacks camped for the corroborees of the wet season, to say nothing of its *multum in parvo* half-castes. At its one little picture show, 'The Sun,' on Saturday nights, you pay according to colour—white people 2s. 6d.; Japanese 2s. 6d., but behind the whites; Chinese and half-castes 2s.; Koepangers and Malays 1s. 6d.; and the humble black Binghi 1s. Manila cooks are selling their *saté* on the verandahs, Chinese gramophones and Asiatic cats wail in the by-ways. Announcements are made in four languages, English, Chinese, Japanese and Arabic. Un-roofed to the wide sky, the auditorium commands the beauty of the tropic night. Meteors fall and moons rise on Tom Mix riding on through the chaparral, and in the sudden downpours of monsoon Marlene Dietrich airs her charms and emotions to one of the most polychromatic collections of humans on earth. I am deliberately out of date. The big features come round to Broome about five years after their first screenings.

CHAPTER VIII

BROOME is very variegated. The dear, patient, white-robed sisters in the walled convent look after all the half-caste girls from babyhood, guard them like dragons, teach them to do fine needlework and cook and read and write and pray for grace, and, even so, most of them have a baby of a different colour every year.

Brian Taylor, the shell-packer, a negro from Jamaica, expressed it best, when sitting on the verandah at the Sunday School picnic—'I'll back a West Indian half-caste to race any other —— half-caste,' he shouted.

Brian's wife was a lubra with a dash of bitters. He was an expert shell-packer. With his crippled, withered hands, that had been paralysed with frost bite when he was the nigger of some Narcissus up in the Sea of Okhotsk in his windjammer days, he could pack a three-hundredweight case in less than ten minutes, in perfect symmetry and with no danger of chipping, a bearded Binghi to hand him the graded shell. Brian made good money, but he was a doomed man, and he died soon afterwards. He believed that his countryman, Con Gilmore, 'had the blight' on him. Con, the yardman at the Continental, was a keen reader and a keener philosopher, and a great friend of mine in his spare time. His mother had kept a Roman tavern in the Barbadoes and I loved to listen to him, forever crooning a little Creole lullaby to the tune of his bucket and broom, as I typed away. He told me the story himself.

'Brian's got it all wrong, Miz' Hill,' he explained in his pleasant negro drawl. 'One time we had a row over a half-caste woman, and I put a chicken-bone on his doorstep with a bit of Voodoo to it, and his son got killed and his lugger sank and his wife went mad, all in a few weeks—but I don't harbour any resentment now.' Con had the reputation of the village wit.

One day he set me a human equation typical of Broome:

Tommy d'Antoine and Robin Hunter are half-brothers, same black mother, different white father. Nellie Hunter is Robin's sister by father. Tommy d'Antoine married Nellie Hunter, and Nellie's sister Wobbili by another father married Robin Hunter, so Wobbili's children call Nellie Hunter auntie because their mother was her sister, and also because their father was her brother. Q.E.D.

Behind the barred windows of one Asiatic shop sits T. B. Ellies, the Cingalese jeweller and pearl cleaner, with untold fortunes hidden from time to time in his iron safe. Son, grandson and great-grandson of filigree workers of Point du Galle, Ellies came to Cossack as a boy, and is now recognised as one of the pearl-authorities of the world. Thousands of pounds' worth pass through his hands each year, milk-white jewels of the sea that in those subtle dark fingers glow with a pure barbaric splendour that white shoulders can never reflect.

In the little room, for forty years, have been unfolded the biggest secrets of the most secret industry on earth. Famous pearls, unlike the beauties who wear them, lose their lustre by being talked about. Here are brought the riddles of Fate for the dark master-jeweller to unravel; the 80-grain stones that peel away to nothing, the brilliant double-buttons that are flawed right through, spheres of roseate light that set the agents of Paris houses rubbing their hands in glee, and the blisters that hold mud—or a fortune. A monocle lens, a light file, a down brush, and a gold scales in a glass case, so exact that it will weigh dust or an eyelash, these are the only tools. Happy the pearler, breathlessly waiting, who hears at last the quiet: 'I t'ink you have luck, my friend.'

'You can't turn your head to spit when Ellies is working on a stone,' said a pearler of Broome to me. Four hours' concentration on a gem of serene lustre a few years ago secured the pearl-cleaner £200 and the owner £4,000.

From his lifetime's experience, Ellies told me the history of many a famous stone, the 'Rajah's pearls,' always a faultless round, of 100 grains and more, that he has skinned and polished for Oriental turbans; the seed-pearls graded into necklaces; the worthless baroque—the pearlers pronounce it 'barrack'—that has attained celebrity from its freak shape. The synthetic product of Nippon pearl gardens appeals little to this scientist. 'Colour very nice, shape very nice sometimes,' he said, 'but never last, family to family, same this pearl. Skin crack one place, come all round. Nature do better.' In 1917, Ellies returned to his native Point du Galle, and to his dead parents' memory erected a Buddhist temple of much magnificence, set softly among Cingalese palms. The interior is a shrine of white ebony, with a Buddha of 700 ounces of silver carved by the craftsman's own hands. Some day he believes that he may go back to live in an Eastern house that faces the temple and the dawn, but, in the meantime, in that little room of big memories, still patiently working, he is content to be a cleaner of pearls.

Honesty, humour, kindliness and discretion have made T. B. an outstanding character. He took me to his home at the back of the store, and showed me all his treasures, the stones in his keeping to sell, the diamond filigree that is his leisure-hour delight, the exquisite Chinese tapestries, 1,300 years old, from the Holy of Holies of a temple in Pekin, looted in the Boxer Rebellion, and presented to him by a Buddhist priest in recognition of his munificence. He had married a Japanese woman in Cossack, his two sons had been educated at one of the best colleges in Perth, and he was justly proud of them. They were the only coloured people admitted to the Residency parties, or allowed to play cricket with the whites.

One of them was already married to a Cingalese of high degree. The younger had incurred his lenient father's displeasure by falling in love with a black and white half-caste with almond eyes. T. B. paid a call on the girl in his glossy big sedan, complimented her on her beauty and virtue, but made it clear that she was not for his son. A marriage was immediately arranged in Point du Galle, and I saw Charlie depart, carrying as a wedding-gift a necklace of graded seed-pearls valued at £600. But the bride was not his type. He returned on the next ship, dutifully restored the necklace to his angry father, married the first love, and took her to Darwin, where he established a jeweller's shop of his own. When I last met them, they had a dear little Cingalese-Japanese-Chinese-black-white son, who will be quite at home in Darwin.

In the leafy lanes where painted signs in English proclaim French and Chinese and Jew and Persian pearl-buyers

—Habib, Zoumeroff, Lew Tack and Bargurdjian—in the half-caste shacks and the blacks' camps, I made many friends, all so generously interested in the note-book and pencil, finding me 'characters' in all colours, introducing their friends, Malay and Manila and Mahommedan and Ming, who had been in willie-willies or murders or the finding of a gem. 'Might be you tellim this one that time you catchem big stone?'—and how they delighted to watch my shorthand. I collected all the old dramas into a story, and a Sydney paper made it a full-page, 'WHERE GREED LAUGHS AT MURDER,' with artists' impressions of naked submarine beauties and bubbles and knives in their teeth. It was scarcely as bad as that. They are a kind and harmless people, and more law-abiding than most whites, except in affairs of—shall we say the heart? The lemon-drinks that the little Japanese ladies brought me, shuffling along in their wooden slippers with many a bow, I shall remember every summer of my life. They were a foot long, all crushed ice and deliciousness, with a whole lemon and a syrup-secret from Osake.

One morning, writing up the dawn on Dampier Creek, the Kullarabulloo tribes trailing in to Mass at the Catholic Church, and the Oriental market in Sheba Lane, all together, I heard music in a foreshore camp, not the usual meow of Chinese music, but the 'wailful sweetness' of a 'violin—lilt of Hungarian dances, the allegrettos and elegies of Mendelssohn and Massenet, the wistful double-stopping of the Schubert Serenade. I explored. I found a dark-eyed, dark-skinned fiddler with a dinghy strung above him and a coil of diver's tubing at his feet. He was Johnet Alie, sail-maker, from the islands of the head-hunters, and as his leather 'palm' and his big sail needle flew over the canvas on his knees, a strange tale he told me.

At Samarinda, on the east coast of Borneo, nearly sixty years ago, Alie was born to native parents in the employ of one Hermannbach, a German professor of music who travelled the East Indies giving violin lessons to the children of Dutch Colonial parents. Perhaps it was an experiment, or a freak of generosity that prompted the old professor to take the native boys, Johnet and Alien Alie, under his musical wing. At the ages of nine and fourteen they played excellently, with a long repertoire, and when the Hermannbach family returned to Leipzig, the little black prodigies went with them.

'My brother, he plays always more better, long way more better,' Johnet told me. 'Lady in Europe have big reception, they like Alien play. Pay very good. One time in Amsterdam, Kubelik, big musician, hear him. He play one t'ing he make himself, call him "Javan Air." That one Kubelik like so much, he write him down, play his own concerts. Alien play even in America, make much money. Professor Hermannbach he die. Alien and I sent back our own country, Dutch Indies.

'That time I thirteen years old. Queen Wilhelmina come to throne in Holland. At Batavia great pleasure, great affair. Concordia Town Hall, I play for many t'ousand people, soldiers, ladies, officials, all ver' nice. I play that "Allegro" I play you now, with little song "Farewell Melinda." Second time I play, all singing, and Dutch lady cry tears, ver' good. That song "Farewell Melinda" I not hear now thirty years.' The hand of the sail-maker paused a moment in memory of an old song, then he took up the thread again, to tell of how love and tragedy lay in wait for one of the troubadours. Alien Alie returned to the work of his master, with many pupils on the Dutch plantations. At Olehleh, on the north coast of Sumatra, he fell in love with the Sultan's daughter. Night after night, outside the royal kampong, he serenaded his dark lady, with rondo and canzonetta, winning his way to her heart only too easily, in that a former suitor, perceiving that all was lost, invited the unsuspecting lover to a cup of tea in which he had carefully steeped a deadly poison. The murderer was brought to justice. 'But what good?' Johnet asked me sadly. 'My brother, who play so well, was gone.'

Twenty years ago, idling in Singapore, Johnet was induced to come to Australia, a land of fable where one was paid in 'real gold money.' He brought with him a treasured violin, eighty years old, that had been his brother's. The gold money proved 'all same hard work,' and the violin was stolen in Carnarvon. Gradually northward, along the west coast, he has made his living, sail-making always, with a little coterie of music pupils, guiding

small fingers, white and brown, through the mazes of the
'Cavalleria Intermezzo' and Offenbach's hackneyed 'Barcarolle.'

The evening meal over, while the other coloured men
are gathering in the gaming-houses, he plays over on his
gramophone a record of Kreisler, Heifetz, Menuhin, with
his own fiddle painstakingly following every phrase and
flourish, sometimes slipping into harmonious seconds—Alie,
whose brothers in Borneo forests are blowing yet upon the
karu-ling, the painted gourd that is their one crude music,
duetting with the world's great!   As the belated footsteps
shuffle homeward in the Oriental village, one of the last
sounds you will hear is the dreamy diminuendo of old Alie's
violin.

But there were many artists in Broome.   Hurrying about
in the heat I could call in upon Murokami, the Japanese
store-keeper, devoting years of his life to perfecting a new
scientific divers' gear—a helmet, a hundred miles of rubber
tubing like a dugong's inside, no suit and no leaden boots;
or Fife, grandson of one of the first steamship builders of
the Clyde, whittling away in a foreshore camp at fragments
of pearl shell and native ebony and sandalwood and tortoise
shell and dugong ivory that he picked up on the beaches, of
which he made the most delicate inlaid boxes, a marvel of
handicraft; or old Skipper Scott—Kippacott, the blacks call
him—who once rowed 400 miles in a dinghy through
the reefs of the Buccaneers to save the crew of a wrecked
lugger, and out on the high seas had compiled a dictionary
of his own as the words occurred to him; or dear, white-
haired 'Koko' Forbes, the local barrister and solicitor.

His legal office, a tumbledown shack between Tonan
Shokai's Eastern warehouse and a colony of half-castes, was
always littered with tomes and dust, for to 'Koko' the law
was only a means to an end.   His grandmother was a
Castilian grandee, and his brother is an R.A. in London.
Always I would find him, immaculate in complexion and
attire, his sleeves rolled up, patiently modelling, hour after
hour, the most delightful figures and groupings of the
Binghi, the beauty of attenuated forms and half-baked Stone
Age faces, emotions and camp gatherings and posturings

brilliant in their interpretation and something new in the world of art.

For no one has as yet chosen the aboriginal 'smockless Venus,' child of the woodland, as a model. The muddy pigments and the 'mine-tinkit' Jacky jokes of city galleries and comic newspapers are a libel and a death-mask. Forbes is a genius undiscovered. For the lack of anything better all his masterpieces are modelled in ephemeral plasticine, which bends and sways in the tropic heat and loses contour in a week. Being a true artist, the joy of his work is its own reward. Litigation of pearls and murders only bothers him unnecessarily. A brief is nothing but a brief, and an interruption, and when a trial is over at the little tin-roofed court-house by the tamarind tree, how gladly Praxiteles makes back to his Phryne, her languorous eyes half-shut against sun and flies, an ebony baby in her coolamon, and a digging-stick in her hand.

As he works, he loves to listen to the very musical singing of the myriads of half-caste children in the laneway. They are the Hunters, fifty-seven to a family, very direct descendants of Harry Hunter, the 'Old Man of Cape Lévèque,' who was once a silk-hat manufacturer in London, and became a patriarch of the North. For some reason, Hunter came to Cossack in the bad old pearling days, scoured the islands for black ivory divers and trepang and turtle-shell, founded a bit of a cattle station, helped to build an outpost lighthouse, and finished up lying in the sands with his lubras feeding him on crabs and native tucker. Nevertheless, he was a pioneer, and every one of his half-caste sons was a skilled craftsmen. I asked Robin how his father, alone on a wild coast where the natives were notoriously hostile, subdued the wilderness in those early years.

'I suppose he take up plenty pipes, tobacco, plenty turkey red and beads and tomahawks, make friends with those natives?' I suggested. Robin surprised me with a healthy contempt of his own dark blood.

'Not on your life!' he said frankly. 'He just went out with a riding-whip, and whipped the niggers in.'

In those narrow Eastern thoroughfares, where old Manilamen, twisted like gnarled trees from divers' paralysis, carry round the mangrove crabs and dugong steaks strung on a shoulder-pole, in the foreshore camps, or at Wong's chop suey in the evenings, strange tales are told, of snides and schooners and sudden death. The best are not published abroad, but it is known that a harrowing percentage of Broome pearls have been handed over the bars of the 'shy-poo' shops, or negotiated in a cake of soap, a coil of rope, a parcel of dried fish, or even swallowed in emergency. In one pearl-stealing case, a valuable stone was sent to an agent in Roebourne, carefully stitched in the binding of a book. Pearls are so easy.

The exciting history of the pearling port will never be written now, for one by one the old hands are setting sail for even farther westward. Four of them died in Broome, even as they were telling me their best stories. There was Captain Harry Talboys, who lost a £1,600 pearl in the Indian Ocean, and miraculously found it again; 'Frenchy' d'Antoine from the Seychelles, who blackbirded the coast in the 'seventies, and lived among the natives in perfect amity ever after. He had just come in from the islands, and waiting on the verandah of the little hospital to tell me more, I heard Frenchy breathe his last.

There was Pat Percy, policeman, pearler, publican, politician, and patentee of a puzzle pearl-box, who in his young days chased Malay and Manila murderers through the maze of the Timor Islands, and, with his wife Anastasia as mate, lived on the schooner *Gwendoline* tied up at the jetty for years. I went to see him on Sunday mornings, with an old schooner bell hanging in the pandanus to ring me in at the door, and the dark rooms crammed with Virgin Maries and grinning heathen idols he had picked up in the Indies. They say that Pat Percy made his fortune in snides. He died of pneumonic influenza that raged among the blacks and the whites just at this time. A nun and a barmaid laid him out, and for a long time they could find neither a will nor a relative. We adopted his cockatoo at the hotel. '*How*-ly Mary, Mother o' Gard—an' phwat about a drop o' beer now?' it would shriek with flapping wings when the Angelus rang. Recently I read in a Western newspaper that Pat Percy's real name and his aged mother had been unearthed in Ireland. So a poor old peasant woman has inherited a pearler's wealth from a son she thought long dead.

Then there was Tommy Clarke, who found the 'Southern Cross.' Sold ultimately for £27,000, and at one time in the possession of the Pope—where is it now?—that freak jewel, the Southern Cross, so the story goes, was a gigantic hoax. A remarkable arrangement of eight baroque pearls in the form of an almost perfect crucifix, Tommy picked it up in 1874, when he was a boy of twelve, dry-shelling with an old lubra on the reefs at low tide. Clarke's father sold it to Shiner Kelly of the Lacepedes for a bottle of gin. Kelly passed it along to Frank Craig, a Cossack publican, for £10, and from him Frank Roy, a Natal buyer, bought it for £40, and sold it for £100 in South Africa, to set out on its career as the gem of the century. Those who know say that it was Frank Craig, with a clever Roebourne pearl-doctor, who mended the Cross and interposed the missing pearl that made it perfect, and Tommy Clarke admitted to me that it was in three pieces when he found it.

Tommy led a charmed life. From early youth to old age, wandering among the blacks of a coast then wild, he knew the tribal customs and languages of two thousand miles. For ten years he walked the streets of Broome with a broken neck, a surgical marvel. A temperamental Irishman, while I was in Broome he took poison. His wife it was that died, a gentle invalid who collapsed as a result of the shock, and Tommy was fined 5s. With a world of romance at his finger-tips, it was his pet vanity to avoid writing and writers, determined that 'what I know will die with me,' but, being Irish, by a cautious strategy of contradiction, mild and polite, I could always make him talk.

Tales of the sea, and its wonder down under—in Broome you will hear them, on balconies that look out on the moon-rise, sails of incoming luggers etched black on the silver; the lifelong enemies that went to their deaths in a stricken schooner, fingers knotted about each other's throats at last; the lugger that rose from the waves in the swing of the south-easter, all sails set and not a soul alive aboard her; the Thursday island woman whose body went down to Davy Jones with a Rajah's pearl in a bottle strung round its neck —true stories, with names and dates for every one.

To-day the lustre of the little town is dim. Crippled by the war, and the scattering of ancestral necklaces in the Russian Revolution, with restricted fishing and pearls unfashionable, its population has been reduced from 6000 to 1000, white and coloured, and its fleet from 400 to 50 ships. In an age of gimcrack and elastic, helplessly yet hopefully, because the mind of man is forever fascinated by the glamour of a pearl, Broome waits for the turn of the tide.

SNIDE

Onoto and Ipana were a happy Jappy couple,
Ipana strong as steel and Miss Onoto small and supple;
Their latticed cottage was in Broome, beside the peacock sea,
And they had *huîtres aux naturels* on pearl shell plates for tea.

Ipana went down diving, and he found a gorgeous pearl,
And he put it in a cake of soap and sent it to his girl
With a note in funny squiggles, which a Jappy understands,
Saying, 'Dear, be careful when you wash your honourable hands.'

When Miss Onoto found the pearl, with one ecstatic look,
She very neatly sewed it in the binding of a book;
But a friend of hers, Hi Wata, casting round for things to read,
Happened straightway in upon it, and was very pleased indeed.

So now, whenever Hi went out, the priceless pearl would go
In a hollow of his slipper underneath the little toe,
Until, in his elation, he unwisely chanced to stop
For a private celebration at Hop Wi Lee's shy-poo shop.

He went from beer to *sake*, and from *sake* on to rum,
And it wasn't very long before this Hi was overcome,
And, smoking in the corner, Mr. Hop Wi Lee arose
To investigate the gleaminess of old Hi Wata's toes.

Just then a customer came in. Hop, winking at himself,
Pushed the pearl in a potato going bad upon a shelf,
And then, while he was called away, his wife, who never smiled,
Went and sold the bad potato to a little Binghi child.

The Binghi ate it going home—they haven't learned to mash—
And his little gullet closed on eighteen hundred pounds in cash;
But valuable pearls are never worn on the inside,
And with a frightful shriek that night the little Binghi died.

His black relations wailed for him, and put him in the ground,
And now they cannot understand why, always grouped around,
Onoto, Hop, Hi Wata, and Ipana home from sea
Day in, day out, all sit about, to watch the other three.

Some evening in the shadows by the little graveyard gate,
There'll be Orientals cut up small—which ones it's hard to state;
And a very gracious marchioness will wear the pearl serene,
And never even make a guess at places it has been.

CHAPTER IX

GRAVES OF A THOUSAND DIVERS

HELL'S GATES, Fantome Pass, and the Graveyard!
'Up east' of Broome, on the western shores of
King Sound, lies the Graveyard, so named, to quote
the Australian Pilot, 'from the number of pearl-divers who
have lost their lives there,' the strangest phenomenon of
the Australian coast. For the Graveyard is a graveyard, of
ships and of men.

An irregular lagoon on the north-east side of Strickland
Bay, eight miles long by a half to one mile wide, studded
with islands, of sudden shallows and sudden depths, it is a
weird white kingdom of the dead. Hell's Gates and the
Whirlpool Pass lead into it, in the sweeping ten-knot tides of
King Sound, with a rise and fall of 34 feet twice a day.
'On account of strong tidal races and deep channels,' says
the ever-helpful Pilot in no uncertain terms, 'this locality
should be avoided.' That was why we sailed into it.

The gates of the Graveyard are two steep white cliffs
150 and 350 feet high, 100 yards apart. Hills of pallid
quartzite fall sheer to its waters, where the grey roots of
the mangroves writhe in the grey mud—ghostly, ghastly
hills that are a monumental mason's nightmare of broken
columns and shrouded angels. The dirge of the tides is a
fitting requiem for those whose graves are there. There
is even a graveyard bell, a balanced rock at the entrance
that, when the tides are running, ebb and flow, makes no
sound, but, swinging in the slack, is heard in a hollow
deep-sea boom.

Not a blackfellow haunts its shores, for its shores are
waterless. Long ago the pearlers have given it best.
Christian crosses of wood, and the sandstone slabs of the
Japanese on Aveling and Robinson and Hidden Islands
tell that story. The ominous name, the eerie aspect, and
the souls of the dead who are said to haunt the place have
driven away the superstitious Manilamen and Chinese.
Even the Japanese, the stolid, commercial little Jap, always
a fearless diver where there is money to be made, refuses

to enter its waters. To-day the pearl shell that abounds there, never fished since 1920, is probably wormy and worthless with age. Before that, its divers died like flies. Murder and mutiny among the Malays, repeated epidemics of beri-beri, a life-line snagged or a hose torn upon those jagged submarine precipices, but, above all, the menace of divers' paralysis in those suddenly varying depths, were the explanation.

Luggers dared not drift nor sail in those tides, but lay secured by a double anchor. The divers' gear was reinforced with 240 feet of coir rope. Even so, they frequently went over the edge of a cliff into a crevasse down under, or, crawling up a steep bank, found themselves unexpectedly beside the lugger. The toll of uneven pressure was enormous. In the swirl of the waters, few bodies were recovered. Fishing there in 1917, the lugger of Captain Talboys reclaimed a rubber suit in two pieces, a whitened skull grinning through the helmet. With a superstitious horror, Talboys' divers refused to go down again in that locality. So much for the Graveyard, a fantasy of unearthly beauty with a bad name, its natural vaults and its leaning stones a suggestion more of memorial statuary than of death.

Since the inception of the Australian pearling industry in 1865, literally thousands of men have given their lives for the treasure of the sea. It takes a fatalist to fish for pearls. Almost as soon as a dead man is out of a suit, another is in his place. To the Oriental, death is destiny, and the dark journey nothing more than a soul-migration. It is an extraordinary fact that these aliens come to a strange land only to make money, and, incidentally, if so it be written, to die. They have no link with Australia and its people. Most of them make their homes on the pearling-luggers or in the foreshore camps near where the fleet is anchored. They have no interest in this country beyond the bank drafts that they regularly send to Kobe, Koepang and Singapore.

So great are the odds against the pearl-diver that no insurance company in the world will grant him a policy. As a safeguard, he claims, and receives, an advance sometimes equivalent to his whole year's earnings before he begins his work. In Broome the divers demand advances of hundreds of pounds before the fleet sets sail.

Tip-toeing about the ocean bed, up hill and down dale, through coral forests and deep-sea gardens and deserts of level sand, peering through the glass for the half-opened grey lips of the oyster, that immediately snap shut in suspicion of him, the diver is imprisoned in his rubber suit with its 40-pounder boots, a 14-lb. metal helmet, and 20-lb. leaden weights on back and chest. He stands a poor chance in a hurry. The shark and the giant groper, with its mighty, cavernous maw, are his most fearsome enemies, but happily they are both cowards, and a few air-bubbles released from his cuff rarely fail to frighten these monsters away. Even so, no diver, if he values his life, will attempt to bring up a crayfish, as popular a delicacy with the big fish on sea as on land. Not long ago Tommo, one of the best of the Thursday Island divers, working only in the helmet, felt violent convulsive movements of the tube and lifeline. Looking up, he perceived a 15-ft. tiger shark entangled. How securely entangled he did not know, but he took his chance, slipped out of the helmet, and swam naked to the surface, within a few feet of the tiger, and saved his life. That was courage!

In another instance, hose and lifeline were severed simultaneously by the blade of a sawfish, cutting off both air and communication. Minutes elapsed before the ship could be turned and a second diver sent down—to find the first still living. That was quick work. Fumbling about the reefs for the pearls of greatest price, hose and lifeline are frequently cut by the corals. Giant clams, four feet long and three feet across, may snap shut on an arm or leg without warning, holding a man down helplessly to drown. At any moment, in North-west seas, a whale or a giant ray rising can cause the upset of a lugger, yet so skilled are the Asiatic fishermen that the ship is righted and the work continued without even a report of the mishap. In Broome, the *Bintang's* diving-line was caught in the crab-like semi-circular head of a powerful diamond fish. The tender paid out more and more line, thinking that the diver was going deeper, until he came to the end of it, and lugger and diver raced away in the wake of the gigantic fish until the line was cut and the amazed diver hauled aboard.

Hurricanes sweep away hundreds of men in a night,

but the greatest menace to human life in the sea is divers' paralysis. If you would learn of the men who found the famous pearls of the North, seek among the thousand Japanese and Malay and Filipino graves, row upon row, in the polyglot graveyards, and among the poor, twisted cripples of the Asiatic quarter.

The diver may be seized, in the middle of the night, by that merciless grip of the left shoulder, sometimes so intense that he can scarcely move or speak. He is immediately sent into the suit and sent below to be 'staged.' Before the science of staging was discovered, air-chambers were installed in the pearling ports to regulate the release of the pressure, but the lugger might be days on the return journey, and numbers of men died on the way in.

Sometimes the diver is too far gone to manipulate the valve that controls his ascent and descent. A remarkable little story of devotion in such an instance came under my notice in Broome, when the diver of another neighbouring ship, after his own long day in the waters, donned the suit and went below with a countryman who was black in the face and utterly helpless. Throughout the night, these two strange friends, silent, fantastic figures goggling at each other through the glass in the dark waters, remained for hours at different depths, the second diver controlling the valve of the almost unconscious man, and watching for every move of the eyes that told of relief or pain. After nearly twelve hours below, the paralysed diver recovered.

Many are the tales told in the little lost ports of the North-west of the men who have died for pearls, black men and white. The most dramatic of all was that of Lieblid, a Jewish pearl-buyer, who came to Broome in 1903.

On the fishing-grounds out from the Eighty-mile Beach, a Swedish pearler found a pearl in his first year out. In amateurish delight, he made for the nearest white man to celebrate his prize, a lugger owned in partnership with a shrewd Manila diver, named Nabos. Glass after glass of squareface was raised to the luck of the new beauty, and when the Swede pulled off in his dinghy, practically incapable, it was a bit of baroque that rattled reassuringly in his cherished tin matchbox. The story is that the pearl remained behind with Nabos, who, for safe hiding, on his next night watch, wound it round and round in a strand of rope near the tiller. When the Manilaman returned to Broome, the pearl had gone, but he was arrested for stealing it.

It was then that Lieblid, a traveller in gimcrack jewellery, in reality a buyer of snides, heard of the missing pearl, offered £500 for it, and became the eager, credulous prey of Pablo, a Filipino, Simeon, a Patagonian sailor of gorilla strength, and Charlie Hagon, a Scandinavian of sorts, barber and saloon-keeper. Clandestine meetings on the sand-hills and the dark jetty, in which the glass marble of a lemonade bottle-stopper, wrapped in a handkerchief, masqueraded as the pearl, and Lieblid was killed by a sling-shot in the cabin of the derelict schooner *Mist*, lying opposite Broome, his mangled body left by the tide in the mangroves. Mystery surrounded the murder, until, through the influence of a priest in the confessional, who refused absolution till the crime was disclosed, the Manilaman turned King's evidence, and the three murderers were hanged. Thus four men went to their deaths for a pearl which not one of them had seen.

Week by week for many years the dead were borne in on litters from the sea, Koepangers and Malays and Timorese who had died in their bunks of beriberi, divers up to the number of fifty and seventy in the year, and sometimes 300 in one day, victims of a sudden willie-willie. On all of the islands and beaches of the North-west are to be found tilted stones with a line of Japanese writing, Mahommedan crosses of the Malays, ornate graves of Manilamen, each bearing a Spanish name. In the thousand graves of Broome's cemetery, the history of the coast is written. Here, within a few brief weeks, I watched the Chinese placing the paper-money on the tombs of their countrymen, Mussulmans crying a bismillah of woe, blackfellows patting the mounds of the aboriginal dead with boomerangs, and lighting the smoke signals that carry tidings of death to the tribes. There are monuments to missioners and explorers and sea-captains who met tragic deaths in the early days, to East Indiamen and West Indiamen and Afghans and South Sea Islanders and Spaniards, and the shrines and sheds of the Oriental banquets in honour of the departed. The Japanese ground is the largest Buddhist cemetery south of the Equator.

Percy Anderson has the last word in Broome, an under-taker in white, never a top hat or an umbrella to his name. Like Hamlet's clown, he has been 'sexton here, man and boy, for thirty years,' and 'sings at grave-making.' Master-pearlers that have looked upon their last stone, Jews and Chinese, priests of many religions, his own old school-teacher, all in turn have followed in Percy's wake, and Percy ever cheerful. 'Perce and the hearse' are a standing joke.

Born at the lighthouse at Granthèaume Point, as a promising lad he was apprenticed to old Tom Newlands who 'ran the hearse' in those days. A fearsome hearse it was. One old lady is still alive who, when they told her she was at death's door years ago, flatly refused to go through it in such a vehicle.

'It had broken doors that flapped and banged when she rolled,' said Percy, 'and old-fashioned church windows, and it was one of those cold dead blacks. The fowls used to roost on it between times, and when it went out it looked more like a wedding-cake than a hearse. Washing it down only made it worse. It turned pallid. There was a funeral of one of the civic fathers; I realised I had to do something, and I hadn't the money to give it a coat of paint—half of them here don't pay to be buried. 'Give her a rub with anything black,' they told me. The half-caste boy and I fossicked round and found some black stuff in a bottle. We glossed her up with it. It turned out later to be Stockholm tar and oil.

'It was only a few hours to the funeral, and not a hope of it drying. In any case, Stockholm tar never dries. We hitched up a couple of ginger horses, and the funeral was a big success. But what with pall-bearers and mourners and all in their white suits, we finished up like a herd of zebras.'

The worst accusation ever levelled at Percy was that he buried eight men in one coffin, with a collapsible floor. 'The Malays didn't mind,' he told me. 'Mahommedans prefer it that way, that's what gave us the idea. Wood was dear, and diving and beriberi deaths were frequent. It was the Japs that made trouble. They appealed to the authorities, and we decided to put the coffin away for the time being.

We buried it in the bush, and when we went back for it for the next Malay, the white ants had eaten it.'

'Perce' has a new hearse now, but the vari-coloured populations of the little town still follow him home. Some of the grimmest jobs in history have come his way; to crawl into aboriginal mias two feet high after a customer, to uproot and pack Celestials for transplantation to the Flowery Land —'I'll bury a good fat Chinaman, and a couple of years later they send him home in an attaché case'—and, a few years ago, to attend the transference of a dead jockey from the Fitzroy Crossing, from plane to plane. A cut from the tin coffin, leaving Percy with a blood-poisoned hand that was nearly his own funeral, and the death-plane went its southward way, flying out of balance and strangely erratic, with a dead man beneath the undercarriage.

Tales that for hair-raisers make Ambrose Bierce a byword Percy Anderson can relate when he is in the humour. There is one of a Koepanger, four days dead in a lugger bunk, that suddenly sat up from muscular reaction, and of a wallaby that attacked him in a newly-dug grave on a dark and windy night—'It was all claws and a kind of slimy downiness and eyes shining until I got the lantern to find what it was.' Once he got 'the wrong nigger.'

'We just had him in the box, and he threw one leg over the side. By Jove, it gave me the crickets for a week. But I got him a couple of days after.' It is Percy's favourite jest. 'I'll get you yet,' he laughs. Kindliest of souls, he laughs his way through all the gruesomeness, and through an even darker shadow, for in the early forties Anderson faces the terrible truth that he is going blind. As the result of measles in childhood, his sight is steadily failing. Knowing that, we can forgive him the valour of a wicked merriment, and the yarns he tells that nobody would dare to write. 'I'm sorry you're not staying on in Broome,' he said to me. 'We can do things nicely here if you'll pay the price—latest consignments from Perth, cypress pine, polished oak, Spanish walnut, anything you fancy. The white ants enjoy them all just the same.'

Every year, in the full moon of August or September, the Japanese hold their Bon-matsuri, Feast of Lanterns— breath of Eastern incense blowing across the Australian bush, a populous corner of the dead that glows like a street in Kyoto with its coloured lanterns. For weeks beforehand they prepare, and on the night of the festival, when the luggers come in from sea, the graveyard is a picture. Every tomb is bearing the libation of the Japanese dead, and hung with paper lotus-blossoms and festival lanterns, little luggers a-sail against their candlelight. Even the loneliest and longest-forgotten has its tomatoes and biscuits, its baskets of manju-rice-cakes, its *sake* bowls and joss-sticks and garlands of rosy oleander blossoms. In earlier days bottles of gin and whisky accompanied the repasts, but the good Australian blackfellow, waiting outside the fence, invariably filled his tin billy-pots with the grog, and held an impromptu corroboree on the spot, so now that part of the programme is omitted.

Towards twilight the graveyard is filled with mourners, and the women's prayers begin. Under the Aliens' Restrictions Act, no Japanese woman has been admitted to Australia for years, and the dancers are a little wrinkled and long in the tooth, but the ceremonial kimonos and the silver praying-bells, and the heaping of the propitiatory rice to chanted prayers, make a delightful pageant. Now and again one of the mourners will spit backward over her shoulder, or sit on a tombstone to light a cigarette, which mars a little the purely devotional atmosphere, but is delightfully human.

At nightfall the lanterns are lit, to flutter softly in the virginal white of the moonlight, and Broome's Jap graveyard becomes a poem of the dusk. Later still, from the foreshore camps of the Asiatic quarter, tiny luggers are set to sea, that bear the souls of the newly-dead. Laden each with a lantern ghostly-blue, and with repasts of fish and rice and sweetmeats, they are carried out on a full tide to the muffled chant of the mourners kneeling on the sand. Lucky those little soul-ships that, unimpeded by the rocks and snags of the channel, sail clear of the mangroves to the open sea. Then the mourners go back to their latticed houses. Bon-matsuri is over.

Only the blue signal light of the Buccaneer Rocks remains, and the yellow moon, serenely sailing, lantern of lanterns, above that quaint white village steeped in sleep.

CHAPTER X

YOU'RE all right so far,' said the West Australian pilot, wind-burnt scarlet from a thousand miles flying in the day, 'but wait till we get you into Kimberley, up among the cavemen. There's a Chinese woman keeping the pub at Derby, and *wait* till we get you to Turkey Creek!' A few weeks of lazy luxury among the pearlers, and I was off again on the plane. The fish-traps and sapphire seas of Broome merged into the paler seas of spinifex. There is a river between Broome and Derby, the Logue, but you have to go down on your hands and knees to find it.

To the north-east of Broome lies the cattle-kingdom of Kimberley, closed in from half a continent of desert by the circle of two great rivers, the Fitzroy and the Ord, a subtropical country of 1,000 square miles or so, well-watered by their tributaries. Derby, at the mouth of the Fitzroy, and Wyndham on Cambridge Gulf, each with a permanent population of about fifty, are the capitals of East and West Kimberley, the only settlements that could be dignified by the name of towns. For the rest, there are two or three crude bush stores, a couple of hundred miles apart, two or three police stations and post offices, and the station homesteads, each with its million-acre 'garden,' built on the billabongs or the bank of a river, with a white man or two in charge and a camp of blacks to work the cattle.

All day in the saddle and most nights under the stars, the white men are a lonely lot up there. Some of them never see a white woman in a year, or maybe five, for there is not more than a handful of managers' wives scattered round on the nearer stations. In the year's work of mustering, branding, droving and shipping its cattle, Kimberley is a country of wanderers, stockmen and 'ringers,' swaggies and saddlers and well-sinkers and prospectors, men 'out dogging' in the wilderness. 'Over the ranges,' the rugged King Leopolds to the north, lies a magnificent coast unknown and unsurveyed, where later I was to sail 'over the rim of the map' in a little yacht, to find havens that could shelter a navy, rivers alive with game and fish, agricultural areas and the traces of gold and other minerals that the white man has yet to find.

The blacks were fairly ferocious up this way thirty years ago, but they are a genial lot now. Half of the white population died at their hands in the very early days. Great lusty fellows, they knew no white man's law. They speared the cattle and drove them from the waterholes. To some of the first white colonists, particularly the multitude of the gold rush, they were just niggers, the boys shot at sight, the women used brutally. It led to complications, and the innocent suffered for the guilty on both sides. Even to-day there is an occasional tragedy, not often the black man's fault. But most of the natives are working happily on the stations. The manager provides the whole camp with rations and clothing and medical attention, and there is a protector in every two or three hundred miles to see that these children of Nature are well-treated, as in almost every case they are. The man who persecutes or ill-feeds his blacks is a pariah among bushmen. Flogging is forbidden, and unnecessary, and unknown. With no care for to-morrow, riding round the cattle in the daytime and dancing corroboree at night, each tribe still camped on its home billabong, the natives of Kimberley are merrier and more contented than in any other corner of the Continent where they are in contact with the white man. Where there are only two classes, whites and blacks, and the bush breathes the melancholy of its loneliness, humans are too glad at the comradeship of each other to quarrel about it.

You see no suit-cases in the wild and wide. Swags are the furniture of the bush, and neither man nor woman ventures out without one. Slung over the pack pony, hanging from the camel, or thrown into the back of the truck, with a quart-pot dangling from the strap, they stand for house and home and life's achievement.

I have met Don Quixotes of swags, lean and cadaverous; fat little Sanchos of swags; swags brand-new, with bright leather straps, swags grizzled and elderly, double-bed swags, swags that had been to England and back, swags heavy with gold, and swags pathetically empty after the gathering of fifty years.

Everyone that wanders Kimberley has a story to tell. You cannot do justice to that country from an aeroplane. So at Derby, with the aid of the pretty and hospitable little Chinese woman who certainly did keep the hotel, I threw away the suitcase and took lessons from the bushmen at packing the swag.

They don't count time by the calendar in far North-west Australia. Up there, where life's a long vacuum, the years and months are 'wets' and 'Koolindas.' 'The house has been up for four wets,' a station manager will tell you, or 'I saw him in Derby three "Koolindas" ago.' The wet is the continuous monsoon downpour of summer that cuts every homestead completely off from communication. The *Koolinda* is the State Government's mail steamer, that hurries up and down 5,000 miles of coastline twelve times a year, the Nor'-wester's lifelong friend. To the exiles of nine or ten ports almost off the map, and the blank bushland that lies behind them, she brings all the necessities of life, from flour and potatoes to wedding rings and the bride. Every soul on the electoral rolls, and a good few who are not, are known to her. She carries them away to be born, to school, to marry, and to die.

The only regular caller at some of the ports, and the only sea-traveller north of Derby, on her two-monthly run of 1,500 miles to Darwin, with 1,200 horses to help her to stem the big tides and to fight through the willie-willies, the *Koolinda* is 2,000 tons of sheer kindliness, the homeliest ship personality of the Australian coasts, and the only thing in the far North-west never known to be late, Christmas included. So sure as the schedule date of her arrival, there is a wisp of smoke and the hoot of a whistle off-shore. 'The *Koolinda's* in!'—the news goes round by wireless, by telephone, by smoke signal and mulga-wire, and by the time she is alongside, the whole population has scuttled miles to the jetty to meet her. Even the bagmen, asleep for years under the baobab trees, wake up once a month to watch the trucks go by and wonder what it feels like to get a letter.

While the ship is in port it is a red-letter day—greetings of friends sometimes years and thousands of miles apart, the opening of parcels, fruit from her freezer, dancing under the electric fans to her wireless gramophone, friendly gossip of the Never-Never, the births, deaths, marriages of a country without a newspaper, and the only really cool drinks north of 28. Towns blown down by the hurricanes are all rebuilt from her hold. Wool and gold and cattle and peanuts and pearls and hides are her principal cargo, and empty beer barrels. Passengers range from baronets to blackfellows, with many an old bushman who has lived on flour and tea and bully beef for fifty years getting used to civilization on his holiday to the south, with a steward to answer every wish.

A mile or two from the head of King Sound, Derby is just a barren little cattle-port of the marshes, two 'pubs' and as many streets, in a fantastic setting of the mirage and the baobab trees.

A Caliban of a tree, a grizzled, distorted old goblin with a girth of a giant, the hide of a rhinoceros, twiggy fingers clutching at empty air, and the disposition of a guardian angel—such is Kimberley's baobab, friendly ogre of the great North-west. Food for his hunger, water for his thirst, a house to live in, fibre to clothe him, fodder for his flocks, a pot of beer, a rope to hang him, and a tombstone when he is dead—these are the provisions of the baobab for man. In all nature there is no ally so kindly, with the possible exception of the coco-nut palm.

Adansonia Gregorii, first cousin to the African monkey-bred, the 'boab,' as it is familiarly known, belongs to a zone of 1,000 square miles skirting the coast between Broome and the Victoria River. Magnificent specimens are to be seen in the streets of Derby, and along the banks of the Fitzroy and the Ord, and between those rivers and the sea it grows in profusion, the dominant personality of the bush. As one travels northward and eastward it loses in girth and becomes more of a symmetrical bottle shape, of which it runs the whole gamut—squat little Benedictine bottles, graceful hock bottles, stone ginger and rum and plain beer and sherry magnum, and keg and cask and barrel, appropriate in that many a time it has saved a man's life from thirst.

Water preserved in its knotted hollows from the wet season is found fresh and clear after weeks, sometimes months, and when that source fails, in the merciless dry, the pith, ripped from beneath the bark and wrung like a cloth into a pannikin, provides a clear draught, cooling and tasteless, that is often the wanderer's eleventh-hour salvation. The rind of the pods, chopped and stirred with water, makes an acrid but nourishing food that the blacks enjoy, and that tides over the tuckerless white man to the next out-camp or station; and the flower, a waxy white bloom, possesses medicinal values, particularly in allaying fever. Stirred with sugar, it makes a refreshing drink. Some of the bushmen have succeeded in concocting spirituous liquors from this mixture, well-fermented, which they insist have a fine 'sting' if made from the flowers of young trees. But they are the old incorrigibles, who can smoke pituri.

The pollen gum furnishes the blacks with a most efficient glue and a stringy pitch for the sticking of spearheads and stone tomahawks, the fashioning of hair-belts, and the feather-tufts of corroboree gear. From the stranded bark of the tree a rope superior to Manila hemp can be manufactured, and the natives carve the velvet pods with goanna, bird and fish designs, making tobacco money from the sale of these curios to tourists.

But it is as first camp and last camp, station homestead, pub, prison, store, post office and bagman's rest that the boab has twined its roots deepest into the history of the country. That gigantic girth, very often 30 feet in diameter, hollow in age, provides a natural 'home from home' for black pilgrim and white. At Calloman Yarda, in Lennard River country, I saw the boab homestead where Harry Layman tended his 16,000 sheep for twenty years, with his sister as housekeeper. At Mayall's Well, outside Derby, there is a tree-vault 25 feet in diameter, a native burying-ground; the Hillgrove Baob at Wyndham was once a gaol, thirty native prisoners at one time being chained inside it, and along the Ord River is the Boab of Patterson's Prayer, still fairly legible, a De Profundis of the Never-Never in the days when the Ord was the biggest cattlerun in the world. Here it is in its entirety:

> Oh, Heavenly Father, if you please,
> We pray to Thee on bended knees
> That you and your blessed son, Our Lord,
> Will keep the 'cockies' off the Ord.

O paralyse the duffer's hand
When he lifts up his flaming brand,
Keep poddy-dodgers from the glen.
For Jesus Christ's sake, Amen.
Now, O God, forgive our sins,
And may every cow on Ord have twins.

A spring cart beneath a boab tree, with a peg driven into the trunk to hang up the stores from the white ants, has been the nucleus of many a station that is flourishing to-day, and in the shade of the tree many an old wanderer has settled down to his last sleep. There, when they found him, they buried him, and scrawled his name on the tree above. The boabs of Kimberley and the histories they tell!

Letters graven into that gnarled grey bark will never fade. On the banks of the Victoria, a few miles below its junction with the Baynes, Gregory's famous boab yet bears as clearly the cut inscription of the explorer: 'July 2nd, 1856. Letter in Oven.' A little farther along the river-bank is the 'autograph tree,' every inch of its bole and branches covered with names and initials and dates that go back to 1884 and the Hall's Creek gold rush, in which it played a tremendous part as night-camp for the first Round-Australia travellers. Near Forrest River, a boab monument commemorates 'Mrs. J. Wilkes, first white woman in Kimberley,' and her baby daughter, who was born and died beneath it. Scrawled and re-scrawled with names that have become famous and names forgotten, hundreds of these memorial trees tell the tragedies and comedies of outback, waking many a memory. Even yet they are the post offices and grand hotels of the wilderness, rendezvous of years ahead for drover and teamster, to whom days and years are much the same. A billy to boil, an idle hour, names scratched deep with a clasp-knife in this living register, and with donkeys and packs and swags the bagmen wander on, bound for the shelter of some other boab far away.

It is a legend of the North that for its kindliness, the gods have conferred immortality upon the baobab, and that except when destroyed by fire or lightning, or other act of God or man, no one has ever come across a dead one. Botanists estimate the ages of some of the trees in centuries. Immune from the ravages of the years and the white ants,

it is a patriarch.   To all the wayfarers of that splendid
empty country, where for fifty years men have been fighting
a hard fight alone, with its misshapen body and its writhing
limbs, the baobab is universal friend, and in the battle with
uncompromising Nature, a mighty ally.

I arranged a 750-mile journey through Kimberley with a
passing saddler and a mailman, and out from Derby, in
the white blaze of tropic noontide, bounding merrily along
on the front of a truck laden with station stores for the wet,
we made straight into Eldorado.   Behind us were the white
roofs of the little town, before us the illimitable marshes,
beaches of a dream sea.

Fifty yards ahead, and ever receding, the mirage began—
great lakes blue-gleaming, rimmed afar with capes and
bays that were the darker groves of the paper-barks, set
here and there with a little island of downy trees, or the
spread sails of a windmill, and all reflected in the infinite
and dazzling blue, to beguile the senses and to cheat the
soul.   How often, on these lonely marshes, they find the
few poor belongings, and all that is left of the wanderer
who believed and followed.

Mirage, Nature's day-dream, that lends the loveliness of
seas remembered to parched grey plains of drought, that
clothes the stark awfulness of hills bled white by the sun
with the glory of tenderest colouring mirrored in shallow
silver at their feet—waterholes that a thirsting man will
never find, hills that recede and recede.   Throughout
Australia, in the salt lake or clay-pan country, where the
sand-hills are bare ribs beneath a blazing sun, and where
man and beast have lain down glad to die, there are the
big green rivers, the rock-holes and the ripples, and the
sweet tree-shadowed pools of delirium that led them on
and on.

Everything is exaggerated in that unreal light.   A goat
from fifty yards away might be a camel, a camel a shed.   A
station homestead dwindles, as one approaches, to a humble
tin shack.   All men are giants, moving in a kind of
crystallised slow motion.   An Afghan teamster, until we
were within ten yards of him, was a turbaned djinn of the
Arabian Nights, twenty feet high, and away on the clay-
pans we could see a ship upside down on the eastern horizon,

stereoscopic in detail, so clear that there was no mistaking it, the *Centaur* from Singapore, loading cattle at the wharf at Derby 70 miles behind.

A grim country in drought, and a devil's grin to the man who thinks he can defy it. For it is an easy thing to die of thirst—too easy. A dozen do it every year at the end of the dry. Most of them of them are old hands, and heaven knows why, except that they follow the mirage. Generally it is a 'foot-walker,' a bagman after a bender, a cook going back to his job.

He starts off from the pub cheerily enough, with the whole town to see him off. 'Good luck for the thirty-six-mile dry!' they shout, 'and don't forget, there's water at Morgan's Grave.'

He doesn't like the sound of that, so he goes back for another bottle of beer to keep him company. The first mistake. Beer is thirsty stuff in the long run. Still, he knows the track.

He carries a water-bag, or it may be a gallon can. He fills up at the billabongs and the station tanks, and he meets friendly blacks, who show him the soaks and the springs, or how to wring it from a baobab tree. A couple of days and he leaves the course of the river behind. Across the spinifex ridges and the clay-pans the air is light and mirror-like. You get thirsty early in that country.

He finds no water at the Broken Wagon—never seen it so low in his life—and at the Native Well the stuff is putrid, a bit of slimy mud. Bad luck! The bag is getting lighter. Still, it ought to last out, with care. A man gets drier when he knows he has little, and the air of the clay-pans is salt.

He turns off the track four miles or so, to a soak that a native showed him a couple of years ago. The blacks and the water are both long gone, and the soak as dry as a bone. Another mistake. That makes it a 44-mile dry.

The hours run on. Sip by sip the water-bag grows limper. The mirage is dancing before him, and the road runs straight into it, two slight ruts across the clay-pan. Queer how he misses it sometimes, and has a job to find it.

Paper-bark clump and clay-pan, paper-bark clump and clay-pan—an insanity of sameness. There used to be a windmill along this track—no, it was at Ooberguma, out the other way. His head is getting a bit light. He can't remember.

Morgan's Grave, they said. Stick to the road. Always make up a creek, not down it—or was it down a creek, not up it? Looks like a creek over there, where that bird is now, that deeper line of trees. This is mirage, of course, but over there, that liquid greeny blue . . . hell of a word, liquid, to a thirsting man!

Subconsciously his feet strike the tangent, the tangent that will become the reeling circle of death. Across the clay-pan the mirage dances tantalisingly on . . . fifty yards . . . not here, just over there . . . can't you see it's water, smell it's water? He goes down on his hands and knees and tries to sneak on it. Still it recedes and recedes, till his eyes dance. He pulls his long hair and laughs, laughs at the cunning of it.

His own shadow, squat as an ape, leers back at him.

It is not long after that before the swollen lips begin to whisper. He licks the water-bag, bone-dry for hours. Horribly he licks his own salt sweat, and bites his lips for the blood.

Then he staggers back to the road and camps for a bit—but it is not the road. Another mistake, his last—he sets off across country to look for it. Now and again he stoops to dig, dig till his finger-nails are gone, and the fingers bleeding.

The sun goes down and the moon comes up. He scarcely knows which is reeling above his head. The red dawn rises, like a blood-shot eye, on a world of emptiness, and a madman, naked and gibbering, with froth on his lips, circling foolishly on the plain.

Noon, and the mirage, and nothing moving.

A blackfellow finds the swag and a policeman rides out to bury him in a few weeks—or it might be never. It all depends on when they miss him at the stations, or how high the rivers rise in flood. Not long ago they found the skeleton of a man who had been dead for fourteen years. They reckoned the time from the white bones, rotten with sun, and the dates on a couple of sovereigns that shone gold among them.

There are some shocking tragedies of thirst to be found in the records of the outback police stations, and you hear the word 'perish' often enough in that country. There it has a meaning all its own. Just as I passed by, there was Foghorn Foley, whom they found under a tree at Rosewood, completely mummified in six weeks in the dry heat; Paddy Kearney, who had left his swag and water-bag for us to find by the roadside, and wandered up the bed of the Margaret River, to die within half a mile of a pool; and another, a stranger, whom the mounted trooper found sitting on his swag, naked as the day he was born, with a scattering of little yellow-backed novels all about him, and one in his hand. He had elected to go out reading.

Quite often they find them in the last long sleep, lying naturally as to a night camp, their empty water-bags beside them, and their sand-shoes under their heads. Some of them die raving mad. There are others who in the last moments scribble a note in pencil on a stone about the ownership of a pack-saddle. Some of them fight to a finish, vainly trying to dig themselves a soak—a soak that becomes a grave—and there are others who shoot themselves in the first day rather than go on with it.

For death, as life, is merely a matter of temperament. What is either but mirage?

CHAPTER XI

WHISKY CROSSING

I SET out on a truck from Derby on a blazing day in October. At Yabbagoodie, a well in the paper-barks, we found a bower-bird's playground and Bullocky Johnson. Camped beside the big wagon, the donkeys out at water, Bullocky made me welcome to a shade beside him, a poor half-blind old teamster who in 1882 had cut across the desert with his team from Charleville, and for fifty years now has travelled the trails of Kimberley, 'water to water,' forty or fifty stubborn little grey mokes in hand.

Bullocky buckles for the donkeys. 'Never run out of petrol. Pull all day an' live on anything. I've seen a couple of them fighting over the last bite of a year-old *Bulletin*. But teaming ain't what it was. Five hundred pounds the lot when I bought these, and now, with these 'ere motor-trucks, y'can't give them away. Shootin' 'em for pests, they are.'

'Got a plate?' I asked him, bringing out the lump cheese, tinned sausages and black tea that were my first real Kimberley lunch.

'Mobs,' he replied cheerfully, 'but I've had mine. A goat chop and a yam. Livin' rich.' Fifteen years ago Bullocky was eligible for the old-age pension, but with the splendid independence one meets so often among the old bushmen, he 'don't bother his country.' 'So long as me nigger don't go bush on me,' he said, 'I can get along. If he did—well, me eyes is gone. Even then, I've got Sanko' —a whistle, a fossick under the wagon, and he produced a pocket-poodle-terrier of doubtful breed. 'More grass-seeds than dog, but nine years we've been together, and I wouldn't take £100 for him.'

'I believe the water's putrid along at the Native Well,' the young driver asked him. Bullocky was indignant.

'Fresh and clean as any I seen in me life,' he reassured us. 'Only there ain't none there now.' True to all the traditions of bush hospitality: 'Have a donkey!' he offered me, with a magnanimous wave of the hand. It was all he had to offer. But there is trouble enough in life without a donkey, so I thanked him and left him there outlined in the bright sunlight, with Sanko in his arms, a sad yet gallant old figure in his blindness, half his beard burnt off through lighting his pipe with a fire-stick, and a hole in the top of his hat.

On we swung through the pindan, fairy bush of the light sand country, young gum and wattle alight with the blowing yellow of wild cotton and the green moth wings of bauhinia. Now and again our way was canopied with parrots, flashing flocks that flew screeching before us, green and gold and scarlet, and dawn-clouds of galahs, black cockatoos with their crimson tailfeathers, blue-bonnet and golden-shoulder, and the brilliant little love-birds, flying two by two. As we passed the big Meda billabong, a daddy pelican watched us from the rushes, and a thousand brolgas rose on leisurely wings into the blue.

Fifty miles and the station gates went by and we turned a corner at dusk to the homestead of Kimberley Downs, nestling in the lee of Mount Marmion. In the last gleam of day an old black Phyllis was shepherding down from the heights her flock of half a thousand goats, running among them a Cupid piccaninny. Across the twilight came the tonging of a dinner-bell, the only human sound in a couple of million lonely acres, and there waiting for us all the warmth and kindliness that are the heart of the Australian outback.

Pleasant meetings there were in the lamplight, stockman, storekeeper, and the manager's young wife, housekeeper and ministering angel to the wilderness and all its wanderers. Lubras, soft-footed and dusky, were carrying up trays from the kitchen, balanced wonderfully upon their curly heads. As we turned to the telling of many tales on the wide verandah, from the lower slopes of the hills came the click of the gil-gil, music-sticks of the blacks, in the night's corroboree.

'Piccaninny daylight' found the whole station awake, and we were early upon the track, the endless trail of the ant-hills and the baobab trees, through 'Pigeon country' along the Lennard River, ravaged years ago by a police black-boy 'gone bad,' who shot a trooper stricken with malaria, ran away with his rifle, and murdered four white men before they caught and killed him in a tunnel of the Winjina Gorge. By noon we came to Ellendale, the station that stands in West Kimberley as the epic of a woman's faith and work. Some twenty years ago, Ellendale, the property of Mr. and Mrs. 'Joey' Bell, was a spring-cart beneath a boab tree. To-day it is a cheery homestead, an 80,000-head sheep-run, with top prices in West Australian wool sales to its credit.

For years, while her husband earned their living on the adjoining stations, Mrs. Bell lived alone in the bush with a black girl named Tanjee, 70 miles from the nearest whites. Fencing, digging wells, riding round the sheep at night with a rifle to ward off the dingoes, tending and nurturing the flock, helping to shear, to build a homestead, crossing flooded rivers on the shoulders of befriending blacks, and on rafts made of pack-saddles, and riding alone, in necessity, the five-day trail to Derby, are only episodes in the story of those long years of building that this little bush woman has faced alone with her husband—kindly years for all their sternness, in that they have taken no whit of her youth and vigour and loving-kindness.

A day at Ellendale and we took the pindan plains again, through unending cemeteries of ant-hills, past Boab Tree Bore, Mad Gap, Chowalkutta and Kalloman Yarda. Thirty-five miles from the Ellendale homestead we passed its letter-box, a tin nailed to an ironwood tree, surely the longest postman's whistle in the world. Nowadays, Ellendale hears as much of the cricket as it did of the war.

With the sun high overhead, we dinner-camped at Broken Wagon, a billabong of the Fitzroy rimmed with dark and glossy chestnuts, with a name that goes back to the Kimberley gold trail of 1898. The saddler and I ate our good fresh bread and cold mutton from Ellendale alone in a mighty stillness, and set off again by a rough road across it. In the afternoon we passed Tragedy Gate, where even yet they believe that the sad ghost of a woman goes crying through the night. Nearing Noonkanbah, we pulled in beside a big donkey-wagon camped on the plain, and reclining beside it Lofty Larkin, the highest man in the Kimberleys, where the average height is six feet three. Lofty touches it at six feet seven, and takes fourteens in boots. He has to get them made to order in Sydney, and down there they don't believe it. It is something of an achievement to look upon Lofty, but he would not stand up. The offer of a drink, the desire to take his picture beside the wagon, all failed to move him, yet they are chivalry itself in Kimberley. It was not until we were well on the road that explanations came on his behalf.

'Lofty says to apologise to you for him not standing up. He knew he should, you being a woman and all that, but the back of his trousers won't permit.'

'Drink o' tea-time,' as the blacks call it, found us at the homestead of Australia's farthest-north sheep run and the crack station of West Kimberley, that passes its 90,000 through the shearing shed each year. Excellent outbuildings, well-trained blacks, a fine billabong, and nine white men living in good fellowship that is proverbial for miles, also the fact that the Kimberley plane puts down for lunch there, make it a shining light of the Fitzroy—not forgetting the famous Noonkanabah cocktail, first welcome to visitors, lime-juice and fruitsalts and whisky to taste, a stroke of genius in that country.

The twilight horizon deepened to an intense and living blue, then faded to tender amethyst. A 'big mob' of horses, shining brown in afternoon light, came down past the blacks' camp on the hill to the waterhole, driven by a half-caste stockman in an outsize sombrero, a spotted neckerchief, and a cartridge belt—a movie Mexican to the life—and after dinner we sat out on the tiny patch of lawn that is the pride of the station, listening to the unexpected sweetness of a woman's voice in No-Woman's-Land—a soft contralto, on the gramophone. There are eight stations in 250 miles along the Fitzroy banks, and not a white woman upon one of them. The men up there grow old and grey without them.

Next morning, by a muddy pool of the big river, we stopped for a chat with 'Bendy' Wilson, soldier of outback fortune, who regaled me with the doings of forty years spent in the land of gold and pearls. Shell-opening in 1911, he had discovered the biggest single stone ever found in

Broome waters. 'I was always lucky,' said Bendy. 'They reckoned if I fell off the lugger, I'd come back with a pearl.' But there are no white shell-openers in Broome now, and Bendy's big days are gone for ever. In a bough shade all alone, he sits thinking of them through the long, long days of nothing but sunlight, so motionless that the old man crocodile that is the evil genius of that pool comes to the top and watches him with a thoughtful eye.

We came in late and tired to Quambun, the travelling saddler, Mr. George Inwood and I, after the five days' journey through seven million-acre cattle runs, and not a soul but he and I to be seen save at the stations. Certainly we had sighted a few roaming natives in the distance, but they flattened themselves in the landscape as we passed. The line of the big river was but a deeper shadow of the dusk, and the homestead buildings a few rectangles black against the red wreckage of a sunset, as our lights slewed round and found the horse-paddock gates.

Already the blacks were singing by their camp-fires, eerie minor harmonies descending and ever descending, and their clicking sticks waking the night with the voice of a million cicadas. In 'Government House' a single kerosene lamp was burning, and we were welcomed by a solitary owner-manager sitting out smoking on the verandah, but the Chinaman cook was in a good humour. With relief, we unrolled our swags, found the soap, and made for the shower-room. Happily we shared cold meat and the store-room's best pickles, a lubra waitress standing behind us in the shadows, smiling. The meal over, we settled down on the verandah, with the contentment of weariness come home, to the evening yarn that has been day's ending in the North-west ever since it was the North-west.

The owner was Mr. Rose, an old hand of the Fitzroy, for forty years building up a prosperous little sheep run in country where once they said that sheep would not live. 'He can tell you a tale or two,' they had told me farther down, but it was scarcely a night for abusing hospitality by hunting copy. Far more pleasant a casual yarn under the stars.

And what stars they were! A very curd of stars, poured from the cornucopia beyond the suns across the night-skies of Kimberley; surely the brightest circle of the spheres. Stars in their courses wheeling and marching to the horizons; stars burning steadfast and yellow as the oil-lamps of a shrine; little stars that skipped and twinkled like mice through the granaries of Heaven to be lost in the silver winnowing of the Milky Way—and above them all the Emu, totem of the tribes, the great bird cut out in inky blackness from sparkling clouds of nebulæ. Lovelier than all, a young moon in its beauty, hung low against the paler curtain of the lingering twilight, shone the great blue lamp of the evening star.

They were paling in the dawn-red west when, after a good night's sleep and a hearty breakfast of Quambun lamb chops, we romped across the clay-pans and the river-flats, bound for the Fitzroy Crossing. From the air, the Fitzroy Crossing is three shacks in the wilderness. At ground level, it is three shacks and a swaggie or two, and a camp of blacks. Yet there is no dot on the map that holds more of the distilled essence of the real Australia.

There is the 'pub' on the bank of the river, the great winding Wallaberi that before the white man came was the happy hunting-ground and corroboree haunt of all the tribes of West Kimberley. There is the police station, two miles up, with a solitary trooper whose beat is 500 square miles of bush, and there is the post office, four miles away, on a flat safe from the floods. To send a telegram, you borrowed a truck or walked the four miles through the ant-hills, but they were putting a telephone across, and Horace, the linesman, 'layin' off' on the verandah, assured me that it would not be long. 'They began it in 1924,' he explained, 'and if they had started from the post office, we would have been through in three weeks about. But they began the pub end, so we haven't got across the creek yet.'

At the Fitzroy, they dress for dinner with a brand new cattleman's handkerchief in a rakish knot round the neck. You take your plate to the kitchen, to have it piled with meat and fresh vegetables from a garden that is the pride of Kimberley, and bring it to a stool and table, looking down through the window to the still pools of the river forty feet below. When you are ready for sweets, you wash the plate under the tap if you are particular, and take it back—but a more wholesome meal you will go far to find, or a companionship so hearty.

The 'plane lands on a flat two miles out in the bush, and the pilot and postmaster hand out letters from the wings. When I arrived at the Crossing, I found about six people there, barman, storekeeper, postmaster, policeman, and a couple of bagmen 'layin' off,' and through the blinding heat of daytime nothing stirs. But with the cool dusk they begin to straggle in, eighty miles by truck from the stations, from teams on the plain, camps on the fences, holes in the river-bank, swags under the coolibahs, in for a drink and a yarn, until the place has a literally floating population of two or three hundred—men that have not slept in a bed for thirty years, and never want to again. They tell a good story of the Fitzroy Crossing Inn. An overland traveller of birth and breeding one day arrived in a high-powered car, carried his neat leather suit-cases up on to the verandah, and asked for a room.

The proprietor spat in derision. 'Room!' he echoed. 'Room? Ain't there enough —— room out there?' He waved his hand to the great wide spaces, and went back to the bar.

For epic yarns and epic 'benders,' the Crossing stands alone. The only pub for over 200 miles each way, it is the one respite from the eternal loneliness of the bush. Men that have 'gone dogging' over the ranges, cooks and saddlers and teamsters, cattle-barmen in from the wells, old miners living in kangaroo warrens in the hills, and drovers who know the stock-routes of the Continent by heart, in they come, across the jagged Leopolds, or up from the desert, 'swamping' with a bullocky, staggering behind a pack donkey, or on Shanks' pony with a blackboy, striking the Crossing once in a couple of years, or it might be ten.

Cheques that run far into three figures are handed over the bar to buy friendship and forgetfulness—lukewarm beer and razor-edged whisky at fabulous prices. 'But it's not the drink,' the young barman told me. 'I've seen them fighting mad before they reached the bottom step coming in. They ain't used to company, and it goes to their heads. When the money's gone, four or five of them go out every year, and finish themselves with a gun, or perish on the track. I reckon it's the lonely life.'

Great names they have, for nick-naming amounts to genius in Kimberley. When I was there, there was Billy the Bull-tosser, the July Bun, the Asbestos Beetle, the Galloping Thistle, the Singapore Ant, the South African brothers, Inspan and Outspan, Hot or Cold, the station cook who had given his victims corned beef for forty years, and Bangtail Billy—a battered little crowd of Nature's gentlemen that the Australian bush has taken to itself to make or break, mostly to break. They gathered there in the evening, about me on the hotel steps, vieing with each other in the telling of the good jests of Kimberley, the humour and good-fellowship that helps them to carry on through the empty years; and as the Fitzroy moon came up, silvering the wattle-trees and the wild lilacs, and dropping little patens of gold in the river-pool, they broke into a long-drawn and beery part-singing:

'What the world thinks about us don't matter . . .' and with the world so far away, I knew they were right.

In the dry, the Fitzroy at the Crossing is a few shallow waterholes where the blacks congregate, with a long line of whisky-cases as stepping-stones, between precipitous banks. In the wet, it is a sweeping Mississippi 14 miles wide, and fathoms deep. The yearly coming down of the big river is one of Nature's dramatic moments. Sometimes, uncannily in the bright sunshine, swollen with rains from higher up, a little lipping wave creeps from waterhole to waterhole, the brimming creeks rush in, and the river becomes a raging torrent, a mad welter of surging waters, and fallen timber, and bush creatures alive and dead. Rising 36 feet in a night, it surprises camps and camels in the creek-beds.

They will tell you of how a wayfarer passed a dry crossing at eleven o'clock on a fine night, and an hour later the flood there was running at six knots; of the big donkey-wagon overtaken when it was laden with cement sand for Moola-bulla, the cement set in a solid millstone block and the donkeys drowned in harness; of old Dan Lynch, the teamster, three days in a tree, his body the refuge of snakes and centipedes harmless in their terror, and Findlay, five days straddle-legged on the top of his tin camp, sharing a bit of salvaged bully beef with a rooster—when he came in to the Crossing his hair had gone dead white. They will tell you of how the boys, marooned in the big flood on the hotel verandah, roped in a live bullock sweeping past in the torrent, and killed him on the spot for fresh meat.

'You'll have to get up at piccaninny daylight for your bath,' I had been told farther south. 'It's a shower in a tree.' But, thanks to the innovation of a woman cook at the Crossing in recent years, the shower had been fenced in with roofless tin walls, and only a white cockatoo in the tree above bent an inquiring eye.

The presence of a woman had changed things considerably. Up till a few years ago there was nothing in Texas could run the Crossing second as a Wild West shanty town. Fourteen men out playing marbles in the dust, with nothing on but their boots; gladiatorial contests that left the vanquished almost skinned alive; white corroborees that through the livelong night challenged the yelling revelry of the black, bullets biting the dust at the heels of a prancing stockman, and trails blazed with a six-chambered Colt through a man's hair, are some of the good times of not so long ago that they like to look back on. Mrs. Cashan, the proprietor's sister, changed all that. A quiet, motherly woman who rarely left her kitchen and admonished them little, it was her very presence that counted, for to the true bushman, no matter how dilapidated and reckless he may be, on all women falls the glamour of worship and tenderness that he felt for his mother and sisters, or the little lost sweetheart of long ago.

Billy the Bull-tosser was in on a bender, shaggy hair, wild eyes, recklessly wandering, looking for something to shoot. Gallantly the Crossing kept him out of my way, but 'he's funny all right,' they said. 'Last week the Bishop was here—first bishop we've had in years—and Bill got his dead-lights on the gold cross. Sort of fascinated him.

' "Ye better look out," he told the Bishop, "or some o' these cows'll dong ye for that!" '

They 'don't charge for ladies' at the Fitzroy Crossing Inn, so rare and so much appreciated is the passing of a white woman in the far North-west. Even the washing was given in, by Miss Australia, a dusky local beauty, spindly black legs beneath a gorgeous frock of perished yellow taffeta that I passed on to her. Sinister local rumour credits Miss Australia with having eaten her youngest son and daughter, but the evidence was purely circumstantial, and because she had such a merry toothless smile, I gave her the benefit of the doubt.

There was a big influx of strangers at the Crossing, a missioner and a travelling dentist in a caravan, as well as me, quite a crowd of tourists. The missioner was giving out Bibles marked in red ink to the savage in his nearly nakedness—the blacks will accept anything, but they prefer tobacco—and telling them the story of the Crucifixion. I asked Miss Australia about it. She obviously had to think hard. 'Him bin talk,' she explained slowly, 'white-fella, brudder belong him, bloke been peg him out longa forked-stick. That poor old —— been deadfella now!'

The dentist was dealing exclusively with the whites in his caravan under the baobabs and by the wells. He was the first to take this road, and business was brisk. 'There's a beautiful outcrop of teeth in the Kimberleys,' I was told, 'and gold fillings—25 ounces to the ton! Coolgardie was nothing to it.' Men who had never worried about molars and bicuspids in a lifetime were riding 70 miles to waylay him on the road, and 'break down' their cheques on dentures. Whisky was the universal anaesthetic, and one man shouted his mates £250 worth of teeth!

The next morning Miss Australia came along with a suggestion: 'You been catchum me tchope, toe-bacca, I been wadjum longa you!' she offered pleasantly, and took my laundry down to the river, so that I was packed and ready for the Hall's Creek mail, which is a story in itself.

Before I left the Crossing they told me to watch out for a 'foot-walker,' one of the scores of long-distance hikers that, in a strange, aimless energy, are continually circling the Continent, on foot, on sixpence, on baby food for a bet, on the generosity of whites and blacks. They subsist by means of the station 'hand-outs' to travellers, or on the goanna-tail of a tribe by a billabong, if nothing better offers, tempting Providence over the long, waterless distances with nothing but a suitcase and a gallon can. Ostensibly looking for work, some of them keep it up for years in the ever-trustful, ever-welcoming outback, making Australia a mighty merry-go-round.

This 'foot-walker,' as the blacks call them, was unusual. He intrigued the cattle-men, because in a country where bread and beef and a fig of nigger-tobacco are the only hand-outs, he was a vegetarian and a non-smoker. At the Margaret station he had asked for cheese.

'Cheese,' repeated old Jack Cameron, and fell into deep meditation. 'I haven't seen cheese in thirty years!'

When he arrived at the Crossing after a 260-mile walk from Derby, hurried into the bar and asked for a needle and cotton, his success was complete. 'He'll make a story for you,' they said, and then with a dash of real Kimberley humour, 'he's either a woman or a half-wit. You'll pick him up to-morrow.'

But we did not pick him up to-morrow, nor the next day. On those poor, eager feet, that now travelled mechanically, he was making thirty, and even forty, miles in the day, miraculously keeping ahead of our tyres. It was at Darwin, five weeks later, that he told me his story, and in that five weeks he had walked 1500 miles—Albert Raine, printer's apprentice from Vancouver, making from Sydney to Singapore, the long way round. It was nearly two years since he had come to Australia to make his fortune—and most of it spent in walking, from Sydney to Melbourne, and Adelaide, and across the desert to Perth, and again across the deserts northward. Until he came to Kimberley he had never seen a blackfellow or a kangaroo, but he had learned what it is to be thirsty. Once, under a threatening storm-cloud, he tilted his gallon can against a stone to catch the drops. A passing boundary-rider thought it a good joke. 'We've been watching that cloud for three years,' said the boundary-rider.

Albert Raine was a quaint character. A fresh pink complexion shone from beneath a floppy little panama hat with elastic under the chin. Shirt and shorts he wore, mended all over with stitches neat as a schoolgirl's sampler, neatly gartered black socks and the flapping rags of what once had been sand-shoes. 'I'm not a roamer, I'm a seeker,' he told me. 'You'll laugh, perhaps, but I've carried a little book of poetry in my pack all the way. Any beauty that came along I gathered it to my mind, and some day I'm going to write about it.' At Darwin, the Territory police found him relief work, and he saved his fare to Singapore, the Mecca of all those lonely nights and days in the Australian bush. I trust he found good luck there.

CHAPTER XII

THE Wyndham mail to-day is a de Havilland, silver-winged, that takes a swallow-flight through from Broome on Sunday mornings, with a dip to Noonkanbah, the Fitzroy, Hall's Creek and Ord River, a round 700 miles. Five days from Perth, they know now when there is a war on, and have tasted grapes for the first time where the coongaberries grow.

Before the age of hurry-up, it was a horse-team, a buckboard, and a motor-truck, in order of chronology, always changing back, in the nightmare difficulties of the wet, to the patient little pack-ponies, slow but sure. In those days the mailman was the guardian angel and monthly newspaper of a thousand square miles, gathering news and blessings all along the way, with bush poets writing odes to him in their spare time. Far and wide they are remembered yet, Mick O'Connor, who followed the gold escort mail of the 'eighties; Dave Edgar, who had half his foot bitten off by a crocodile, wrapped what was left of it in a saddle-cloth and the toes in newspaper, rode 200 miles to the doctor at Derby to see what could be done about it; Billy Smith, who perished of thirst at Dead Horse Creek. One day Billy, dinner-camped at a water-hole alone, was threatened by a dozen wild blacks with their spears levelled. Girding on his leather bag of 'jewellery'—knives and forks in Kimberley—he advanced with a menacing jangle and a fierce countenance till the savages changed their minds and fled.

It was Ted Stutland, boating the mail across the Fitzroy, who was caught in a snag and tipped perilously, just as the river came down, wafting him 20 feet up and on to safety. It was Jack McDonald who swam the horses across the Laura, and then had to sit down and re-write the whole sodden mail in lead-pencil—either that or lose the lot, he told me—and it was Gordon Whale, 'The Big Fish,' who, in a truck tied together with string, made the record long journey from Hall's Creek to the Crossing and back, a month for a four days' trip, thumping home at last through the gorges to the cheers of the population, his tyres stuffed with blankets and wearing apparel, and a horde of blacks pushing.

Even with the aeroplane droning over, the back-track mailman still is faithful, bringing the heavier regular mail, matting through sandy river-beds, thrashing along with the pack-horses up to their girths in mud, and rolling his camp-sheet at the billabongs of evening mostly alone. So it was with young Jack Knox, famous for his smile, that I made the round of good-byes at the Crossing, shipped a miscellaneous cargo, and collected from the postmaster, 'Dad' Cunningham—23 years in Kimberley and 23 stone of good humour—certain canvas bags with quaint addresses.

'Colorado Jack, Hall's Creek,' 'Ryan, Kimberley,' 'Scotty Johnson, Station Cook, Nor'-west,' read the top three at a glance, and there was one among them, covered with the scrawls of re-direction, that had been from Ireland round the world and out again, to find its mark somewhere on this borderland. We picked them up all along the lonely route, on forked sticks by the wayside, on prongs of wire in the fences, in niches of the station gates, or in the dust with a stone on them, a plucked branch or a petrol tin to mark the spot—love-letters and bills and reunions after many years, His Majesty's mails of the great outback, some of them carried for 200 miles by a blackfellow on foot, and left there for our passing.

The Kimberley mailman delivers them all, somehow, sometime. Friend and confidante, the only certain traveller of the road, to him are entrusted the closest secrets of life, wires to send, shares to barter, dingo-scalps and eagle-hawk claws and tobacco-tins of rough gold to be exchanged for clothes and tobacco and 'shin-plasters' at the nearest bush store. With a commission at every stopping-place, he battles along, private secretary and bush lawyer and nurse and doctor and Santa Claus. Riding in wet clothes for many days, menaced by malaria, and shooting the horses when they bog too deeply, he takes it all with the subsidy, part of the job. He knows that if he is overdue for more than three weeks, they are sure to come out to find him. Sometimes they come too late. In that lost country the

'Fizzer' is not the only one who has given his life for his mail.

Out past Fossil Downs, the station to which the McDonald brothers made an early trail of three years on a bullock-wagon, across the Continent from New South Wales, we began our ups and downs through the network of creeks and rivers, the Laura, Mary, Margaret and Louisa, with all their creeks and tributaries of the Fitzroy. Before the coming of the now impending wet, they were all sand-beds, and down on my hands and knees, stuffing spinifex under the wheels, merrily I helped the mailman to mat through them.

We passed a big team with natives and dogs asleep in the noon-day under the wagon, on its yearly journey carrying out the Christmas stores to the stations. 'Buryin' bones for the wet,' the teamster told us, and when we admired the physique and intelligence of one of his blacks, 'Yairs,' he agreed. 'Tiger. He's done ten years in Broome for twisting his gin's head off, and then sticking a spear through her to make sure, but he's not a bad boy.' Across the river the country opened out, misty grey, coolibah and ironwood and Daking Hart pine, splashed over with the bright red berries of mistletoe parasite. We threaded again the desolate cemeteries of anthills, no longer a wilderness of small gravestones, but a crude Rodin sculpture, weird groups of unfinished statuary into which the imagination can weave a thousand interpretations, classic, grotesque.

Flat-topped limestone hills came into view, like Rhineland castles. We dived into the Mont Pierre Creek that divides West Kimberley from East, when the rivers are up a raging of rapids, but at present a steep and stony bed. The hills were black-capped now, with bright green bushes thrown into striking colour relief, and the gum-trees and spinifex carpeted the valleys between.

Gold country. Here they travelled forty years ago in search of Eldorado, men and women with hand-carts and horses, with covered wagons and donkeys and just swags, the saddest trail of death and disillusionment in the whole story of Australian gold. Every stone has its sermon, every mile its tragedy, could we who run but read—Minnie's Pool, with its huge balanced rock, a geological wonder;

the Sandy Billabongs and Hall's Pot; Poison Camp, where
the splendid draught horses of the New Zealand contingent
died in their hundreds, and Morgan's Grave, where they
found the old prospector rolled in his blanket, pinned
through and through with spears—and as we rose to the
Pond Springs Jump-up, before our eyes was unfolded the
pageant of the hills of Kimberley.

On our right were the jagged peaks of the Mueller
Range, their red-gold slopes magnificent in afternoon light,
dredge-nets of purple shadow thrown over cleft and hollow; before us, the Slatterys, ridge upon ridge of broken
ochre, rising in prismatic cadences of colour, vivid rose and
mauve and blue, a harlequin patchwork cut into the sky;
to southward the bosomy hills of spinifex hazed into sunny
gold, undulating away across half a continent, empty and
unknown. Ranges of glory, and never a white man to
find their secrets. Through the long afternoon we threaded
them as they changed and glowed like milky opals, on the
'forty-mile dry' to Louisa Downs, pulling in at nightfall
to a gaunt homestead of livid blue standing stark in the
mighty plain. 'It was the only paint we had when we built
the house,' said Mr. Billy Cox, old-timer, very wistfully.
' "The Blue Lookout" we call the station now.' For forty
years he has faced drought and fire and flood alone in
Kimberley, winning through where so many times it has
been a blue look-out indeed.

A yarn under the stars and we were off across the spinifex,
as the red rising moon grew silver, to camp at the Margaret
River Station, a shack on the river-bank that some cheerful
soul at the end of its tether had papered throughout, every
square inch of wall, with the startling stories, race-horses,
poems and pretty girls of twenty years' newspaper pictorials,
so that even at the Margaret it was hard to be bored. I
was the first white woman to arrive at the Margaret, and a
guest of honour they made me. I unrolled my swag in the
saddle-room that night, with five strange bearded men, who
had ridden in seventy and a hundred miles from 'over the
ranges' for their mail, sleeping in their blankets about me,
and the wurlies of a horde of scarcely-civilised blacks a
stone's-throw away by the billabong. It was a hot night,
and I slept with the door wide open. I slept soundly, and

I never thought of the gun. I was beginning to know my Australia.

Next afternoon found us at Lambo, where another lonely man, graduate of one of England's best-known universities, has spent forty years in the wild bush, losing not one whit of a rare intellect and fine philosophic humour; and the next afternoon, at the pocket-handkerchief, goat-and-brumby-and-cattle run of yet another, who surrounded himself with all the d'oyleys and delicacies of a woman's home, and rang the bell each evening, in all solemnity, for himself to go in to dinner. They found him dead in the well there soon after I passed through.

So we came to Moolabulla, thirty miles from Hall's Creek, the big State native station of East Kimberley, established by the West Australian Government for the welfare and training and general feeding and supervision of the aborigines. All the tribes of 500 square miles drift in and out of Moolabulla—which signifies in their language 'plenty beef.' Greetings from a little army of practically naked warriors, amiably waving their spears from the crest of the rocks, and there was a mad scampering of piccaninnies under the very wheels of the truck. We were given royal welcome by a manager's wife, a true bush woman, dainty and sweet after twenty years in the back country, and her small daughter aged seven, who goes to school each morning with thirty-five ebony play-fellows; little Olive Woodlands, the first white child I had met in the length and breadth of Kimberley.

Moolabulla is the only native school in Australia, other than those of missions and institutions, and in its little tin shack schoolhouse, Young Black Australia, delighted with the things of his generation, shows an unbelievable aptitude in grappling with the Three R's. Each morning the school-bell brings an excited straggle from paper-bark wurlie and pandanus camp, flutter of vivid gina-ginas and trousers a riot of patches, the unruly frizz plastered down with creek water, all tidy as may be, to recite little poems about robins and the snow, and other things undreamed in their philosophies.

With melting, fascinated eyes, Bingi Junior listens to tales of Red Riding Hood and the dingo dog, and Horatio

keeping the bridge. He has never seen a bridge. Valiantly
his black fingers struggle with pen and pencil, writing
'millee-millee,' but dearest to his heart is the singing lesson,
at which he discloses a soft and mellifluous vocal tone, a
faultless ear, and a sense of rhythm and harmony that
would be the envy and the joy of London choir-masters.

No prouder parents' association could be found anywhere
than that ramshackle camp gathered in the light of the
spinifex fires, to ponder the marvels of education, as such.
I interviewed a smiling mother of three piccaninny scholars.

'Which-way that fella been talk longa school?'

'Been talk big mob all-about,' she told me proudly. 'Been
makim millee-millee yabber longa jam-tin. You savvy?'

I did. To these simple souls marooned from the Stone
Age the pageant of English letters is 'yabber longa jam-
tin,' because the only printing they see is that of the labels.
Queen Mary was 'lubra belonga Ole Man George,' and
Joseph's coat 'big mob pretty-fella patches.' The multi-
plication table they had borrowed for the libretto of a new
corroboree:

> 'Tchebben tchebben porty-nine,
> Tchebben tchebben porty-nine,'

I heard in the weird wail of native singing that night, as
I lay in the first comfortable bed for a week in that pretty
station home.

All day long at Moolabulla the bower-birds were telling
droll stories in the poinciana trees, the piccaninnies singing
in their school, and the old women squabbling in the creek-
bed camps. House-lubras, sleek-haired and tidy, hurried
in and out; boys of the stock-camps and the tanning-sheds
went leisurely about their work, for the great station, three
in one, 1,500,000 acres, is haven and feeding-ground of
many tribes as they wander in and out at will.

Darkness wakened a fantastic world of 'blackfella night-
time,' for there was an initiation corroboree in progress.
Into the shrill treble of evening crickets crept the steady
high ringing of the hard-wood music sticks, underlying it
the bass droning of the 'didgeree-du,' a pulse of primitive
rhythm, the big hollow smokewood pipe that is the native's

only attempt at a musical instrument. Spinifex fires sparkled on all the hills. Round and round them went the weird painted figures of the black men, stamping and hooshing to chase the debil-debil; Spider and Mailman and Ginger Harry, who had parked their tattered trousers and old felt hats behind a coongaberry bush, to become Jungaburrie and Milbinya and Weeringoora, witch-doctors of the Chambidyena, human kin of the leaping firelight and the tree-shadows. What dramas of the darkness were being enacted out there?

Safe in the custody of three or four of his 'mothers,' I was introduced to a thin, weary little chap some twelve years old, with pride in his eyes, and a little fear—Joogoolgu, in other words, Casey. Casey had been walked 48 miles in the day from Alice Downs, to spend the night in corroboree dancing. For another day and two nights he was allowed no rest, and the next day, as the stars and spinifex fires were paling in the dawn, and the deep sleep of outraged Nature that is the black man's anæsthetic overcame him, at the hands of the old men he received his first degree of initiation. 'Good luck corroboree, make him big fat one, all same Gubmint fella,' old Rosie, his 'aunt by skin,' told me earnestly.

This was my first introduction to the complicated relationships of the Australian native. I asked a piccaninny if a man of the camp was his father. 'Little-bit father,' he qualified.

Everyone had four or five 'muddas' and a 'brudda belonga me not proply-fella,' or a 'piccaninny belong my boy, no more belonga me,' and it was very, very difficult to sort out a family. I later learned that it is all part of an age-old aboriginal mysticism that the white man cannot possibly comprehend in one lifetime.

The language is a ripple of Italian vowels and bird-calls that retains its own characteristics throughout the Continent, though vocabularies change every fifty miles or so. Very pretty and appealing spoken in those caressing voices, is pidgin-English.

'Little bit long way, not far close up,' means that it is a fair distance. 'Which way sun!' is the clock, and 'how many time sleep?' the calendar, while 'I been sorry longa my binjey' conveys the fact that dinner-time is overdue. 'Dry water' is low tide, 'dark moon' means that there is none, and one boy described to me a bald-headed man as 'little-fella race-course, big-fella plain.'

Next morning we were off again from Moolabulla, through the vast blank melancholy of the Australian bush, its dreamy vistas, its silences so tense that they can be heard. Half-way in to the settlement we passed the oil-drum of water they left under a tree for an old stager who perished just there a few weeks before, and, because my own little 'bluey' was deemed inadequate, they gave me the one he had left. From Hall's Creek to Katherine I carried a dead man's swag.

A hail to Doughboy Tom who, with the sky above him in the dry and a camp-sheet in the wet, had camped on a windmill for nine years without moving, and our way led up through the gold hills of grim memory, now cadences of light in the cloud-shadows, with the crest of Mount Pandora caught in a noose of bright sun, and passed the lower slopes gaping with the wounds of old shafts and gold diggings into Hall's Creek. Forty years ago a town of 5,000 people, to-day it is but a few tin roofs gone blue with the heat—police station, post office, A.I.M. Hospital, hotel and store, a store that has not its counterpart in Australia. Donkey-teams, camel-teams, packs and buck-boards and travellers by boot, parsons and governors-general and braves on the warpath, everything that wanders Kimberley comes to Ernie Peel's store in time, and a merry little Cockney with many a laughable coster phrase, Ernie does his best.

'Miles' of treacle and 'mobs' of onions, blackfella's hats and whitefella's hats, pack-saddles and pump oil and eye lotion, the old earth-floored lean-to is packed with the needs of a thousand square miles, but within its walls real money is rarely seen. Little tobacco tins of rough gold from the prospectors, dingo-scalps, shin-plasters, and eagle-hawk claws are the common currency. You can plank down a few dog-scalps on the counter, and walk off with a shin-plaster and a couple of eagle-hawk claws in change. They don't like real money in Kimberley, for the only pound notes they ever see, they will tell you, come out of the toe of an Afghan teamster's boot.

I was a guest at the police station. There was, strangely enough for Hall's Creek, a white man in the cell, awaiting police escort for trial at Wyndham, and Mrs. Archibald, our happy and hospitable hostess, invariably included him in the morning and afternoon tea. He was a good soul, his imprisonment was only a matter of form in the kindly outback, and each night he regaled us with 'The Rose of Tralee,' at the top of his voice, the old song echoing through the empty hills. Each day, sitting on petrol boxes and barrels, I foregathered at Ernie Peel's store with the old hands to hear great tales—of Russian Jack, who wheeled a dying mate in a barrow 210 miles over the rugged ranges to Wyndham; of Paddy the Flat, who preceded Ernie as the storekeeper, and, not being able to read and write, drew his book-keeping; of Mrs. Dead Finish, who ran a horse-team by herself in the wild days of the gold rush through black man's country, and charged £120 a ton for her freight —histories and 'characters' unending, and among the tale-tellers I found 'characters' still, as comic and tragic as any that were gone.

From Hall's Creek we took up Harry Cameron who, a week before, lost in the ranges out near the Turner Station, killed his pack donkey and drank its blood to save himself from perishing. We dinner-camped in the bed of the Baynes, a 'thumb-piece' of Wyndham's tinned meat on bread and a billy-can of black tea, a stone's throw from Frog Hollow, where Sam Muggleton and Jack Mackenzie were mates in death. It was a trail of tragedy now, every few miles a nameless grave by the wayside—Barnett, a teamster, killed by thieving blacks, who defended himself from their spears for three days behind a stockade of flour-bags; Billy O'Donnell, dragged to his death with his foot caught in a stirrup iron; men who died of spear-wounds, of fever, of thirst, of delirium tremens, unremembered save for a post and rail grave or a name on a baobab tree.

Past Pompey's Pillar, a majestic stone needle in the ranges where a cattle-stealer hid from the police for fifteen years, we called in for the night at Turkey Creek, a wild little corner where an Irishwoman, Mrs. Ratigan, lived mostly alone for thirty-five years, the only white woman in 250 straight miles. Still she retains her sweet Irish dignity and a County Longford complexion under all the suns of Kimberley. I learned what the aviators meant when they talked so knowingly of Turkey Creek. Two white wanderers of the hills there had recently fought a duel. One of them had shot the other through the head, and he was lying at death's door in Wyndham. 'Over a little yella-fella,' said the bushmen. 'One of the lubras has had a half-caste kiddy.'

'And each one blamed the other?' I suggested, with my southern reasoning.

'No, each one reckoned it was his!' they corrected me.

Past Paperbark Springs, Cow Creek, Hell's Gates, Cheese Tin, Black Flag—the weird litany of bush names passed us by, nothing but names in a wilderness of semi-tropical beauty, camps long forgotten, permanent water, or bottle-tree meeting-places, but never a human dwelling on a 200-mile road. Through the magnificent heights of the Cockburn Range and the tall grasses and the dream world of the marshes, we came at last to Wyndham.

CHAPTER XIII

THE JOCKEY IN BLACK

THE thermometers, and the mosquitoes, are three feet high at Wyndham. In the world's humidity stakes, Darwin and Wyndham run a dead-heat with the Gold Coast.

A picturesque spot, in more ways than one, is this far-north cattle-port, 2000 miles north of Perth, only 260 miles by sea from Darwin, but nearly a thousand overland—you have to go a long way to get round.

The best story they tell there is of the publican who died on a Sunday morning with the key of the bar in his pocket. They buried him with some haste—they must in Wyndham—and they dug him up on the Monday morning to retrieve the key of the bar. Blame the humidity, the blazing sun and the rains.

The regular population is about seventy, but while I was there, there were five weddings and five births in one week. In every one of the hotel bedrooms is a huge white thermometer tacked to the wall, so that you always know the worst, waking and sleeping. From October to April, the mercury seldom falls below the century mark.

For 200 miles south straggle the rugged and beautiful ranges of East Kimberley, and for 70 miles north the equally rugged and beautiful Cambridge Gulf, both an apoplectic purple in the haze of the heat.

Surrounded by marshes, the town, which consists of a jetty, store, post office, and a double row of shack shops, mostly Chinese, hangs on grim death to a narrow fringe of mangrove shore at the foot of the Bastion and Mount Albany. These two majestic ledged hills rise a thousand feet sheer from the houses in lofty disdain, as though they were about to kick them off into the sea. Crocodiles occasionally show an expectant snout along the waterfront, and over at the big State meatworks, a mile across the marshes, in sluices that are a crocodile's heaven of blood and mud, inert and ugly they lie, to use a Kimberley phrase, 'in mobs.'

The *Koolinda* puts in with the necessities of life every two months, on her extended trip to Darwin—and calls back for the empty barrels. In April she brings up an army of three or four hundred meat-workers for the season, managers and their wives and families, cashiers and carriers and canners and clerks and *sans-culottes* of slaughtermen, wading to the knees in blood. With picture shows, cricket matches and a refrigerating works, Wyndham becomes a busy suburb of Perth. But in September they all sail south again, leaving the marshes and the purple gulf to a few old hands, and the finest sunsets this side of Paradise.

There is magnificent prairie country behind Wyndham, and most of the million-acre runs can muster 20,000 head. A good many of the settlers rode over from Queensland, or were three years on the track in the early days with cattle. A heroic country, even if the salt marshes do make it a thirsty one. Is it any wonder that when Wyndham sends up an S O S that it has run out of beer, ships go speeding round Australia on a 4000-miles non-stop from Adelaide or Sydney, both engines full ahead?

A few years ago the *Koolinda*, on her last trip before 'the wet,' ran on a sandbank north of Derby and had to put back to Fremantle for repairs. Wyndham was appalled. The year's work with the cattle was over. Stockmen and drovers and station managers were riding in from hundreds of miles away, and there was nothing in the pub but cherry brandy! Nobly Bill Flinders, six feet or so, and a hard-bitten son of the country, leapt on a truck and set out for Derby by the fire-ploughed road through the ranges and on across the pindan. As he was loading up at the hotel there, the monsoon swept down upon him. Did he quail? Not he. In storm and stress, those 690 nightmare miles whizzed under his threadbare tyres in thirty-six hours. As he thumped in across the home marshes with a thunder-cloud behind him and the wet clay flopping into the truck, from the parched throats of all Wyndham rose the strains of 'The Conquering Hero,' and even the Methodist missioner could scarce forbear to cheer.

The meat-workers had all gone south, but there were one or two 'stories'—a man named Riddell shipping eight tons of birds to London. With a few whites and blacks employed to help him, he had been snaring them at the billabongs at the end of 'the dry,' when the desperate little things came in for water.

A throw-net at a pool in the early morning snared as many as seventy dozen of the brilliant little painted finches and love-birds and doves, and the lubras caught emus and brolgas for him. He sold them to Continental bird-merchants, to be caged as curios in London fogs, and for over twenty years they had provided a trip to Europe for him every year. He told me that before the psittacosis scare, the glamorous parrots of the region had netted him a revenue of £400 per annum.

Another character was a prospector, Dan Hooley, bound for Mount Dockerill, about 300 miles away, with a huge white bull-terrier and her half-grown litter of six pups, trained to be savage. He said 'the gold was good and the blacks was bad' at Mount Dockerill.

Wyndham is off the map when the big wet comes down between December and March. The aeroplane cannot land north of Derby. Christmas is carried out to the far stations by donkey-teams, and sometimes, with the rivers in flood, arrives in March, the plum-puddings mouldy, the three-tiered cakes long stale, and all the cards and presents, and maybe the mailman, covered with tropic fungus. They hold Christmas when it comes. The Government cannot help it. The mailman cannot help it. It is just—the wet.

I arrived at the end of October, and announced my intention of getting through to Darwin. There is no mail road in this remotest corner of the Continent—800 miles of melancholy bush scarcely tenanted, the thermometers up in the hundreds, a network of creeks and rivers before us, and the monsoon threatening. All Kimberley was dubious but hopeful. Nothing is impossible or out of the way to the bushmen, not even a woman's whim.

With the eager co-operation of the whole population, I was immediately offered (a) a trip through with Vestey's mailman, Mr. 'Piggy' Williams, and his packhorse team, travelling six weeks to Darwin at 20 miles a day, a camp-fire every night in the wilderness, provided it was dry enough to light one. I had never met Mr. Piggy Williams, but that makes no difference: all Australian bushmen are knights-errant; (*b*) a helter-skelter flight through with a North Australia policeman and four Chinamen, one of them under arrest for smuggling opium or stealing pearls, or some other purely tropical offence; (*c*) with the best luck in the world, half a trip through with one of the finest and oldest pioneers of the north, Mr. M. P. Durack. Mr. Durack had received an S O S from one of his border stations that, with sugar and tobacco running short, the manager could not keep the blacks to the brumby muster. He decided to make a swift dash out to Auvergne, 160 miles away on the rim of the 'wild nigger hills' across the Territory border. The Victoria River Depot Races would soon be held, and there was 'sure to be something' to carry me on, 250 miles to Victoria River Downs, and from there another 250 across to Katherine, from which it was a safe 200 up to Darwin by rail.

It was a chance, and a good one, providing the rains did not catch us. If they did, we might be marooned anywhere, with food and shelter or without it, for a month or more. My only alternative was to go home with the downward *Koolinda,* or to remain for two months in Wyndham; but now I had the tang of the wild and the star story in my blood, so it was with one of the first white men to set foot in Kimberley, and a member of one of the bravest pioneering families in all Australia's history, that I triumphantly set out. To M. P. Durack, every mile of the way was a picture of the past of fifty years ago, when he, with his uncles and brothers, landed from a little boat on these uninhabited coasts, and later had helped to drive some thousands of Durack cattle 3000 miles and three years overland from the settled Australia to the stark wilderness. In those days the blacks were bad indeed. Four of the Duracks within a few short years had given their lives to the colonisation of virgin soil.

Through the hills and the limitless pastures, past the Bend of the Ord, a gorge of glory, and on through the grey quietness of the bush, we travelled the first hundred miles to Argyll, the head station, where, after a night's rest, with the best hospitality from everyone down to the smallest pot-bellied piccaninny, who could give us nothing but a smile, we crossed the Territory border, a string tied round a tree, and made on, past Newry homestead, with its suspension bridge across the Keep River, and another seventy miles to Auvergne. Auvergne has collected in its history many a native murder and sudden death, and every station from there on had its tragedies, recorded in the baobab trees and the post and rail graves that were the only sign of the human presence.

A woman lives out there, often alone for months, one of the most remarkable women in a Territory of remarkable women, Mrs. Harry Shadforth, with a Continental education and a ready wit, and not a soul to talk to sometimes for a year save the blacks in the homestead camp. Not only has she droved cattle overland for 2000 miles on occasion, but she has made a pretty home on the edge of beyond. With the lubras watering the garden on the bank of the Baines, she has charmed up roses and carnations and sweet English wallflowers just because every tropical agricultural adviser in Australia said that it could not be done. To the north of Auvergne is the kingdom of the wild blacks, the only outpost being the Fitzmaurice Station on a tributary of the Victoria. Last year two prospectors were murdered out of hand up there, and it took the police three months to catch the guilty natives, an exploit that goes down in North Australian history as one of the most dramatic chases on record.

Hardly had we settled to the home-made cakes and hospitality of Auvergne than there was another dust on the plain, Mr. W. R. Easton, a Surveyor-General of the Territory, making a dash for Darwin before the wet, after a patrol of most of the unexplored country of the Continent. My luck was in. His kindly offer of transit to Katherine whisked me across the remaining 400 miles, through the unnamed ranges, through the Jasper Gorge, a spectacular scrap of scenery where the savage tribes lay in wait for the teamsters not so long ago, their spears hurled into the gully from the towering cliffs—and through Victoria River Downs, the largest cattle-run in the world. Victoria River consists of 13,000 square miles of country, nine out-camps, and 150 black stockmen, with 150,000 cattle year by year being turned into Bovril. A night there as the guests of Mr. and Mrs. Martin and their family, and we were off in the early morning, another 250 miles across the crudest roads within imagination, past the two isolated stations of Willaroo and Delamere, a solitary manager on each of them, with the wet close upon us, to Katherine. We did it in a day. On the way, we met the straggling population of about a thousand square miles—and there must have been nearly a dozen—making out to the Victoria River Depot for the races.

The bush races! He staggers out of the spinifex on a fire-ploughed road through nothingness, wild-eyed, wild-haired, suggesting waterless distances and a tale of the nick of time. He drains the water-bag, and then holds out a torn and dirty envelope that has been clutched in his hand all the way from Mad Gap.

'£5 straight out and £2 for a place on Gun-shot!' he gasps, and romance goes down with a small sighing sound. It is only another Cup bet.

While the fever of spring meetings is raging in Australia's cities, the sporting enthusiasm burns just as brightly in the pindan deserts of the North-west, and along the great rivers of the Territory. With no spring to speak of, the outposts of civilisation have their annual bracelets and cups and handicaps, and the increasing heat of the end of the year finds them arguing in bars and camps over a sure thing, talking in their sleep of weight for age. In the lost places where Christmas goes by unnoticed, race day is the event of the year.

The outback race season begins at Onslow, works upward through Roebourne, Hedland, Marble Bar, Derby, the Fitzroy Crossing, the Ord and Hall's Creek, across the Territory border to the Victoria Depot, Katherine, and Brock's Creek, on the way to Darwin. Horses are hacks and grass-feds from the drovers' plants and the stations. Jockeys are stockmen and black boys, wearing the satin jacket and flying colours for a brief hour in the year of workaday.

The day before the races sees the people of a hundred-mile radius, black, white and variegated, making in to the Mecca of the moment.

Up through the dazzled mineral hills, over the tide-flats, or through the wooded gorges and crocodile crossings they come, men, women and children on buggy, donkey-wagon, truck, motor-car and motor bike, with cartloads of blacks in the rear, a Darktown joy-ride.

For many it is the only trip in twelve months, for some, in five or even twenty years. Conveyances pull up anywhere in a scattering of shade. Horses are tethered, and swags unrolled and camps pitched in the creek bed under the trees. A hundred and ten at a meal outside and inside the bush store make a crowded hour for the store-keeper's wife, and all is beer and merriment.

Race-course accessories have come from Perth and Sydney on the aeroplane, record cargoes of frills, c.o.d.— you never know what the frock is like until you open the parcel. The women are fine and festive enough to move to band music on any metropol.tan lawn, but, alas! there is neither a band nor a lawn in the whole of the North-west —just a track worn round and a bough-shade grandstand.

The lubras, full of laughter, are wearing bright gina-ginas, with sunshades and gay scarves, but never with shoes. Bucks with scarlet neckerchiefs stalk proudly beside them. Everybody, white and black, brings the baby.

The saddling paddock, the flat and the St. Leger are just part of the great wide spaces, and the judge's box the frame of a windmill or a donkey-wagon. There is always a bar, and plenty of billy tea.

In from the boundary fences, the bores and the homesteads they come, trotting along in the pack-teams, in all humility, Dingo and Pretty Lass and Bony Bream, the favourites and forlorn hopes of the great event.

Larger towns make up their own totalisator, but along the Territory and Kimberley courses a bookmaker collects the lot. Big cheques are 'knocked down' without a tremor. Up to £1000 changes hands at one race meeting of seventy people, and £50 bets on each race are recorded from men to whom years of work and wandering suddenly seem a detail. There are some who come to the bush races with a swag and go home in a motor car—and *vice versa*.

The police trooper or the nearest doctor is invited to be judge—at Oodnadatta recently it was the visiting clergyman!

The horses file out, Irish colours in the ascendancy, the

clerk of the course on one of the left-overs, or maybe a mule. The handkerchief goes down. The fun begins.

Quite frequently the whole field goes bush after a brumby leader. Quite frequently one of the horses meets a remembered friend of the pack-team, and in all docility slips into line behind him till the race is over. In the last mad rush down the straight, a too-anxious black jockey has been known to pull up, wheel round, study the prospects, and stir up again for the finish.

In the places where there is no pub, the day closes with a grand ball to accordeon music, on a spread tarpaulin by the headlights of a truck, and a corroboree to a didgeree-du, down by the creek.

Jim Maloney is the Knight of the White Lettered Bag, the one and only bookie of the outback, shouting the odds from a beer-case. In the large towns, like Darwin and Alice Springs, where there are registered clubs, he employs a clerk and penciller, but out in the bush he depends on himself and Billy-Joe from Argyll. It is mostly pencilled chits and dingo-scalps that go into the bag out there.

Strange things happen at bush race-meetings—engagements, and elopements and funerals—and sometimes the odds are long. Beer and the heat are a hard argument for men who have lived hard, and a prompt bush burial is part of many a day's festivities. They take it casually enough.

North-west of Convention, the grave has no victory. When a man is through the last gate, there is little energy for mourning. A few planks are rigged up about him, or maybe he is wrapped in his camp-sheet, and out on a truck he goes, a mile over unmade, stony roads, to the blazing ironstone patch they call a cemetery. Where there is a settlement within a hundred miles, coffins are made at the blacksmith's shop, mostly of petrol cases. Freights make living too difficult to allow of dignity to the dead.

An occasional missionary travels the roads, but he never arrives in time for a valedictory somehow. Twenty minutes out and back is ceremony, an 'Our Father' and 'May the Lord have mercy on your soul' the usual service. Then it is 'all hands back to the pub' for a send-off, the strange unspoken homage, expression of pent-up sorrow for a mate that is gone.

There, where life is just a greeting in passing, they know how to die. In Broome I heard of the man whose last words were a shout for all hands, and at the Fitzroy of the world-weary drover who plunged into the flooded river from the hotel verandah with a casual 'Good-bye all!' At Derby, funeral services go solemnly and according to the book, but there it has been a tradition for years that 'Last man back shouts for the mob,' and the whole cortége, including the donkey-team, comes back at a gallop.

But Hall's Creek tells the best story, the story of a race-meeting a few years ago when Harry Hopkins died—but his name was not Hopkins. Harry was all 'cleaned up' after a 200-mile ride to the festival. He arrived early, drank deep, and lay down in the shadow of the booth before the first race. The sun shifted round and found him. His breathing grew heavier, his face a darker red. The babble of race talk did not wake him, nor the sound of the galloping. In the blaze of afternoon somebody put a camp-sheet over his head, and it was not till a horse he was backing won in the second last race that they remembered him again. Old Hopkins would not wake.

They tested him out with a pin and a mirror, then Barney O'Leary went for a bottle of whisky, and opened it at his ear. 'He's dead all right!' they said.

They put a couple of pennies on his eyes, tails up. They rolled him up in his camp-sheet and carried him over into the shade near the grave of Moosie Khan, the Afghan. Nobody knew his religion. Most had forgotten their own. A few prayers petered out half-way. Then someone at the back of the little bare-headed crowd had an idea:

'Fo-or
            He's a jolly good fellow!'

the old tune rang out, beery but heart-felt, the song of good mateship Australia over. Every man there took it up, and, to the long-familiar swing of it, the last rays of the sun slanting in on his last camp, old Harry Hopkins went on.

Book II

ROYAL MANTLE OF THE TROPICS

CHAPTER XIV

THE APEX OF AUSTRALIA

IT is not until you cross the Territory borders that 'the royal mantle of the tropics' falls upon the West Coast. The far north of Australia comes as a splendid surprise. There are no infinities of crocodile mud-flats and deserts of desolation that wring the heart, such as one would believe from the vagueness of the map, but a country of wonderful permanent rivers, some of them 250 miles long, rising ninety feet each year in flood, breath-taking in their beauty—Nature run riot in fertility to a dense tangle of jungle extending 200 miles south from the sea. Rankly tropical, the very far north is a stranger to the rest of Australia. Had the coastline extended for another hundred miles, we would have had the jaguar and the monkey.

Blessed with prolific tropical soils and sub-soils, with a mineral belt of potential wealth that extends for 10,000 square miles, and the most extensive cattle-breeding country of the Continent, to-day all unexploited, the Territory is that saddest of all prospects, a country without a future. The great need is population. Census returns disclose that there are 3306 Europeans in 553,000 square miles, and 744 full-blooded non-Europeans, and 800 half-castes, and, roughly estimated, 25,000 blacks. So that the black outnumbers the white at nearly ten to one. When it is remembered that at least 10 per cent. of this European population consists of Government servants in residence for three years, that the half-caste population has doubled itself within the past decade, and that the increase in the white is about seventy persons per annum, the future of White Australia in the north looks very black indeed.

Wandering there, I stumbled upon all the traces of a century of failure. I heard everywhere the stories of white men taking on a job too big for them. Too many of the deaths are grim, untimely tragedies, of thirst, and fever, and suicide. The only country of its latitudes where a determined and sustained endeavour has been made to colonise exclusively with the labour of the white man, as yet, because there are so few of him, the jungle wins.

Outside Darwin, that 'gateway to the East' that never opened, and the tiny settlements of a railway that straggles away into the bush, are but a scattering of cattle stations, 50, 100 and 200 miles apart. Each a million acres of empty bush, they nearly all belong to the great English firm of Vesteys, with a manager and a few blacks on each to hold the country, and a white woman in residence here and there. Wives are not encouraged in the wilderness. The reason given to me was that the men hang round the homestead too much when there is a woman to keep it comfortable, instead of getting out with the cattle. The results of this virtual martyrdom of segregation are often obvious and regrettable. For the rest, a handful of buffalo-hunters and prospectors for gold, and old pioneers, 'just sitting down,' as they told me, by a billabong, hoping for the best, and letting the dreamy tropic days go by. They have done their bit, but the youngsters will not follow.

Mines of gold and tin and lead and silver and wolfram, that yielded hundreds of thousands of pounds' worth in the 'eighties and 'nineties, are deserted. Cotton of a hundred plantations is now practically indigenous. Coco-nuts and bananas and blue maize and millet and rice and vanilla and indigo are threaded through the native bush, and the bushmen are lighting their pipes with what once won prizes as the finest cigar leaf, plucked wild at a gilgai. The buffaloes, Brahma cattle and sturdy little Timor ponies that the early settlers brought to the yoke of colonisation are galloping mad along the flats of the Mary and Alligator rivers, and at Port Essington, the shy little English deer, never molested by the black tribes, still peer between the leaves of the pandanus. For the Territory is too generous. Everything flourishes far too well, making it difficult for a few white men to cope with. Superstitious old hands, reviewing its history for seventy years, told me that the country was cursed, but it is cursed only with the mistakes of misunderstanding and the hoodoo of its loneliness.

The dominant need is for the great national stimulus of home life, a blessing it has never known. In a word, its crying necessity is more white women, who will share the lives of their own white men so patiently plodding on through the years, and rear children who understand and love the country for its own sake. Statistics show that there are less than 1500 white women in the Territory, one to every 360 square miles!—and most of those in Darwin. Wherever there is a white woman on a station—and sadly few there are—that station is a pleasant and prosperous one, and her influence is deep and illimitable. The blacks are clean, the homestead is clean and pretty, the stockmen are cheery—they have a home to come to, someone to listen to their troubles, and see that they change their shirts, and write to their mothers, and jest with them, and keep them human. In a climate that is perfect for most of the year, and, at its worst, little more trying than the summer heat of Sydney and Melbourne, these women, making home for their children in the health and freedom of the bush, are holding the North for us, which without them must slip back, ever and again, to a haunted, homeless loneliness. Far greater than the need of £15,000,000 railways and naval bases and garrisons and aerial expeditions and the discovery of gold is the Territory's dire need of the white woman.

After a pretty hard day, the Surveyor-General and I pulled in to Katherine township at nightfall, to be met by a hearty Irishman surveying the world in company with a lean and lanky pet brolga from the front verandah of the pub.

'Where's your otto-mattick?' he demanded of me. 'Ivery sthranger that comes to the Katherhyne has a camera in wan hand and an otto-mattick in the other, kapin' th' wild men covered while they take our phótygraphs.' But the wild men were anything but hostile, the boisterous cool shower a joy, and the great glass jugs of goats' milk on the dinner-tables a good refresher.

Katherine township is a few angles of tin roofs among the trees on the banks of the beautiful Katherine River, winding a hundred miles down through the jungle to join the Daly. The blacks are numerous and picturesque all along that river-bank, bodies of wonderful symmetry, skins of silky texture and black as boot polish. All they wear is a scarlet naga and a few bamboo armlets, except when they come in to the town to do odd jobs.

There were a few railway cottages, a one-roomed school with three white pupils and eleven Chinese, and a good few camps of old white wanderers 'retired,' spending their pensions on flour and tobacco, each with a nigger as gentleman's man to catch him kangaroo and barramundi.   One of them, Raparee Johnson, was living in an ingenious adobe home he had made of ant-bed reinforced with bottle-tops.

Tim O'Shea's pub was the centre of attraction, with a festoon of home-made electrics picking it out from the Chinese shacks at night.   It was said that Tim had taken £90,000 in the railway extension days of 1926, when thousands of men of all nations were camped in gangs on the line.

Some epic cheques dissolve, like Cleopatra's pearl, in the beer glasses of these outback pubs.   The men of the bush watch them fade away without a twinge of regret. Katherine boasted the record, £700 in a scrap of paper that one Len Adams, once passed over the bar.   He was a young English teamster from the railhead out to Wave Hill, 800 miles there and back.   Finishing up five exemplary years, he sold the horse-team, drew his cheques, and set out for the lights of London.   At Katherine he stopped for a whisky, and forgot where he was going.

The cheque and the celebrations lasted six months, and then Len Adams went out to Victoria River to find a job. He rode in to the station on a January day, and walked over to the well for a drink of water.   The pannikin fell from his hand—and Len Adams was a bar-room yarn.

A tragic country, with the need of women to care for its men.   Of all those commemorated in that graveyard in the grasses, very few had 'died in their beds.'   It isn't done.

A day later, I left for Darwin on the Sentinel.

'First Ladies.'   A bunch of lubra faces framed in the carriage window, all with a tooth or two knocked out, and all laughing, passengers on the Birdum-Darwin express, that stops every time a bushman leaning against a swag gives her a hail.

There is a train a week in the Territory, and it runs practically the whole gamut of Territory history and scenery, one of the world's best for interest and diversion, though it carries more swags than suit-cases.   All the blacks of the countryside put on their dungarees and Mother Hubbards, and straggle down to the sidings to watch it go through, and old settlers, camped on the creeks, rectify their calendars by its whistle. They call it Leaping Lena. One terminus is Birdum, three shacks in the bush, and the other the first breaker of the Indian Ocean. The northern section of the trans-continental railway begun in the 'eighties and never finished, it has taken the little 3 ft. 6 in. gauge fifty years to struggle down 300 miles, and there are still 700 miles of wilderness to cross before it links up with the southern section at Alice Springs. But there are grey-headed optimists who believe that one of these years they will see it completed, to bring population and prosperity to the North.

In the pungent wet season it was here that I began to smell the Territory, Chinese scents of lancewood and steaming lagoons and jungle grasses, blacks and pandanus, and later the reek of the mangrove creeks and the crocodile rivers. The Sentinel—Leaping Lena's official name—is a string of scarcely glorified cattle trucks that never fails to provide a good jest at the expense of overland travellers. So uncomfortable are its narrow wooden seats that those who know them always prefer to sit on the floor. But there is a humour and a hearty democracy about it that no other train in Australia can boast. The guard has been known to bring round 'beer for all aboard' on the Sentinel.

Passengers are as varied a collection of human oddities as the world can offer—buffalo-hunters and anthropologists, mining agents and half-castes, A.I.M. sisters on errands of mercy bent, white men seeking medical attention for spear-wounds, native murderers, globe-trotters and stockmen, Russian peanut-farmers and Chinese women in their national dress, with frequently a tribe making down to Darwin for 'bigfella corroboree' in the compound there. A number of native prisoners from the Centre were aboard, to be tried on a charge of murder. Passing a good patch of melons, the Sentinel slowed up, and the natives were freed to go and collect them. Well under way, they struck a better patch of riper melons, threw the first lot overboard, and let the natives off the chain again.

Past the few Chinese shacks of Mataranka, and Marranboy, nothing but a sign-post leading to abandoned tin diggings twelve miles away, we left the Katherine for lunch at the inn, kept by Mr. Tim O'Shea and his seven pretty daughters, a galaxy of Irish beauties unique in the Territory, and pulled in for the night at Pine Creek, where the grasshoppers are as big as birds and the frogs have voices like goats. Howley and Union Reefs and Zapopan, Rum Jungle and Grove Hill and Brock's Creek are tiny settlements with two or three whites and half-castes and blacks, ghosts of the once-great gold mines. At Stapleton I met the Sargents, a Canadian family, who demonstrate just what the right type of settler can accomplish in this country. Mother and father and a large family of mostly girls came to Stapleton twelve years ago, and they now grow and manufacture everything for their own sustenance—cassava and rice-flour for their bread and buns, an excellent garden of vegetables, of tropic fruits, millet for their brooms, horsehair for home-made halters and upholstery, raw-hide for their bed-mattresses, strung across saplings. The only commodity they find it necessary to buy is tea. These girls ride round the cattle, erect their own fences—thirty miles and more of wire hand-twisted round bush-posts—and descend fifty feet in the earth to dig for lead. A remarkable little group, content in their isolation, they are all well educated by correspondence, and not one of them has ever been as far from home as Darwin.

On went the little train, almost in the towering grasses and swamps of the wet season, past the Adelaide and the Darwin rivers, and then twenty miles through a thick jungle of eucalyptus and milk-wood and fan-palm and sago-palm and screw-palm, to pull in beside a pearling-camp on the Indian Ocean, and wake Darwin from siesta with its shrill little whistle, in time for afternoon tea.

To come into Darwin in the wet season is to tiptoe across the bounds of possibility into an opium dream. The personality town of Australia, vivid, illogical, fascinating, the population, of about 2000, numbers some 43 races, each one distinct and sometimes all blended up in one, with complexions that range from gun-metal to old ivory. Government officials, immaculate in white; Larrakeahs and Wargaits, their skins gleaming like glossy black taffetas, riding bicycles about under the banyan trees; Chinese ladies with pantaloons and blue umbrellas; swarthy Filipinos, Fijians fuzzy-wigged, and grave Doric beauties, their fair hair parted above 'the brow that launched a thousand ships' —these are some of the characters in Darwin's musical comedy. All through the winter months, when the tourists come by on the Singapore ships and the overland chars-à-bancs, to find a little huddle of latticed houses in bareness by the sea, Darwin is demure and not nearly so intriguing. You must catch it in the gipsy moments of monsoon, when the electric storms sweep over and the tropic trees are in blossom, a background of barbaric glory for its thousand coloured faces.

Built out on the extremity of a small forked peninsula, north, south, east and west, dense jungle headlands drop a sheer eighty feet to the corroboree-figured rocks of the sea, a tangle of chartreuse sunlights making a harlequinade in green. Lining finger-nail curves of beach, tall coco-nuts toss back the sunlight like a juggler's knives. Against bamboo lattices, yellowed with sun and rain, are painted the poincianas.

> 'Wickedly red and malignantly green,
> Like the beads of a young Senegambian queen.'

the dragon limbs of frangipani, crowned with creamy per-fumed flowers, lanterns of the cassia, leopard crotans and trailing purple bougainvillea, the soundless golden bells of alamander, tasselled hibiscus, and deep crimson cluster of quis qualis, the Japanese jasmine, that changes colour at dusk.

From beneath the deeper shadow of tamarind and ban-yan, those lattices shine mysteriously in the evenings, suggesting romantic intrigue, but really merely bridge; and along the jungle-tracks, lost in grasses fraily coloured as a lunar rainbow and fourteen feet in height, there comes the acrid, heavy-sweet scent of—might it be opium, or just the dusk-scent of the flowering henna?

In the harbour, beneath the splendour of high-piled cumulus, the tide of the tropics is hurrying in and out like a live thing. Whole beaches move before the eyes, with flocks of indeterminate grey sand-pipers and the crawling of a million million hermit-crabs. From every lily-pool rises a vibrant symphony of frogs, and in the bush foliage, alight with the flight of butterflies, finches and parakeets of brilliant plumage forever writhe and flutter, restless and watchful as the bright-eyed mottled lizards.

Such is the fantastic setting for the drama of Darwin, solitary jewel of a black man's country, an alien in Australia. What can be its future? Already it needs an ethnologist-biologist to sort it all out, a Darwin himself, intent on the origin of human species, for its genealogical trees are grotesquely twisted and intertwined, even as the creepers of its jungles, or as the writhing mangrove roots of its fœtid salt creeks.

To overlook the vestibule of its one picture show on Saturday night is to gaze upon a kaleidoscope of humans that surely no other town of its size in the world can boast. Eagerly taking their turns at the ticket-windows, and the barrow where a Chinese cook sells hot potato chips and *sate* on sticks, you will see stockmen in sombreros, men of the donkey teams and the pearling-luggers, Chinese women in embossed silks, Melville Islanders who have paddled sixty miles across turbulent crocodile seas in a ten-feet bark canoe to see Greta Garbo look pensive in a divorce drama they cannot possibly understand—'Plenty shootem, no more kissem' is their idea of a good programme—while waiting on the corner for a Don Jose from the unemployed camp strolls Carmen herself, with graceful swinging hips and flashing eyes. Romances of that silver sheet, open to the skies, are pale to the romance behind all those dark eyes watching.

But that is only one act. Out in the native compound, on a curve of beach a mile away, a hundred tribes are gathered in their season, foot-pilgrims of 2000 square miles of territory, never speaking nor mingling with each other in the tin lean-to and paperbark huts of the camp. All the week, in frocks and trousers, they perform the menial tasks of the latticed houses, but the walkabout of week-end finds them 'noble and nude and antique,' queer, savage figures painted with the vivid ochre stones of the seashore, hooshing in corroboree.

There is the football match of Saturday afternoon, with barrackers in twenty-five recognised languages and the 'yacka-hoi' of the tribes in all the unrecognised languages from Cocos Island to Thursday Island, with swarthy half-castes in bright blazers, the majority of the teams, leaping ten feet into the air to catch the shining, rain-wet ball, and running with the swift grace of a deer-hound. In the town of Upside Down, they play cricket in winter and football in summer, for one reason because it is cooler! From December to March the monsoon blows cold. A downpour of three inches in one shower is powerless to hold up the game, for what are rain-squalls to those who truly love the bounding ball? The game from a distance may appear more like water-polo, but to that motley crowd of 1000, only outwardly limp, it is good stuff.

All Darwin loves the football. It is the great democracy of Saturday afternoon. By diagonal tracks from China-town, motor-roads, bicycle trails, and blackfellow pads through the bush they come, wearing everything from red handkerchiefs only to the regalia of the Greek priesthood. The blacks occupy, by right of concession, the whole northern side of the oval, where the lubras are pulling at their cutty pipes, the piccaninnies straddle-legged in the trees, and the wild myalls, after one glimpse, ready to hand over all the rain-stones and hair-belts in camp for some-body's old cast-off blazer. A foul or a rough-house is greeted with hoots and shrill hooshings guaranteed to freeze the debil-debil off the face of creation, and when the bell rings the quarter, his cart parked under a flowering calo-phyllum tree, the old Greek ice-cream man dispenses his wares to coolies in oiled straw hats, Government Residents, Patagonians, and Maltese and naked piccaninnies and all and sundry, principally sundry.

Then there is the monthly visit of the ship from Singa-pore, from the headland a spangle of lights between the trees, with the whole population of the town aboard her for one crowded hour of glorious life, gin-pahits and danc-ing to the wireless in her panelled saloons for the white people, and the Chinese eating mangosteens down on the lower deck. There are strange ceremonies of life and death, Greek weddings with their wailings and their wine, Manila funerals with a dinner and dance to conclude the ten-days' mourning, Chinese processions, the constant coming and

going of the pearling fleet—white sails against the blue—
and of pack-teams from the eastern rivers and swamps of
No-man's Land, laden with buffalo hides. In the main
street, on a sunny morning, I would meet, consecutively,
a special magistrate riding his bicycle to the court-house, a
buffalo-shooter in from the Mary, a French Roman Catholic
missioner, for twenty-five years a voluntary exile on an
island miles away, a Gilbert Islander who was smuggled in
years ago in a beer-cask, and Apergis the Greek, round the
world from isles Ionian to slather up the posters and ring
the auction-bell.

So the daily drama goes on, with many a curious life-
story, white and black, the tragedies, the farces and the
drawing-room comedies of Darwin, played out in secret
behind those shadowed lattices, the mazes of the jungle,
and behind the barred windows of the Asiatic shops. And,
as a grand finale, the last triumph of the great scene-painter,
splendour of tropic night follows the glamour of sunset
along the headlands, and the white moon rises, to silhouette
the pearling-ships in silver, and above the shack roofs of
so much huddled humanity, to waken the moaning of a
didgeree-du, the reedy music of a Chinese flute.

Against the seas of Fannie Bay stands the modest stone
monument that Darwin erected to the memory of the late
Ross Smith. Fifteen years ago, all Darwin stood on the
beach there to watch for a speck in the clouds, a speck that
was to put the name of the little tropic settlement, a
thousand miles from anywhere, on the map of the world
in big letters as Australia's first airport. What Government
failed to do, the aeroplane achieved in a twinkling, and they
can never forget Ross Smith. His huge Vickers Vimy
thrilled the whites and frightened the blacks and the chickens,
and as the first four navigators of these aerial seas stepped
from the 'plane, an inspired Resident greeted them with
congratulations upon the 'marvel of reaching their native
land through space.' Many tales there are to tell of the
men and women who have flown in since. A few months
after the arrival of Ross Smith, in 1919, a second 'plane
taxied feebly to a standstill with two pilots, Parer and
MacIntosh, who still hold the 'long record' of 207 days
from London, through every known kind of bad luck. They

landed with their 'crate' tied together with pieces of wire, after a 470-mile nightmare crossing of the Timor Sea, with a pint of petrol left. Cobham and Hinkler followed, and Scott and Mollison and Kingsford-Smith, and Amy Johnson, bearing her first blushing honours thick upon her. In 1929, Darwin lit oil-flares and watched far into the night for Moir and Owen, to find that they had landed on a northern promontory, saved from the sharks and the crocodiles by the skin of their teeth, on a reef by the lighthouse at Cape Don. It was when C. W. A. Scott came through with his first record, that he and I sat up with the moths and the winged things of a sweltering night, by lamplight in the post office, till three in the morning, to send a 3500-word story, via the Australian newspapers and London *Times*, to the world's breakfast-table.

The years between have seen dozens of young men and women in caps and goggles climbing out of the cockpits under the banana palms, and Darwin is well-educated to the bird-men now. When a 'plane was signalled through from the Dutch East Indies, we perched a blackfellow on a post to keep watch throughout the day across the seas to north-ward. As the 'plane hummed over, there was a scamper of the whole town out to meet him in Chinese taxis, and the gaol-prisoners were hurriedly sent down to chase off a veteran white horse always grazing on the aerodrome, and the ubiquitous goats. Valuable machines were left to soak in the heavy night-dews, and wilt their wings in blazing sun. Now there are modern hangars and oil-tanks and engineer-ing workshops, and a beacon that sheds its kindly light for a hundred miles on a clear night to the aid of aviators belated in the crossing of that formidable last hop, the Timor Sea.

At last Darwin is a port on the twentieth-century's trade routes, and the aeroplane has put it there.

DARWIN

Man Fong Lau and Wing Cheong Sing—
　All the names along the street,
　Sound an Eastern music sweet,
A guitar of single string,
　　Ping of lute and tang of 'cello
　　Plucked by little nails of jade.

Scarlet poinciana shade,
Cassias drooping, lantern-yellow,
Veil a hidden byway where
Eyes oblique and blue-black hair,
Squats a trousered Mongol maid.

Frangipani, white with flowers,
Altar-candles in the gloom,
Lights the dimly purpled bloom
Of the bougainvillea bowers,
Blows soft-petalled on the wind
By the shuttered balconies;
While with tangled traceries
Of bamboo and tamarind,
And palms that tropic suns caress,
Far and bright and shadowless,
Gleams the blue of dazzled seas.

Where the curve of jetty swings,
And the pearling-luggers ride
In the ripple of the tide,
Quietly, with folded wings,
Comes a snatch of island tongue
In across the water blown,
Or the sleepy monotone
Of a Koepang chantey sung,
Or swift oars, with dip and flash,
Break the silver with a splash,
Where a black man rows alone.

Latticed windows in the night,
Slippered footsteps in the day,
Shuffling down a devious way,
Lead to some unnamed delight,
And the sun goes down in gold
Panopling of clouds and sea,
And the moon's a wizardry,
Subtly young and slily old,
Where quick Love, with yellow eyes,
Crouches waiting, leopard-wise,
In the shadow of a tree.

CHAPTER XV

A LIVING JIG-SAW PUZZLE

MEN take strange brides in this lonely land.

'Wilt thou have this man to be thy wedded husband, to live together after God's ordnance in the holy estate of matrimony?'

The bride gives a frightened glance about her as of one who would flee, rolls the whites of her eyes, and with a nervous gesture of long black hands, murmurs something that sounds like 'Might Be!'—the nearest approach of the non-committal aboriginal race to a promise. The white man beside her stands with bowed head. It may be he is thinking of a first love, long ago.

Of all the grotesque love stories ever told, there is nothing in fact or fiction to surpass the weird unions of Australia's Ultima Thule, that last land north of the desert, with rich green jungles reaching to the lips of the great rivers, jewelled with many a lily-pool, but land of a fiendish loneliness, that eats into a man's soul. Many of its strange marriages are forever unwritten save in the mad hieroglyphics of those 'debil-debils' of despair and desolation that bide their time out there. Some of them are registered in Darwin, where he who runs may read.

Within the past few years, a planter of one of the peanut-settlements, an immigrant colonist with a fine record of pioneering work for the Territory, married by all the laws of Church and State a sixteen-year-old girl three-quarters black, reared in a black's camp; the errant son of a church dignitary applied for licence to a similar marriage, and, on an outpost of wilderness farther south, an aristocrat of Southern Europe has wed the mother of his homeful of half-caste children, thus endowing an Australian aboriginal woman with the title of Countess, did he or she ever care to claim it. At Pine Creek, just as I passed through it, a white man married a half-caste girl. They held a wedding-breakfast at the one little hotel, and the bride's mother, not being allowed on licensed premises, under the Protection of Aborigines' Act, had her share of the party on the wood-heap.

Katherine had a story to tell me. It came from the vicinity of Victoria River Downs, where the tribes 'going walkabout,' demanded a lubra from her friend and benefactor. Loth to let her go, the white man dared not refuse, until the wags in at the station suggested the only way out —legal marriage. To their amazement the jest was taken in earnest. On a truck, 200 miles to the Katherine settlement, the bridegroom drove his bride, returning her in a week or two, proud in the possession of a brand-new wedding-ring, suit-case and marriage certificate. Down in the camp, there was great 'yacki' as all three were passed along, 'paper yabber belonga Mista Gubmint' held mostly upside down and sideways, proving unanswerable. As the baffled tribe shipped spears and billy-pots and swam the crossing, the lubra, now 'proply-fella missus' sat upon her suit-case, and howled for good times gone.

Just across the bridge at Katherine, I found a rough stone 'In Memory of Maggie B,' a black woman who tended a lonely white man through long and desperate illness, to become his faithful wife for many years. These piebald unions are not rare. There are still living in Darwin at least two lubras who have been legally married to white men, and they are by no means the only unusual nuptials of the Australian north. Of the far-fetched blends and complexions there are even stranger stories to tell.

A full-blooded aboriginal woman who is rearing a Greek child; a sixteen-years-old white boy who has lived all his life as the adopted son of a Chinese family, thinking Chinese, living Chinese, and speaking his own native language in pidgin; a Greek wedding with Chinese bridesmaids and a Manila string band in attendance, and a Chinese-Filipino and a Norwegian-aborigine who are Australians and first cousins—where in the world would you find such a weird interweaving of race and colour as that of the outpost capital, a stranger to White Australia?

The population of Darwin to-day consists of, approximately, not quite a thousand British, 600 Australian-born Chinese, multiplying rapidly, 100 Japanese and as many Koepangers, indentured men of the pearling fleets, and between two and three hundred Swedes, Slavs, Swiss, Germans, Russians, Ionic and Doric Greeks, Maoris,

Maltese Malays, Manilamen, Siamese, Cingalese and Samoan, with an occasional Chilean, Afghan or African negro, and all or any of these blended for a generation or two with each other and with the Australian black.

Darwin is the scapegoat of White Australia.

Through a hundred years of hoodoo, this Northern Territory, with its lush tropical beauty and lavish resources remote from civilisation, became a more or less happy hunting-ground for some of the world's strangest personalities, and has developed an in-growing population of breeds and half-breeds surely unique. The first chapter in its extraordinary history was written in 1825, when the Imperial Government, at the suggestion of Stamford Raffles, set up a military expedition with 125 male and female convicts from Botany Bay, to found a colony at Port Essington. Blue-coats and colonels, pickpockets and poachers, lost souls from Dartmoor and the down-country and the docks of London, marooned in a jungle of wilderness 10,000 miles from home, they failed dismally. As each of four such settlements was abandoned in despair in the succeeding twenty years, it is recorded that a few remained behind, in a fantastic freedom that nobody in the world begrudged them.

With the foundation of Darwin in the seventies, the discoveries of gold and pearls, and the opening up of an immense cattle-country, came adventurers of the Four Winds and the Seven Seas, from Alaska to the Persian Gulf, miners and beachcombers and younger sons, British West Indian sailors, kanakas from the Queensland sugar-cane fields, Welsh settlers from Patagonia, German peasants and Jesuit missionaries, and men of the East with gold rings in their ears. A trans-continental railway was begun with thousands of coolies imported from Canton. Well-inured to the humidity, they swarmed across a mineral belt that extends for 10,000 square miles, scratching a living of gold and tin, planting their gardens along the river-banks, peaceful and industrious. Deemed a national menace, in the course of time most of them were deported. Their gardens are wild bush to-day, and their descendants, still eating with chop-sticks after three generations, monopolise the main thoroughfare of Darwin, turning it into a street-scene in Canton.

In the decades that followed, the Territory blossomed again and again with golden promise, and attracted millions in capital and thousands of wanderers. But the promise fell with the cassia-flowers to decay, the capital evaporated, mines and bridges and tramways have disappeared in the encroaching jungle, and the wanderers have wandered on, leaving a mottled progeny.

With the beginning of the second era in North Australian history, the taking over by the Commonwealth Government in 1911, came a new influx of strangers, the majority of them Government officials. The opening of Vestey's big meat works in 1915 brought slaughtermen and factory-hands from China to Peru. The railway was extended for another hundred miles into the bush, largely with Greek, Russian and Maltese labour, and, at the revival of the pearling industry, with restricted aliens, came Japanese divers with Koepanger and Amboynese crews. So it is that in a century of strange affinities, the tongues of North Australia have become babel, its genealogies a monkey-puzzle tree.

In an afternoon's walk there I girdled the earth in two and a half square miles, with incidental insight into characters and racial complications that would baffle and delight an ethnologist. Five distinct foreign communities flourish in that vivid patch of Australian bushland on the outskirts of the town. There are the neat Attic cottages of the Greeks, incongruous beneath the poinciana trees; the wall campong settlements of the Malays, and laced bamboo huts of Manilamen, on stilts, and the little bird-cage houses and shops of a village in Nippon, incredibly clean and bare, with their matting beds and tiny shrines and miniature gardens—to say nothing of the paper-bark mias of the aboriginal compound, where all the tribes of the Territory are summer visitors.

In the maze of tin alleys which is Chinatown, where the joss-sticks are forever burning before the tiger-faced gods of Kwong Sung, and barefooted Oriental tailors make the smart drill suits of the white men, I lunched upon salted fish roe, with *soi*, preserved eggs spicy with age, boiled bamboo shoots and sharks' fins, dipping my chop-sticks in the communal rice with trousered women of the East, their

faces a smiling mask. Half an hour later and half a mile
away, I was guest at a Greek wedding, where a grey-eyed
Athene, her hair softly filleted as Helen's own, plighted
her troth to Ulysses Apostopoulis, the fisherman's son. On
the way back I paused to listen to the notes of a sami-sen—
or perhaps a guitar—behind the lamp-lit lattices, and
finished up with a Mahommedan funeral and a corroboree.

The Chinese of Darwin are a curious national problem.
They are multiplying at the rate of from seven to fourteen
to a family in a country where increase in white population
is practically nil. So well-guarded are the women that, in
that fantastic miscellany of half-castes, it is almost impossible
to find one white-Chinese. Slippered and trousered, with
a complexion of frangipani and old ivory, and with the
bright red ribbon of good luck threaded through her hair,
the Chinese girl looks out from behind barred windows and
tin walls to the country of her birth that does not belong
to her. Australian-born, with a public school education and
a vote, she is doomed to the traditional betrothal in infancy,
possibly to a man who already possesses another affianced
wife in China.

Practically none of these alien Australians—alien only
because they prefer to be—is engaged in productive industry.
Ninety per cent. of them are shopkeepers. Two factions
still persist, the War On—ironically enough, Chinese Peace
—and the Young China of the Kuo Min Tang, political
and practical. While one subscribes to send home the bones
of the ancestors, the other bows gravely to the little white
bust of Mr. Sun Yat Sen. Members of the War On daily
answer the mellow brass gong of the Joss House, smoke
their water-pipes on the pavement, adorn their shop-fronts
with the shrines of Chang and Wang and Li, with offerings
of incense, and sweet vinegar, and little bowls of honey-
coloured tea, placed to the honour of Kwan Yin, Mother
Goddess, giver of many sons, and certainly living up to her
reputation in Darwin. Members of the Kuo Min Tang
celebrate their marriages, first at the Registrar's office, and
then under a maze of streamers in their meeting-hall,
affixing their signatures to the certificate with brush writing
and scented inks.

All babies born of these purely Chinese marriages are the

particular care of the Society, and after the day's work at the Australian public school, the poor little souls attend regular classes in Chinese for five nights a week and all day Saturday, until they themselves, bright and intelligent, become an extraordinary study in dual nationality.

Here, too, are half-castes—black and white and black and yellow, Chinese-Greek, Chilean-abo, Cingalese-white-abo, Malay-Kanaka-Greek-abo, double half-castes and criss-crosses and quadroons, octoroons, with red hair and freckles and the lean blackish limbs of the lubra, and one small Japanese-German, a laughable, little square-headed Teuton with almond eyes.

But even more extraordinary than any of these tangled skeins in the web of human destiny are a few individual characters of clearly defined race, whose life-stories seem far-fetched and improbable as the best realistic fiction. One of these is an Englishwoman who married a Manilaman, a 'king diver' of Thursday Island, to become the mother of thirteen children, two of whom gave their lives for Australia during the Great War, and the progenitor of five families of grandchildren who include in their derivation strains of Chinese, Filipino, Scandinavian, Malay and aboriginal.

Another is a cultured little woman of charming appearance and keen business sense, Mrs. Ali Hassan, who is at one and the same time daughter of a Chinese woman who speaks no English, granddaughter of a nurse from Guy's Hospital, widow of an Indo-Japanese-Chinese accountant, acting Consular agent for the Chinese, president of the Kuo Min Tang and a member of the Victoria League.

A third is Henry Lee, a white boy whose father is said to have been an Australian soldier killed at the war. Henry Lee, known to the Chinese as Lee Kim Hong, was adopted in infancy by Mrs. Lee Hang Gon, whose family lives in the Chinese fashion. Throughout his life the boy has been well and affectionately cared for. He has attended both Chinese and English-speaking schools, and has developed an amazing dual mentality. An extremely nervous and sensitive child, torn between the inexorable forces of heredity and environment, Henry acknowledges himself Chinese, and is an exile in his own country, a stranger to the children of his own race.

But perhaps the most unusual case and character of all is Kitty Karlo Pon, full-blooded lubra, evangelist and authoress, widow of a potential rajah of one of the Federated Malay States, mother of two half-caste Malay sons, and foster-mother of a Greek child. The life-story of Kitty Karlo Pon—and in simple sequence of fact and excellent English, she could tell it to me herself, verifying what I had heard from others—reads like romance run wild. Left behind after a tribal fight on the Macarthur River in babyhood, she was adopted and trained by the family of a sergeant of police stationed in the Gulf country —Sergeant Stretton, whose son is Chief Commissioner of Police in the Territory to-day. In charge of the growing children, Kitty taught herself to read and write by means of the Bible, came to Darwin with the Strettons, and married Karlo Pon, Malay bosun of a pearling-fleet. Son of a Sultan in his own islands, Karlo Pon, through his marriage, lost his inheritance and never returned home. Since his death, his wife has employed her time in keeping a little boarding-house for the Koepangers ashore, and in religious works among the coloured people. She took me out to her little Sunday-school in the jungle bush, and to hear her discuss Nebuchadnezzar and the Chaldeans and point the moral of the Prodigal Son was an education in itself. Incidentally, she told me that she is writing the story of her life, *The Red Lily*, named in honour of the totem of her now extinct tribe.

Three years ago, when a tiny Greek child was found abandoned on a vacant allotment, the kind-hearted and cleanly Kitty applied to be allowed to adopt it, and was deemed worthy. She promptly christened the mite Helen.

'Why did you call her Helen?' I asked, very curious.

'I dono, Missus. I just like that name,' beamed Kitty— an extraordinary and quite inexplicable classic intuition? a subconscious mental telepathy between races far apart? Who can say? But certain it is that Kitty, there in her little home that tries so hard to be white, with its air of strict moral rectitude and its cherished rag of a garden, proves the old Kipling quip concerning Judy O'Grady and the Colonel's Lady.

Caste and half-caste, white and black, the uncertain past

has written a strange human story in the north of Australia, that it is to be hoped the near future will unravel. Already white children are far in the minority at all Territory schools. Already the steady increase of coloured and half-breed populations threatens an empty country with the begetting of one of the most illogical and inbred races in the world.

Without the salvation of understanding, without the influx of white settlers in large numbers, its future is a theme unthinkable.

CHAPTER XVI

KINGDOM OF THE CROCODILE

A HUNDRED miles south-west of Darwin, the Daly River runs into the sea. With its upper reaches of the Katherine, 150 miles long, it is the greatest breeding-ground of crocodiles in North Australia. The nightmare beasts seem to rise in millions from the mud. At dawn and dusk, along the Alligator Flats, it is a common thing to see fourteen or fifteen 18-footers side by side on a sandbank, waiting their chance to snap a wallaby or a wild goose in the rushes, or it may be a buffalo coming down to drink, or a fat and foolish piccaninny playing in the shallows. Lying inert for hours among the fallen logs and the twisted banyan roots of the upper banks, or floating idly down in the current, an eye and the extreme end of a snout above the water, for all the world like a knotted stick, the great grey-green greasy brutes defy detection.

Coward of cowards on land, the huge Indian mugger that inhabits the lower reaches of the rivers, the salt creeks and the tepid seas of North Australia is a menace only in the water. Blacks of the Daly, the Alligator and the Roper rivers, on rafts of paperbark, often tune him up from the bottom with their long bamboo spears, and, as he rises to the top, from an overhanging branch they lassoo him and haul him ashore. There they muzzle him with a stout rope of plaited pandanus, and lead him round like a dog until they grow hungry for his tail.

One of the most glorious river-highways of the North, the Daly, with all its potential wealth, has so far defied the white man. Again and again attempts have been made to grow maize and millet, peanuts and even dairy produce along its too-fertile flats, and they have all flourished excellently—for a time, to be swept away in the annual floods or to run wild in the jungle. The lower reaches are the breeding-grounds of millions of anopheles mosquitoes, the little black chap that stands on his head to inoculate you, in a split second, with a lifetime's fever.

On the high, thickly wooded banks east and west live two great myall tribes, Berinkan and Mulluk-mulluk, sworn enemies of each other and treacherous to the white man. Even in these days most of the murderers of colonists in the Territory, other than those of impregnable Arnhem Land, can be traced to the Daly natives.

Seventy years of attempted colonisation have left little trace in these tangles of jungle. A great Jesuit mission, sponsored in France forty years ago, was abandoned in despair. A Government aborigine station, a big copper mine, innumerable plantations, an experimental farm of 3,000 acres, and a community settlement of thirty-five families established by the Commonwealth Government in 1911 have followed it into oblivion. Perhaps the saddest disillusionment of all is the story of this colony of settlers from New Zealand and Victoria. Within six months there were twenty families making their homes in the jungle with Government assistance and with promise of prosperity. The country-side was bewilderingly green, the succulent grasses feet high. Dairy herds and Berkshire pigs and prize Clydesdales were imported, and the prospects of rice and millet and maize were a foregone conclusion. They did not know their Daly.

Within five years the settlement was abandoned. Dairy cattle had died of eating poisonous weeds, or were speared by the blacks, or bogged in the river-flats, bloated with edible grasses one month, starving the next. Pigs and poultry were lost and drowned—they are running wild in the jungle to-day. The bridge built by the settlers for their children to cross to school was swept away in a mighty flood, and the schoolteacher died of malaria within the year. In the tangled bush you can find fallen tin cottages, pumps, a small wharf and tramway, sheds, mining machinery, farm implements—even the remains of a printing-press buried in leafy mould. The big river wins.

Across the dark harbour, the lights of Darwin dipped midnight as we set sail for this Congo of the north on the little ship *Maroubra*. Captained by genial Jack Hayles and Skipper Harry Lawson, an old sea-dog who has sailed Territory waters for thirty years, the *Maroubra* is a glorified motor-launch, oil-driven, 26 tons or so, that carries mails and supplies to the wildest islands and the loneliest missions. This was to be the last of her five trips a year to the Daly before the long isolation of the wet, and she carried four passengers—a rare event, and still rarer, two of them were white women—a girl schoolteacher, me with my note-book handy, and two Government servants on leave from Darwin, with cameras and rifles at full cock.

By dawn we dropped merrily below the lighthouse-top at Point Charles, and were swinging down along the west coast of the Territory in a sea of rollicking blue. With skipper, mate, and a half-caste boy as cook, making six knots, at midday we sighted the shadowy headland of Point Blaze, where a few years ago a trepanger named Renouff was killed with his own shotgun by a blackboy in his camp. At sundown we were within the shallow shores of Anson Bay, the solitary curve of Mount Litchfield ahead of us, and as the first stars blinked ran through a narrow strait in the lee of Peron Island, and slipped anchor in the mouth of the Daly.

Black clouds of geese flew over with their irregular half-musical honking. In the wind-ruffled bay, something that looked like a knobbed stick floated to the surface. There was a sinister suggestion of watchfulness about it. As the rifles barked, it disappeared in a flash. The wide low mangrove shores and the piled clouds of sunset were gradually lost in the darkness, and the ship fell asleep to the lullaby of calm water, broken now and again by the planky snap of jaws.

A gun-shot at dawn, and we were heading up the big waterway against the muddy current, and between far, slimy banks. Mount Litchfield we had left well behind us. A hair-pin bend brought it directly in front again. A buffalo feeding on the lower flats raised his dull head and vanished with a flourish of hoofs. Big grey-green crocodiles, lying in wait for the early kangaroo, splashed frantically to the water 300 yards ahead. Geese, ducks and myriad waterfowl were rising in great crying flocks from the lagoons. The white heron and the jabiru, elegant in black and white, watched us with polite interest. Again and again the rifles rang out, but that scaly, flying tail was always first.

For ten miles there was little break in the reedy banks

of ooze and flatness, except that the river perceptibly
narrowed. A low sand-bank provided the thrill of eleven
crocs., giants some of them, lying motionless in the morning
sun, but at the first crack and ping of the bullets they were
below in a welter of foam and mud. Dead trees, strangely
suggestive of horned back and curven tail, swung down in
the sluggish current. In the greasy warmth of the sun, a
log on the bank or even the mud itself seemed to stir and
move. Fever River!

There was a sudden change. A railway-cutting reach of
high sandstone banks, a picturesque curve in red ochre where
the pink cranes were flying, disclosed the Jekyll and Hyde
of the big river. Below it were the reeds and buffalo-flats,
above a typical tropical stream, shores steep and densely
wooded. For seventy miles crisply our prow cut through
narrowing reaches of silver, cliffs clothed with the living
green of banyan and Leichhardt and native fig, palmy
clumps of pandanus that the black man loves, rich foliage
of vines and creepers tangled in graceful arch and garland,
with gentle geometry of nutwood and milkwood and white-
limbed paper-barks. Blue feather of smoke above the
foliage, and we passed a little paper-bark village of the
Mulluk-mulluk. An ancient king of the Berinkans hailed
us from the other side a little later, paddling his dug-out
with a long bamboo pole, wanting tobacco. 'Gibit myalla!'
—his wailing shout echoed behind us through the aisles of
early morning. Failing a gift, he was ready to trade his
fish for a chew.

At last we came to the old copper landing, to find that
the jetty had been washed away in floods, and that the
Daly River policeman had gone to Darwin with a native
murderer too eager for the kidney-fat of a tribesman. We
rowed ashore, into the leafiness to go wood-gathering and
wallaby-shooting in the twilight, and to tell over a tragic
story of the early days. Four white prospectors were brutally
done to death by the Berinkans at this spot, one of the most
terrible slayings of white men in the history of the north,
for which in their turn 'the natives were severely punished'
—a phrase in old police records which means much.

Tea on the hatch, in a cloudy dusk lit by fire-flies instead
of stars. Bats flew silently over. The boy swung a torch

overboard for the spearing of dazzled fish. Above our heads millions upon millions of mosquitoes tuned in their violins to the evening symphony, vegetarians all, not knowing that we were good to eat. The black velvet of the tropic night came down, and we were but voices and the glow of a cigarette end in the uncanny stillness.

Faint tinge of dawn found us throbbing up-river again to the pea-nut settlements. It was a narrow stream now, all green glades and grottoes, ivy-climbing creepers, the willowy droop of paper-barks over white sand—a scene so sweetly English that one missed the church tower and the old stone bridge. Our hoarse little whistle stirred the cool precincts and set the gum-trees nervously quivering. Trailing clouds of glory, shrill cockatoos flew screaming in flocks above us, white, green, black, crimson, and the dawn-coloured galah. Living silhouettes on the heights, black men were watching the boat go by, clad in scarlet nagas, and holding their long bamboo spears. From wurlies where the first smoke of day was curling came a whoop of greeting, with shrieks of laughter for the white lubras perched upon the prow.

We began the pilgrimage of two or three isolated pea-nut farms, where a few lost souls still struggle on, fighting the jungle single-handed. At every landing the double dug-out canoes, hollow logs lashed together with pandanus fibre, made out for the loading, manned by lithe young natives, their arms and their bodies a sinuous poetry of motion to the swinging of the bamboo pole paddle. Packets of letters and papers tied round with string were flung in mid-stream to a young Apollo in black-bronze. Creepers had been placed in the bottoms of the canoes to protect the stores, and over the side went bags of flour, chests of tea and tobacco, cases of petrol, sacks of seed, iron rails for a little trolley, coils of fencing wire, and multitudes of tinned stores, for in the Never-Never everything is iron-clad. Once we landed at a riverside camp, with its nearby mias walled against the debil-debil, and blacks, quite naked, planting the pea-nuts in the furrows. Once or twice a white man was seen on the liana-ed bank calling a message or a greeting, shouting to his boys in a running babble of their own aboriginal.

Picturesque, indeed, is this pea-nutting community of the North. There are no lonelier white men in the world. In tilling, planting and harvesting, each little farm many miles from the next, they have no help save that of the half-civilised blacks, and their methods are primitive and labour-saving to a degree. A quaint thing it is, in these days of universal machinery, to see a lubra perched in a tree, slowly emptying a bag of pea-nuts into space, for the wind to winnow them. A flat stone, a lump of wood, and half a petrol tin are the shelling patent. With the lump of wood on the stone, they flatten out the nuts and the kernels slip easily into the tin. Promise of tea and tobacco when the *Maroubra* comes keeps the 'factory hands' happy. Territory nuts sell splendidly in all Australian cities, for the river-soils produce two tons to the acre of first-quality pea-nuts. A hard worker, for a few months' graft in the year, can earn a cheque for £800 in a good season, but he takes a risk, with six weeks between ships to Darwin and a month from Darwin down. Many a pea-nut farmer has seen his whole year's harvest lying rotten on the wharf, or swept to the sea in a flood. Patiently, year by year, far away from the normal world, he toils on and backs his luck against the vagaries of Nature that, up along the Daly, is red in tooth and claw. The only friend he ever sees is the *Maroubra*, bringing echoes of his own world once in two months. The patch of tilled fields about his shack rings at night with the descending scale of savage singing. His candle a star in the wilderness, the white man listens. If all is well with him, you may hear the cheery jazz of his gramophone shouting a gallant defiance to that world of sinister shadows outside.

At the police landing on the way down again we picked up a strange item of cargo, the spears and hair-belts and old clay-pipe of a murdered native, to be delivered to the Crown Prosecutor at Darwin. Through all the charm of green and silver down to the wide grey water again, here we made our first bag. In the drowse of a dull, steamy afternoon the banks were alive with crocs. Keen eyes made out two sprawling forms on a sand-bank. The motor was shut off. Stealthily we drifted with the tide to within forty yards of the sleeping brutes. On the sand-bank beyond was a covey of wild geese, six thousand strong. Wild goose is a toothsome dish, but our honour was at stake. A lightning crack of three rifles, the bark of the big Savage, and even as to-morrow's dinner rose in a screeching black cloud, the great scaly opened his eyes a split second too late. He made a lightning dash to the water, and on the brink rolled over dead. His mate, a lighter sleeper, with a whip-lash of the tail, vanished in foaming mud. A noose about the neck, behind the grim, blood-stained jaws, and he was hauled aboard, the half-shut reptile eyes no longer wary. Strung up in the rigging, he was our triumph, and the way was clear to Darwin.

A lower sand-bank provided the roast goose sacrificed to his scaly majesty, to be the deliciousness of a sunny day at sea, and at piccaninny daylight next morning we picked up the lights of a Filipino coal-boat, followed her into port, and passed her as she lay in the roads, signal flags calling for Customs and doctor.

Darwin was not yet awake, but an old Greek fisherman clearing his traps stared at the big fellow in the rigging, and in the antique Ionian tongue shouted something that, in all languages, unmistakably stands for 'Hooray!'

Back from the timeless loneliness of a river of the North, we remembered that in the world of men and women it was Christmas Eve.

CHAPTER XVII

DARWIN COURT

'. . . to be hanged by the neck until you are dead.'

The charge is murder. Outside the little northern court-house the blazing whiteness of the day. Inside, a black-capped judge, in the formal judicial sing-song that robs it of its horror, has just pronounced the death-sentence.

A few of the jury are yawning. A blackboy, barefooted, pulls the punkah backward and forward. A lubra witness on the front bench is suckling her wailing baby. Barristers in magpie black and white, immaculate but wigless, one of them even sockless in the heat, are packing up their briefs. In the prisoner's dock, beside a vigilant police officer, a man has listened to the sentence of his doom without turn-ing a hair. Throughout the case he has said not one word in his own behalf. His downcast eyes are on his hands, folded listlessly before him. He does not know!

The case of the King versus Peanut is at an end. The court is dismissed. As the crowd streams out on the stone-flagged verandah comes Kelley the sophisticated, wearing tattered trousers and a wide grin. 'That boy Peanut him luckyfella!' volunteers Kelley. 'Him no more hang longa neck, him bin stop forty years longa Fannie Bay.'

His Most Gracious Majesty, in a wide Empire whereon the sun never sets, gets into holts with a diversity of creatures, but there are few that provide in a single week more of the unexpected and diverting than Darwin. On Monday you may hear a diver's inquest, where men who speak only in the tongues of Nippon tell of the signal from below that failed to come. On Tuesday it is a coloured man of sorts, accused of theft in jade and rings of red Chinese gold from a woman with sloe-black hair and trousers of coolie-cloth; on Wednesday, a gold-stealing from the trackless ranges; on Thursday an opium-smoker, its throat and cheeks cavernous from the eternal sucking of a pipe, its eyes the hollow of dreams; and on Friday a tribal murder from Berinkan country, tale of an eternal triangle and jealousy and revenge, and black men creeping along the lily lagoons with spears between their toes.

I had never yet 'done' a court in my newspaper days, but Darwin's was copy far too good to miss. My first case was encouraging, a rare little snap of sheer comedy.

A white man was charged in the police court with the common enough offence of procuring alcohol for an aboriginal—only this one happened to be his legal wife. 'It's a queer country where a man can't stand his wife a drink,' was the old chap's protest. The lady was known to Darwin as 'Little-bit Maggie,' and a hard case. She had been found in high spirits, with three-quarters of a bottle of whisky in her possession.

The defending solicitor made the point that a wife adopts her husband's nationality, but this was not allowed. An aborigine is the world's exception. Then the solicitor dexterously shifted ground.

'We hear about this aborigine, Your Worship, but she has not been produced. I contend that for the purposes of this Court, such person cannot be held to exist.'

Apparently this baffled the magistrate, for he dismissed the case. The next one was 'Little-bit Maggie' herself, on a charge of using abusive language to the constable when her husband was arrested. Just having been held not to exist, she made her entry in a flaming print frock, clumping boots, an old felt hat, and a twinkle in her eye. Not only did she admit everything the constable had written down, but she would have said it again had they let her. The husband was fined five shillings, and he and Maggie drove away together.

In all the talkie-theatres in a year is not staged a human drama so poignant or so thrilling as in one session of Darwin Supreme Court. To that little room facing the jungled headlands and the glass-green of tropic seas, its doors guarded by troopers of the North Australia Mounted in snow-white uniforms, come, sometimes from two and three thousand miles away, all the characters in a fantastic comic opera. There are shy old bushmen who have not seen civilisation in years; bearded young stockmen with sombrero hats and concertina leggings; Chinese women in green silk tunic and pantaloons; Malayans, turbaned Afghans, and myalls from central deserts or the swamps of Arnhem Land, with the protruding chins and bushy eyebrows of Neanderthal man, who have never worn a shirt and trousers in their lives before.

The case is called. It is a tribal murder from the melancholy deserts north-west of Alice Springs. The accused are in the box, mystified. In the last three months they have travelled, on bare, burnt feet, a thousand miles with a policeman's camel patrol, another thousand in the first motor-car they have ever seen, to their first association with other tribesmen and their first glimpse of the sea. With faces morose and listless, they look up to His Honour, languidly immune above it all, making 'millee-millee letter-stick' of every spoken word; to the white-clad barristers who amazingly take off their silver curls and lay them on the table, and upon the gallery of intent faces of every shade that lines that little room. Blissfully unconscious that their lives are hanging in the balance, with no word spoken in their own defence, they will listen to the intoning of the death-sentence, in all its terrible mediæval solemnity, with no comprehension.

To them it is some inexplicable 'white-fella wonga' in which they are evidently playing an important part. Back in the firelight under the pandanus, if ever they get there again, 'Bigfella Boss' with all his legal gravity, the popping up and down of the barristers with: 'I object, your Honour,' the quoting of Q.B.D., the tendering of the exhibits, and the taking of the oath will all feature in the theme of a brand-new corroboree, a highly popular burlesque.

A witness stumbles into the box, an interpreter, generally a lubra of his own tribe, beside him. The Clerk of Courts rises to administer the oath. The Bible is meaningless. The Koran, the upturned saucer of rice, the blowing out of a match, and the cock's head, that will feature in the swearing of the Afghans and Malays and Chinese, are of no avail. The myall has no fathers and no faiths. Through the interpreter contact is made.

'What name?'

'Targoolpie.'

'Which way country belong you?'

'Belong Marramaninjie country.'

'You been savvy this boy? Something been happen longa that boy. You been tellem true-fella. No more gammon, no more what nudda-fella been talk-talk, yabber-yabber, belong you. What you been seeum, longa you eye.'

The lubra communicates the gist of it. The witness nods.

'No more gammon, no more lie, him been seeum longa eye,' the lubra promises for him, and the Crown Prosecutor rises to his task of proving the guilt. Evidence is elicited largely by suggestion, and to the slightest suggestion the Australian aborigine is extraordinarily amenable. Child of the world's childhood, he has no gauge of time or space.

'Moon straight up, dinner-time belong moon,' I have heard him explain in the Darwin Court, trying to express his idea of midnight in an unfamiliar language, and 'little bit longa way, little bit close,' when asked from what distance a spear had been thrown. Sometimes a perfectly silent conversation is carried on between him and the interpreter for ten minutes and more in 'finger-yabber.'

Through tedious hours of contradiction and misconception the examinations and cross-examinations go on. New witnesses are called, as confused and inarticulate as the first. The accused show no interest. They do not understand the evidence, they cannot answer it. Moreover, to put a native in the box is to allow him to incriminate himself beyond all hope. A barrister briefed by the Chief Protector bases his defence upon an imagined motive, a possible alibi.

Happily, among the jury are old Territory residents well acquainted with the psychology and the tribal customs of the native, and he is usually accorded a lenient judgment. Even when the death sentence is imposed—and humorously enough falls flat—that sentence is invariably commuted to life imprisonment. For many years no native has been hanged in Australia. If declared innocent, he is immediately set free to return, with his wives and witnesses, to his own country, where, if he has any inkling of their perfidy, he can take it out on them to his heart's content.

Native murders are not purely tribal. The slaying of the white man by the black is another story. Five minutes is the usual retirement period in cases of this nature, and the verdict is a foregone conclusion. If that great empty Territory is ever to be a white man's country, the white man alone in its wilderness must be protected from a mischievous daring and the limited comprehensions of the black. But even then, justice is tempered with mercy.

It was in a case of this nature tried before me in one of the sessions, the wilful murder of William Tetlow by one Stockman Jimmy, a half-civilised station-boy, that the jury brought in a verdict with a curious proviso: 'Guilty, with a strong recommendation to mercy, in that the white man had contributed to his own death by walking in front of a native with a loaded gun.' . Tetlow was an old man who had wandered the Territory for many years, the story of his death a tragedy typical of that country's sordid loneliness. Told in court by Alice, a Daly River lubra who had braved death for his sake, and in whose arms he had died, it was the most poignant story of the 1933 session.

Camped beneath a milkwood tree—his only home—Tetlow had given Stockman Jimmy the rifle to procure him a goose from the billabong. There was no quarrel, no motive of revenge. He had never seen the boy before, and he had shared his dinner with him. But Tetlow made the mistake of walking in front of Jimmy to the billabong. In that primitive brain, the primitive triumphed. Wantonly Jimmy shot his benefactor in the back. 'I been lose him longa my head,' was his only defence. Crawling on hands and knees, Tetlow was found by the little lubra, who held his head up in his convulsions and made him his last quartpot of tea.

'I been talk "You leavem me now,"' she told the court with broken voice. 'Him nod his head. Him finish.' Faithful to the wish of the dying man, this lubra, her life threatened by her tribe, had swum the Daly River, alive with crocodiles, and had walked thirty miles through the jungle to inform the trooper, and to lead him to Tetlow's body and the digging of a bush grave.

But the trial of the myall for murder is not the only diversion of the Darwin Court, where, with the artistry of life itself, the master-playwright, comedy follows close upon the heels of tragedy. Sometimes it is a white face that looks out from the dock, a pilgrim of the outback who has killed or maimed a blackfellow, or stolen his employer's stores, or branded a mob of poddy calves with a hobble chain welded in a camp-fire. Forgery in the south is common-place enough; forgery in the north can be pure drama, an epic of human courage and kindness.

Stealing a bank form, a bagman cashed a cheque with an Afghan hawker camped on a creek, receiving his 'change' in flour and tea and an old pack-saddle, for in the outback real money is unusual currency. This man was arrested some months later at Tanami goldfield. Via Alice Springs to Wave Hill for the preliminary trial, and then back to Newcastle Waters and Darwin, he travelled 3500 miles to answer the charge, perhaps a world's record. He sat in the box disconsolate, knowing there was little hope. But the story was told that on the way in from Wave Hill, the escorting policeman had been dashed against a tree by his horse. The two were alone. Making no attempt to escape, the prisoner not only remained in custody, but cared and tended the wounded man, held him on his horse for three days through a hundred miles of riding, and so saved his life. For in the lonely Territory all men, white, brown and brindle, policeman and prisoner, even one threatened with the incarceration of years, are brothers in need.

My pencil flying in its Press wires, I looked upon the most interesting little crowd of witnesses in this case that I have ever known. To give evidence, a station manager had ridden 700 miles on a pack-horse in the wet season, from Limbunya on the rim of West Australia. He denied the signature. There was a Chinese station cook, an opium addict, interpreted by a Chinese woman of Darwin, in embossed silks and waving a palm-leaf fan. He furnished the cheque form. There was the Afghan teamster, who swore his truth loudly, by God and the Koran. He cashed the cheque for goods, and there was the dashing, young half-caste stockman, who asked the Chinaman to lend him the form. There was also Constable Jock Reid, with his arm still in a sling, who pleaded for one who had been his friend. The bagman was sentenced to two years' hard labour, with one year's remission of sentence for his notably heroic and humane action in saving the policeman's life. With bowed head he shuffled out of the dock, where six myalls in the preceding three days had been condemned to death, to rejoin them at Fannie Bay, where all men, white and black and yellow, are lamentably equal.

Once only, in the Darwin Court, have I seen a white woman, a buffalo-hunter's wife, whose children had all been born in bough shades in the wild bush, coming to plead for the custody of those children in the first case of divorce under Territory law.

Weird exhibits are tendered at times, perhaps the strangest in the world to be filed and tabulated and admitted and bound in red tape. I have seen spears and boomerangs tipped with human blood, a half-smoked pipe, the pierced shirt of a prospector, and the swag and billy-pots that are 'dead men's estate,' and on two occasions I have seen aboriginal heads, unearthed by the arresting policeman, boiled with eucalyptus leaves for their preservation, and carried a thousand miles in petrol tins, in case a doubting Thomas among the jurymen should demand the evidence of his own eyes.

Human dramas in a tragic country, white against black, black against white, eternal triangles, tribesmen's enmities, the grim battle of the pioneer, and the end of it all, perhaps, a spear slanting between the leaves in the grey of piccaninny daylight—such are the themes that, with all the pomp and circumstance of British law, to the scribbling of the clerks and the occasional relief of 'suppressed laughter' are told in the Darwin Court.

Mounted Constable McColl was still in his twenties when he met his death by the spears of the Arnhem Landers at Woodah Island, in the Gulf. He was one of the younger members of the North Australia Mounted. It was only a few nights before I left Darwin that we talked together on the verandah of the Supreme Court, during a late sitting, of the glories of the Roper River, which I was about to visit.

I had heard of its scenic beauties. 'Beauties,' he laughed. 'Naked blacks and 'gators and pandanus swamps, if you call that beauty.' He had just returned from a long quest, by land and sea, of a white delinquent whom he had arrested trepanging at Beatrice Island, out in the Gulf. Myall witnesses that he had brought with him, over 500 miles by native canoe and packhorse, were then giving their evidence in the witness box. A few weeks later I was a passenger—the only one in years—in the little black lugger that carried from Burketown to the Roper stores for his ill-fated patrol. We unshipped them to the care of Mounted-Constable Sheridan at Roper Bar. Morey, Hall, Mahoney and McColl were on their way across country, with a big plant of packs and trackers, to take delivery and make north into Arnhem Land, to arrest the murderers of six Japanese of the *Raff* and the *Myrtle Olga*, luggers that had put in to those savage coasts a year before. McColl never came back.

Amazing is the record of heroism and endurance that is the history of the North Australia Mounted. Even in the last two years these men, some of them still on the sunny side of thirty, have lived the hair-raising thrillers of a schoolboy's dream. I met them all in Darwin, well-tailored and trim, even dashing in their khaki uniforms and outsizes in sombrero hats—hats that have more than once been the target of a shower of spears in the ranges. In from the trail, cooling off on the balcony of the police barracks that overlooks the sea, with their trackers and witnesses huddled under the trees outside it, they laughed with me over yarns that would electrify Zane Grey. Some of them have followed adventure in other parts of the world, but most are Australians from the cities, who apply for the job eager for a taste of the Territory, and are chosen for their physique, pluck, endurance and resource. They need them all.

A few months' patrol of the tin streets of Darwin, watching the Chinese for a possible opium scoop, and they are off on a beat that runs any way for a thousand miles, probably with a pack-team of mules and horses that they learn to manage on the way, and a tracker for company. Following native smokes eastward to the Macarthur and westward to the Ord, rigging a net in the pandanus swamps of a flooded river, and then sitting up all night a hundred yards away from it in a fiendish torture of mosquitoes, living on damper and iron-clads, with native tucker to follow when it gives out, and going barefoot when his boots wear through, there are times in the Territory when a policeman's lot is not a happy one.

One of his jobs is to track up native murderers and cattle-stealers in country strange to him, but an open book to the

men he is after. Such a quest demands tact as well as perseverance. To creep on a camp at daylight with a gun
ready, but instructions not on any account to use it, can be a
dangerous, if exciting, sport. To make sure you have the
right man among a couple of hundred myalls, when not one
of them speaks your language, demands a certain amount
of intuition as well as hard work.

On the way home, the guilty in custody, and likely as
not a tribe or two close following in angry mood, the constable is cook, baking damper and boiling beef for the whole
party after the day's forty-mile ride. In the evenings,
with the myalls about the camp-fire, he indulges in 'a spot
of dress-making', tailoring from flour-bags and pandanus
string a set of neat little nagas, so that his prisoners may
make their first entry to civilisation as resepectable citizens.
There is scarcely one member of the North Australia
Mounted who has not his life-and-death story to tell, but
being a casual Australian, he very rarely tells it.

It was Mounted-Constable Bridgland, of Borroloola,
who, in 1925, looking for the white women allegedly lost
among the blacks in Arnhem Land, spent six months on
the beaches of ill-famed Caledon Bay, with a watch of
three white men day and night. Although they could see
the smokes of the natives, and hear their voices at times,
none of them ever materialised, and Bridgland toasted the
New Year in a tot of medicinal brandy with his associate
constable, who later lost his reason. It was McNab who,
after an arrest of native murderers at Cape Dombey, awoke
one night on the return lugger journey to find the Badu
boatman asleep in the hold, and a native prisoner at the
tiller, steering for the open sea. Mounted-Constable Tom
Hemmings can show you a net riddled with spear-holes,
and Kennett, asleep on his lugger at Blunder Bay near the
Victoria River, in a living hell of mosquitoes, had his right
hand nearly chopped away. 'I had my watch-dog with
me,' said Kennett, 'but he couldn't open his mouth to bark
without choking on mosquitoes.' That job ended in the
grave illness of Constable Kennett at Timber Creek, a
delirium of fear and fever in which he refused to sleep
without his dog in the room.

McKinnon of the South-west Patrol and Tony Lynch of

the North-west Patrol, down in the Centre, have their
stories, too, but those I was to learn later.

Thrilling dashes into the unknown country tracking up
black desperadoes are not by any means the everyday
experiences of the North Australia policemen. These are
only the highlights. In all the little outposts, where sometimes a police station is a tent in the bush with G.R. placarded
on a tree beside it, he is a Pooh Bah in the wilderness,
everything from Registrar of Births to Curator of Intestate
Estates. For months, it may be years, there is no glamour
to relieve the monotony, save the circling after a 'perish,'
or the digging of yet another grave out where the dead
men lie. Giving out rations to the blacks, trading a goat
to eat in lieu of cash for a permit to employ native labour,
counting dog-scalps, certifying wills, signing miners' rights
and marriage certificates and registrations of brands, every
traveller of the track is his guest—and they are few. In
his spare time he milks the goats, slaughters the beef, grows
the cabbages and sets the yeast for his daily bread, and then
eats it alone. Such a cruel isolation, on the trail or at home,
had life become to the long, long arm of the law in the
Territory, that a few years ago the Commonwealth Government issued an edict by which now only the married men
are sent to the farthest outposts.

So it is that the little police barracks at the Roper and
the Daly are pretty homes to-day, the delight of pioneer
women who not only share their husband's loneliness but his
work. Bandaging spear-wounds and making splints from
paper-bark for a stockman's broken leg, baking bread and
sewing for the blacks, and sometimes educating their children by correspondence lessons and the light of a hurricane
lamp in the evenings, these women of the police stations
in the real outback have become outstanding characters,
playing their parts with unfailing courage and cheeriness,
and showing a heroism every bit as notable as that of the
young men on patrol.

CHAPTER XVIII

GOD'S FIRST HUMANS

HIS battered old felt turned down, and his clay pipe tilted up, he sits out in the only scrap of shade in the yard, black arms steeped to the elbow in a tub of murky soap-suds, an occasional puff of smoke to show that he is not quite asleep. In private life he is Winningurri, witch-doctor of the Wargaits, with two or three tribal murders to his credit, commonly known as Nipper, or Nym, or Sandy, or Blucher, or any old name that comes to hand, the universal 'washerwoman' of the North and North-west.

For an hour at a time he sits motionless, watching the bubbles burst, then drifts away to prop his back against the poinciana tree, and doze in its scarlet shade.

'Hey, Nipper, you been finishem up quicktime!' comes an agonised call from the verandah.

'Might be!' says Nipper, trailing back to the tub. Somehow, sometime, this quite unnecessary and all too frequent washing will get itself done. With all the future ahead, why worry? It was at Marble Bar that the hotel-keeper's wife showed me a pair of unbelievably filthy khaki shorts she had found soaking with the d'oyleys and the table-napkins. 'No good, Charlie,' she stormed. 'You been puttim boss's old trousers longa clean-fella clothes!'

'No more boss's trousa,' denied Charlie cheerfully. 'That fella belonga me!'

Through all the towns and stations of the outback, where the aboriginal and the half-caste provide the only domestic service, and the wages are five shillings a week and 'a bit o' baccy,' it is the same old servant problem. In Australia black labour, with its suggestion of dumb, willing slaves that make the white woman a languid goddess, is nearly as disheartening as the white. Certainly, where women of the South are content with one general help, those of the North are blessed with a whole tribe, but it is a questionable blessing —hosts of piccaninnies, friends and relations to be fed and clad, unending family feuds to smooth over, and quite often the said tribe 'goes walkabout' at a moment's notice, back to the nomad life for a week, or perhaps six, leaving a bereft housewife to manage along as may be. His ancestral home a sheet of paper-bark, except on stations where piccaninnies have been caught young and trained from babyhood, Binghi and all his mothers and sisters make poor housemaids. Where natives have been in close touch with the white for a generation or two, it is not rare to find a lubra who can cook, iron, and even machine her own dresses; but few white women will allow black hands to touch the food or the intimate living-rooms. Consequently the heat of the cooking and much of the daily round falls to their own share.

Half-caste girls, well-trained in convents and missions, give excellent service as a rule, but these are restricted to the larger towns or kept at the mission stations, where they are early married into half-caste colonies, so that 75 per cent. of the labour of North Australia is pure black, and black labour is a contradiction in terms.

In Broome and Darwin and on all the stations that lie between, early morning brings them up from camp and compound, the boys with bright headbands round their curly hair and last night's corroboree paint on their faces, the women in vivid frocks that trail to ankle-length above their bare, silent feet, with babies in the coolamons on their hips, and pipes stuck laughably in the back of their beads. One survey of the washing-up, a little dalliance with broom and bucket, and, unless watched with lynx eyes, mysteriously they disappear to the garden, to ponder this endless futility of work that the white man is obsessed with, and

> 'Under the shade of melancholy boughs,
> Lose and forget the creeping hours of time.'

A passing relative calls in, to be followed by others, until the tribe and all its dogs are accumulated, with babble of talk, an animated gambling ring, even a little corroboree singing—and then Mollie and Nubbudda are called back by an exasperated 'missus' to scrub the verandah—that is, to paddle like joyous children in a swirl of well-water.

Rooney is sent to the store with a note for potatoes, which she promptly loses. 'Missus been talk whitefella, puttim longa pot,' she informs the baffled storekeeper. A set of the best spoons is missing. 'Littlefella tchubble? Might be somewhere!' suggests Ngalia hopefully. The appearance of the baby's doll—'piccaninny debil-debil'—is signal for a little holiday of irrepressible mirth. Then a young mother brings up her new baby for Missus to christen, blushing, if it were possible, with pride and delight, when a facetious Boss suggests Narcissus or Billy Musk.

So, with a minimum of work and a maximum of laughter and loafing, the day goes through, for behind those stolid faces is hidden many a whimsical smile and much real humour, conscious and unconscious. Everything that happens in the whitefella's day, travellers arriving, tea-parties, little squabbles between husband and wife, apparently unnoticed, are treasured up to provide merry burlesque in the night's corroboree, and no sooner does dusk come in than lubras and boys and piccaninnies and the old are gathered about the glowing red of the camp-fires, while the tins and the clicking-sticks begin their rhythm, setting the hills and billabongs ringing all the sleep-time through with the primitive music of the 'ninji-ninji.'

A woodland people, strangers to walls and floors, here are your true Communists. Happy and thoughtless of to-morrow as children, to these the things of the world matter little—money has no value for them, and clothes, tobacco, even food to the hungry, all is to be shared. Excellent stockmen, because they love the open-air and riding the white man's horses, which they call yowerda, 'ears,' in Kimberley, as house-servants they have their virtues, an impeccable honesty, deep affection and faithful care of children, a gentle submission, true sympathy in illness— negative virtues all, but those who have the knack of dealing with them, a manner kindly but not indulgent, jocose but not familiar, find them a good working basis.

By the way, they will tell you that a nigger will never contradict you, that he 'lets you have it' for peace and tobacco. Not always. With their quick intuition, they sense their audience, and if he earnestly wants the truth, he gets it. By a casual quietness, a cheery smile, the suggestion of the alternative, and a 'one of the family' manner, I could always get the facts. It was old 'Scotty' Mitchell, of Burnside, who, riding down the billabong with one of his boys, was contradicted flatly. A bird flew by, and Mitchell asked what it was, being a Scot and new to the country.

'Plover,' said his boy Charcoal obligingly in English.

'That's no' a plover!' protested Mitchell.

'Him plover all right!' insisted Charcoal.

'Weel, it's no' the plover I used to know when I was a boy,' persisted Scotty.

Charcoal grinned. 'Oh, that old beggar been dead long time!' he said pleasantly, with the accent on the 'long.'

To rank the Australian native as a moron and a gorilla man is to do him a very grave injustive. Deceived by a physiognomy sullen in repose, the protruding chin and the receding forehead of the ape, and those long, tenuous fingers that are peculiarly helpless with the tools of our civilisation, the earlier ethnologists were hasty in their judgments. To look closer and with kindlier eyes is to discover that the aboriginal is redeemed by the delicate sensitive ear of the true musician, a remarkable gift of languages, the sudden smile and the quiet, quick laughter of a very real sense of humour. Left far behind in the race of the ages, marooned on an island continent of sunny climate, he never bothered to build himself a house because he did not need it. In a country where white ants consume and kangaroos break through and steal, he neglected the arts of agriculture and became a nomad, following the trail of the edible fruits and animals, and carrying the fire to the wood instead of the wood to the fire.

The worst that might be said of him is that he is a child of his environment, but a normal child, not a backward one. If in a sense of handicraft he is lacking, in arts unknown to the white man he is past master. To see a native spearing fish in the rivers and seas of the North that are his own element is to witness a sleight of hand and rapidity of thought remarkable. With unerring perception and a subconscious response in action, he can pick up the direction of those darting shadows far below water surface, and pin them through in the twinkling of an eye. With an extraordinary intuition of speed and refraction, with two separate spears, he can pinion the same fish twice in the hundredth of a second!

Hunting on the plains, in uncanny realism he simulates the hopping of the wallaby, or the stark, motionless branch of a tree, or reproduces in perfect mimicry the cry of a bird to its mate. So close is he to the heart of Nature that he deceives Nature herself. He can track dingoes, a yellow bundle of nerves with yellow eyes ever-open, and spear them sleeping. No white man yet, with all his text-book mathematics, ever made and threw a boomerang as he can do it, and no white man or woman can yandy.

Tracking is a sixth sense—the skill that has made the Australian blackfellow world-famous. Handed down by generations of hunters, it has become sheer instinct. The faster he travels, the surer he is of the trail. The slightest change in that blank and implacable bushland, that covers its secrets so cunningly from sophisticated eyes, are to him easy reading. Like those little birds that refuse to return to their nests when the eggs have been touched, he senses the foreign element.

The native tracks for his daily bread and the safety of his life. He knows if a lizard is fat or thin. He can tell the flying hoof-marks of wild horses from the unshod colts of the station mob, and knows how many there were, and what colour. He can almost tell what mood a man was in, and why and when and where he paused when he travelled that way. He can track over rocks, and along the railway lines where there are any, and, if he loses the track, he circles like a dog, and picks it up again. Question his methods and he becomes uncertain. In deferring to your judgment, he loses his own. One of the most amazing instances of tracking that I know was simple. A white man and a native were crossing the wastes of the Territory, far from the beaten trail, in the country of wild tribes, and came across a boot track. 'A white man!' said the white man in surprise. 'No. Half-caste,' corrected the native. The boots were the good old elastic sides that the whole of the outback wears on the cattle runs, and the boy had never been in this area before; yet, sure enough, two nights later, they came in to a waterhole and found a half-caste camped there. Even a boot-track could tell its individual story.

A self-abasing soul, with yet no sense of inferiority, too quickly has the native suffered the impositions of civilisation, ceding his country, his cherished waters, finding for the white colonist gold and pearls—which he himself never noticed before and never will value—and selling his birthright for a stick of tobacco and a quartpot of tea, with a few old rags of clothing that but impede his movements and impair his grace.

But perhaps the most outstanding of his virtues—and virtues they undoubtedly are—are an innate amiability and gentleness, and an extraordinary natural politeness. Whenever I approached the straggling pandanus camps of the North, where, a mile from the settlement in a sweaty country, he wisely dispenses with all raiment, my appearance provoked a frantic search for something wearable, it may even be a petrol tin or the hastily plucked branch of a tree. Once an old lubra feverishly whipped off her own frock and put it on her husband, and on another occasion two natives walked forth to greet me behind one inadequate old pair of trousers, advancing and retiring simultaneously. Innocent as Adam, they did not mind being naked. It was for my susceptibilities they trembled.

Walking with black guides by the billabongs, I surprised a dozen unexpected courtesies that a seasoned gallant might have envied them, the quick and careful placing of stepping-stones, and the knack of holding back the branches in front of me while they walked behind and accorded me the path. I like these people. I like their ever-ready laughter, just below the surface, at this, or that, or anything; their wide grins and the melancholy in their dark eyes, their graceful gestures, their soft voices, their infinite patience, their uncomprehendingness of life's complexity, their kinship with the lazy Australia that is so much more theirs than mine.

Where do they come from, these children of the sun? Nobody knows. Professor Perry includes them in his migration for gold and pearls from the cradle of the human race in Egypt across lower Asia, Indonesia, Oceania, Australasia and Polynesia to the southern Americas. He quotes kindred characteristics such as the burial of the dead, with their belongings, wrapped in paper-bark. It may be, but if so, they have forgotten what they came for, for the Australian never valued either gold or pearls.

In the past ten years schemes innumerable have been suggested for the betterment of the aborigines, by missionaries and anthropologists and quite a number of other people who are directly or indirectly making a living by them. Public sympathies run high. White Australia is developing the remorse and brotherly love of Jacob for Esau dispossessed. Every year philanthropists who know nothing about them are battering at the gates of governments with new ideas, and most of them absurd. But all our piety and all our wit is wasted. The aborigine keeps on dying at an alarming rate. By the end of the century there will be very few full-bloods left.

'The earth his bed and heaven his canopy,' wrote William Dampier, that globe-trotting journalist of the seventeenth century. Many a time has the beautiful and poetic phrase been levelled at them in contempt, yet it expresses a sylvan ideal of which we, with our lifts and wall-beds and umbrellas raised in a shower, have fallen far short.

Generous to a fault, here is your true Socialist. With no sense of acquisition, no ethics of selflessness or sacrifice, the Australian is content with the fullness and the sunshine of to-day. Nationhood he does not know. Emulation strikes no note in his consciousness. In the great race of civilisation, he is an outsider. Stone Age man, a savage at heart, it is scarcely fair to blame him for the faulty vision of eyes that cannot read sense into our complex codes. Had we white-skinned, adopted Australians been wiser and more tolerant, eager to learn instead of teach, we might have gained much that is of value, a comprehensive knowledge of his life and his languages, his arts and his inmost thoughts, that were never more than half-articulate and that are now irretrievably lost.

Horror and beauty mingle in all the rites of the aborigine. Harmless and likeable for the most part as a 'possum, he suffers surprising reversions to the sheer savage. Even when acclimatised to the white man's ways and the white man's tucker, he is still essentially a primitive. Between his sanity and his insanity there is no margin. So benighted is his mind that it has never grasped the science of life and death.

Death is the deliberate evil magic of an enemy; birth, the permeation of a spirit of the rocks and springs.

Afraid of the dark, he huddles about his tiny fires in the wilderness, and sings at the top of his voice to keep the debil-debil away.

I have studied his life and his beliefs far from the railway lines, where he is still to be found unharnessed with the horrible rags and the half-comprehensions that civilisation has inflicted upon him, and I have stepped into a strange world, the psychology of the savage that, except in a few scientific works of great value but little public recognition, has never been written.

One of the weirdest rites of all is Kurdaitcha, the blood-vengeance. The practice of Kurdaitcha extends throughout the whole of unoccupied Central Australia, westward from Oodnadatta across the Musgraves, the Petermann, the Warburton and the Mann Ranges, north-west almost to Marble Bar.

Technically, it translates into 'man-devil,' as opposed to 'maamu,' the supernatural, and with all the sorceries and secrecies of medieval revenge, resolves itself into a series of Ku Klux Klans of the desert.

Following a wife-stealing on the part of a neighbouring tribe, or a death due to alleged bone-pointing, or sometimes to sheer blood-lust on one pretext or another, the old men of the group put their heads together, and a party of murderers is chosen. Never more than three or four of the discreet and seasoned older men.

For them, first of all, are fashioned the devil-shoes of death—crude little bundles of emu-feathers, matted together with human blood, tied on with a strand of plaited hair. Two inches deep of grey and white feather fluff, uneven in size, these sneaking slippers leave scarcely a mark upon the softest sand, and it is impossible for the keenest tracker to divine whether they are coming or going. In the salt-bush and spinifex country, where the wearers leap craftily from bush to bush, not the slightest trace of footsteps is discernible.

On the night before departure, the men paint themselves in fearsome uncorroboree fashion with straight lines of white eagle-hawk feathers adhering to the sticky blood of the pricked skin. Streaks of kopi distort their faces and bodies from human shape, and the nose is tied up to the ears with whitened hair-string to effect a ferocious disguise. Small special spears are taken, reed-thin and brutally sharp, that leave little evidence of their penetration, with one or two crude white markings on the haft.

During all this preparation, the lubras, children and unchosen members of the tribe see nothing. Kurdaitcha exercises a strange hypnotic effect upon those of the same tribe and on other tribes through which it passes. No word of it is ever sent round in smoke signals. The leader of the ghostly gang has been known to slink through a big camp without being noticed, or to jump into a clump of saltbush and disappear. Little is eaten upon the track; and tiny smokeless fires are lighted behind the bushes and buried. Should a wandering hunter find the traces of such a fire, he immediately lies down and crawls to hiding, and he dare not mention the matter to his own people for months.

Living phantoms of the desert, ready at any moment to 'freeze' into the semblance of a dead tree, or a pile of stones, or even a fat old prenty goanna, the devil-men haunt the soaks and the water-holes and hunting-grounds until they come upon the tribe of the wanted men. Invariably their attack is at piccaninny daylight. Then, with unerring and swift precision, from behind a rock or shrub, the doomed one is pinioned, and the party makes off, lithe vanishing shadows that are but part of the grey of dawn, back to its own country, to the wailing and the scatter of the attacked group. There is little time for planning before the avenging Kurdaitcha is out, sometimes to exact a penalty from a tribe perfectly innocent. So these underhand feuds and ghoulish desert wars go on for generations, never taking toll of more than one man at a time.

South of the Musgrave Ranges and out to the West Australian border, it is often a cannibal matter, for this is the country of the eaters of man-meat. The gangsters secure the collar-bone of the dead as a charm and trophy to be worn at the back of the neck, leaving the unwanted remains to be devoured by his brethren.

Kurdaitcha is practically unknown beyond Tennant's Creek, but the far North can contribute two or three practices of stark horror on its own account. One of these is the kidney-fat rite, known to tribes of the Daly and Alligator Rivers, Arnhem Land, and formerly to the Larrakeahs of Darwin itself. Two years ago a murder case of this horrific nature was tried before me in the Supreme Court at Darwin, and the death sentence commuted to life imprisonment. George or Molyben, the offender, from Manbulloo near Katherine, is at present a prisoner in the Fannie Bay Gaol.

Caught alone in the bush, the victim of this unholy and unwholesome semi-religious practice is slit with a crude knife in the abdomen, and his kidney-fat extracted, generally to be worn in the whiskers of one of the old doctors, to lend increased efficiency to his magic, and sometimes hung in a tree to exert its evil influences upon an enemy camped beneath.

A friend of mine, Mrs. Patullo, of Burnside Station, Brock's Creek, was horrified to learn that the kidney-fat of one of her house-lubras, who had died suddenly and mysteriously in the camp, had been festooned for weeks in her kitchen, to wreak its curses upon the head of old Ah Sam, the unsuspecting Chinaman cook, who had become 'stingy longa tucker.'

Bone-pointing, the evil eye of death in actual fact and a triumph in suggestion, is still practised frequently by tribes of North and Central Australia. Concentrating deadly spite upon its victims, a bone is pointed in secret, but the doomed man, as soon as he hears of it—and he always does—invariably dies. All the hanky-panky of the tribal doctors cannot save him. An Australian aborigine can be bitten almost in halves by a crocodile, or visibly consumed by some wasting disease, or practically burnt to death, and not know about it, quite cheerfully recovering; but in prime of youth and fullness of strength, he cannot survive the curse of the deathbone. He believes that his heart is gone, or that a fire is eating at his entrails, or that his blood is seeping away. Listlessly and hopelessly he sits under a tree, and in a matter of days obligingly dies.

Three or four inches long, sometimes the bone is worn and polished like old ivory from three or four centuries of grisly usage, sometimes even more terrifyingly new, fashioned in the height of anger. To bring about fatal effects, it is always human, generally one of the lesser bones of a man's arm. Attached to two or three yards of human hair string, it is a gruesome little piece of witchcraft unpleasant to handle. Before it attains its potency, it must be 'sung.' The conspirators take it out in the bush and murmur over it some abracadabra of incantation so old that they probably do not know the meaning of the words. Then they bury it.

When the time comes, they bring it in to the vicinity of the condemned man. Perhaps while he is singing corroboree or sleeping in the firelight, they point it at him, never directly, but hiding one behind the other, or with a malevolent and repeated jerk over the shoulder, or bending, with the back turned, from between the knees. No word is spoken, no motion visible to the unthinking tribe, for this sorcery is punished, in its turn, with death, but the sinister whisper comes surely. First the victim, and then the whole tribe, wait with dread for the inevitable, and, when it happens, a bone of the dead man goes with the party to avenge his death.

Sticks and spear-heads and carved pieces of wood ringed with white down, or dotted with red ochre and blood, and euro and kangaroo and eagle-hawk bones are used in lesser magics, while the lubras frequently bewitch their yam-sticks for minor curses. Powdered ant-bed scattered round a wurlie is another 'poison.'

All must be duly 'sung' and doctored with debil-debil. Very rarely do the natives attempt to 'bone' a white man—it is part of their occult 'blackfella business.' But I came across one instance at Banka Banka, where a tribe had passed sentence of death in this manner on a station-manager, who in burning-off had unwittingly obliterated the graves of some of their old men. The whisper of his doom came to him from one of the house-lubras, and he laughed. That is three years ago, and he is still laughing.

But for all that he is admittedly far down in the human scale, tearing his meat with his teeth, frightened of his own shadow, child of an environment of which we have no comprehension, the Australian black is just human, and comparatively few of these purely aboriginal customs are of a revolting nature. Indeed, some of them are instinct with a racial wisdom and a true poetry for which the things of an advanced civilisation make poor recompense to him.

A fascinating study is that of the eight great 'skins' that, with their law and logic, stretch right across the North, from Kimberley to Queensland, protecting the little nomad groups from the curse of in-breeding; the journeys of the corroboree-maker, immune from tribal attacks, in his peaceful mission of collecting new songs and dances. Beautiful are the love-singings of the Centre, where, like Dido of old, a lubra will climb a little hill, making the magics that will bring her boy back to her, and beautiful the simple lullaby that, in a voice soft as an Austral wind, a young mother will croon, her back against a tree and her baby in a coolamon beside her—an Epstein study of Madonna and child.

The proper study of mankind is man. The aboriginal is Australian man, a relic of the world's forgotten past. In teaching him how to live, we have taught him only how to die.

CHAPTER XIX

CORROBOREE

IT rings to the stars in the great echoless emptiness of the spinifex deserts—corroboree, swan song of a vanishing people. Pulsing, primitive, its rhythm is the very heart-beat of the lost Australia, its falling cadences an elegy. The aboriginal is doomed. Child of sunny skies and a sunny philosophy, his ignorance is bliss. He goes down into the darkness singing:

> 'Mana-manaa, mana-manaa,
> Manin-yaa, manin-yaa,
> Ngala-barrai, ngala-barrai, ngala-barrai. . . .'

Boomerangs, reddened with human blood, drumming in the dust . . . a saturnalia of stamping skeletons, wheeling, whirling, whooshing, in the red glow of the little fires . . . and a sweet, plaintive singing, now eerily sinking as a wind among the trees, now strident and clamorous as a kookaburra chorus in the hills at daylight . . . such is a good corroboree, but you have to travel a long, long way to see it.

Not in New South Wales, nor Queensland, nor Victoria, not south of Oodnadatta in South Australia, nor of Kimberley in the West, do they make 'bigfella wonga' now. Shaving with a bit of broken bottle, watching the train come in and the aeroplane take off, going to the pictures on Saturday nights, with a child's short memory they have forgotten.

'Old fella die away, corroboree been finish,' they told me in the camps near the towns, but when I hummed over a stave of that once-heard-ever-remembered music, the same Australia over, the dark eyes would light to laughter and recollection, and the beating tins begin.

For corroboree is not dead yet. I have heard it on the beaches of the very far North-west in the moonrise, by the billabongs and hill-recesses of the ranges, where still they 'make young men,' and by all the lily-pools of the North. There, still, dusk wakens the ironwood clicking sticks and the droning of the didgeree-du with phantasmagoria of song and dance, and throughout the lonely wastes of the Centre that wistful dirge of the choirs of darkness rises and falls and fades away across the sand-hills.

His thoughts and his language lost, his myths and fables a child's immature fancies, and his so-called art a child's first scrawlings in crayon, the aboriginal expresses the whole dramatic intensity of his being, his laughter, his fears, his impressions and his memories, only in dance and song. His footlights are the circling spinifex fires, his green-room the shadowy aisles of the paper-barks. With never a soul to listen, his pantomime is genius, his music one of Nature's own symphonies, the most truly classic native music in the world.

Dark moon. In the mighty starlit theatre of the Never-Never the stage is set, a clearing between the trees. Uncanny under-current of the darkness comes the heavy bass breathing of the didgeree-du, the great native oboe of hollowed smoke-wood or bamboo. A few bars, and the gil-gil sticks chime in with the clear high treble of a million crickets, and the descending chromatic scale of black singing, soft at first, then rising in a magnificent crescendo till the very welkin cracks.

Huddled in a big circle, the whole camp keeps perfect unison, lubras and piccaninnies and old men, eyes and teeth flashing white in the firelight, shoulders swaying to the abandon of the music. Over and over the same meaningless words, the same beat of faultless rhythm. Hollowed hands are cupping naked thighs with the sound of distant tom-toms, boomerangs clicking together, and yam-sticks beating the dust. White-headed and blind, an ancient on the outskirts bangs two tins together, and breaks into an ecstatic yell, the haunted wail of a chained dog.

The singing increases to a frenzy and then stops dead, leaving the echoes pulsing in a deathlike hush. The music throbs again, and one voice takes up the singing, the voice of the 'maker,' thin as a reed and ghostly. The dancers are ready. Timed to the rising of a certain star, corroboree begins.

From the wings of the paper-barks they come, in a mist of dust and firelight, the grotesque dancing figures of the black men. Fearsome faces, daubed and distorted with a grim humour, are framed in pom-poms of cockatoo feathers, gleaming silver-white. Head-dresses rigged of hair and tree-fibres, ochred and waxed to a fantastic erection of sticks, quiver and swing. Bodies painted with pigments of earth and white lines of eagle-hawk down dangle and stamp like bones upon a wire.

In and out in a writhing serpentine between the fires they go, black feet thudding, the rustling of little branches fastened at knees and elbows, and the hoarse, guttural whisper of the dancers making a ghoulish music that is scarcely of this world.

The anguish of a thirsting man and his delirious joy at finding water; the frantic waddle of a fat iguana with the yapping dogs in his wake; great hunts of the past; farewell to an old camp; the graceful strutting of the brolgas in their minuet, or the wriggle of a snake—these are the simple themes of the dance, but so close to Nature that he is at one with her, with an amazing subconscious sense of comedy and pathos, the aboriginal is a master of burlesque, a prince of mimicry.

Trotting through the bush in the night-time, generally alone, for very few of the pioneers have time for the blacks and their screeching, and sitting on an upturned petrol tin under the stars, how much dust and effluvium have I swallowed, but never quite in vain. 'Which-way that one him talk blackfella all-about?'—and there was always something to scribble in my note-book by the light of those crackling fires. Here is a kangaroo corroboree, danced by men of the kangaroo totem—the wild leaping of the hunted, the climax of the kill; or perhaps abracadabra of the rain-maker, with his magic stones from the creek-bed, treasured through generations, wrapped in blood-stained feathers and a spinifex net; the minderee dance of the emu men, 'singing' a little boy's knees to give him the speed of a fleet runner, and safety in flight from his enemies, followed by a wil-wil of the lubras, their feet a soundless chassée in the dust, leaving the track of the turtle, and the sinuous ripple of arms and shoulders that stage-dancers of the world try to acquire, and only a black woman knows.

Of an older darkness, more savage and more sinister, are the manhood corroborees, hidden from all sight and knowledge in the secret places of the bush, with their 'mourra' gods fashioned of human blood and human hair, the totem-boards with crude concentric circles of sex and mystery that is death for a woman to look upon, a mad voodoo revelry that extends over a period of weeks, and rings at the very heart of the night till the last stars are paling, and the dancers fall exhausted with the paint upon their faces in the ghastly grey of dawn.

Sacred and profane, poison-dance and playabout, corroboree is the big 'blackfella business' of life, the armistice of warring tribes, its season a period of plenitude and peace. With the first thunderstorms of the wet, from swamp and jungle, from the cattle outcamps, and the fishing-grounds, and the deserts and the salt seas, the tribes come in, following the smoke signals sometimes for hundreds of miles, over rocks and rivers and blistering sands, carrying their babies on their shoulders and hunting their food on the way, to 'sit down' by a soak or billabong where tucker is plentiful, and 'make wonga' there for months.

For hours and days of preparation, the matinée idols, the producer and the wardrobe-makers squabble and confer, and devote themselves to make-up in their little hidden tree-shelters that are their dressing-rooms. Their props and costumes are whatever the country offers and fancy dictates—ochre and kopi and coloured clay, cotton from the shrubs, feathers of birds, necklets of animals' teeth, or sea-shells, or bamboo, with dangling ornaments and tassels and balls of kangaroo fur and dingo hair, woven and dyed, puffed with the powder of red ochre and fastened with tree-gum. For to this timeless, lazy people, no trouble is too great, no handicraft too tedious, in the cause of the cobba-cobba. To the wild men of the Australian woods, as to the Greeks and the Elizabethans and the talkie-fans of Hollywood, 'the play's the thing.'

Song-hits and dance-successes have their day and go their way, even as the tango and the ukulele and the 'Merry Widow' waltz. Grand operas and musical comedies are passed along, props and libretto and performers *in toto*, on tour through the great wide spaces. A good 'maker' or producer, a long-winded didgeree player or a particularly vigorous or original dancer may travel for a thousand miles, immune from attack in a stranger country, and sure of his tucker for the sake of his art.

That is why, where languages are changing in every 50 miles, nobody knows exactly what the words of corroboree mean, and why you may sometimes find pearl shells of Broome embedded in the sands of the Diamantina, or hear the rattle of the baobab nuts of Kimberley in camp at Alice Springs.

As often as not an impromptu 'singabout' for sheer *joie de vivre* or fear of the devils of night, there are occasions when the corroboree commemorates events in the life of the native even as the baby rhymes of Mother Goose embody so much of the history of England. In the country about Eucla on the Great Australian Bight, there is still in existence a Jennuk-dance, with its sticks carved to resemble muskets, its painted cross-bands, the boat drill and the 'Present Arms' of Flinders, and his blue-coats, who landed on these coasts one hundred and thirty years ago. A time-honoured corroboree along Cooper's Creek is the 'Old Man of Lake Eyre,' tattered and famished and raving with thirst, who pitches on his head into a blacks' camp, to be succoured and restored, with 'yacki' and embraces, to his own kind who come to seek him. This is alleged by the old hands, who have seen it unchanged over a period of fifty years, to be the story of King, sole survivor of the Burke and Wills expedition, who spent three months in the kindly care of the tribes of Innamincka.

But very rarely will you find instances of such long memory among the aborigines of Australia. Corroboree is much more frequently a burlesque of the day's events, or yesterday's—the killing of a wallaby, the peculiarities of a new arrival, or perhaps, with wicked and irresistible humour, the antics of a bagman 'on a bender.' Evidence of many a murder has been pieced together by the police of both the Territory and Kimberley from its gruesome reproduction in mime and music by the camp fire.

Already in the North I have seen an aeroplane dance, great wings of turkey red that sway and settle in the fire-light, the propeller made of a couple of womerahs, or a wireless ballet with its quivering aerials of sticks and fibre, and ear-phones of carved poinciana bean.

Australia is no longer a black man's country, and the twentieth century has no room for palaeolithic man. The old traditional dances are dying fast, sacred dances of the tribes and totems, the rainbow and the rain-stone, and the animals and reptiles that were the great legendary fathers of the race. The nature-voices of the old Australia are fading in the echoes of that wild sweet singing, and for the first of the Australians, the comedy is ended.

A few years, and there will be no more corroboree.

CHAPTER XX

THE MAKING OF A MAN

FIRES in the ranges glittering like the lights of a little city. Shrill frenzy of men's voices in a hidden gully of the dusk. Across the darkness the booming of the big bull-roarer, deepening from a murmur to a roar.

The lubras fly screeching to their mias, to hide their faces in terror in the darkness. A boy, a stripling, stands alone in the tree-shadows, with fear in his eyes.

Till now he has wandered, happy with the other children and all his 'mothers,' to find the honey-bag or a nest of fledgling parrots, learning to track goannas and bandicoots, to tend the fish-traps, to swing the miniature play-boomerang that dangles from his hair-belt. Those halcyon days are over. Now must he keep away from the women under pain of death. Now must he learn the words and signs of skins and totems; eat, from the hands of the old men, the foods as yet forbidden him, and look upon the sacred boards and dances that it is death for a woman to see. Goondabuduri, devil of the Chambidyena, has come to carry a child away, and make of him a man.

Even as the knights of old, with vigil and with fasting, but with certain rites of blood-drinking and mutilation hair-raising in this, the twentieth century—so is the Australian aboriginal initiated into the mystery of manhood. To this primitive race, with no word in its language for love, no regard for its women, and no comprehensions of the physiological beginnings of life, sex is a secret, sacred thing. Rites of the initiation vary considerably throughout Australia, from one 'blackfella country' to another, and between the circumcised and the uncircumcised. In Kimberley and the far North, a man passes through nine degrees from youth to age, in an amazing Masonic ritual of the savage.

It is usually just before the wet season, when the tribes are in from walkabout or work on the cattle stations, that an initiation takes place. For some time the boy's 'proplyfella father' has conferred with his uncles: 'My boy grow bigfella. Whiskers come up belong him. Might be this time been eatum tajee-tucker, makim young man allabout.' As the tribes gather at the billabongs, waiting for the rains, the old men 'gibit word.'

The first step is separation from the lubras. With mysterious whisperings and excursions, the boy is led away to a small shelter hidden in the bush, 300 yards or more from the camp. No longer must he look upon the little girls who were his playmates, his mother, or even his grandmother. No longer must he accept the vegetable food of their gathering from their hands. Even the sound of women's voices is accursed, their track upon the ground. Should he chance to hear their voices in the distance, he must stuff his ears with chewed leaves or wild cotton and fly.

Each night in the ceremonial antics of sacred corroboree, to him are disclosed the totems, his own again and again, kindred totems, enemy totems, the marriage skins and the skins tabu, by the old men and the witch-doctors. Priests, as it were, in this weird woodland religious rite, are the ngungas,' fathers of the lubras into whose skin or totem the boy may later marry.

'Cockatoo catchum crocodile woman, wild dog belonga mopoke,' he is told in haunting sing-song. 'Carpet-snake catchum witchetty grub, that no good, poison, all same skin' —the remarkable racial wisdom that keeps each tiny group free from the curse of inbreeding. So on through pandanus, caterpillar, flying-fox, whistle-duck, lily-root, moon, gull and grasshopper, the great forefathers of the race, until he knows them all. Of the food of his own totem he may now eat for the first time, and is strictly instructed in the foods 'tajee' or tabu. 'Turkey turns the hair grey,' goes the night-long chant. 'Snake-tail make him no more see.'

When he has learned well the totems and foods, comes the knocking out of the tooth, the extracting of the left upper incisor in a crude and painful bush dentistry, generally with a stone wedge and a stone hammer. Should the young patient howl and struggle—and with a healthy, deep-set slab of high-grade ivory he usually does both—the yells of corroboree and a few of his uncles sitting on his head effectively drown the wails of anguish. With tear-filled eyes, and the first outward and visible signs of manhood, the little initiate puts his tongue into the warm salt space and sits up smiling.

Immediately following the tooth ceremony comes the journey to collect relatives and friends for the vital matter of the circumcision. By the men of the tribe, the boy is taken on a long trail of all friendly camps in the neighbourhood, sometimes within hundreds of miles, with invitations by smoke-signal and letter-stick, to his coming of age. As he approaches, his advent hailed by native smokes, he is met far from the camps by the men, never by the lubras. On this journey the name of woman is anathema, not only to the boy, but to all who accompany him. Otherwise he would sicken and die. An offender is swiftly and justly finished by a fatal spear. It is a curious thing that the blacks have no objection in the world to a white woman knowing their secrets or seeing their ceremonies. I think I am right in saying that there has never been an assault on a white woman by the natives in all Australian history, unless in the very civilised areas. They scarcely do her the honour of regarding her as woman, and, right through Australia, I have found no reticence among the old men so far as their tribal secrets were concerned.

The boy is kept on his feet night and day. Fatigued almost to unconsciousness with countless days of walking and nights of dancing, the little chap returns at last to his native country, and, decked with the snow-white down of eagle-hawk and cockatoo, his body painted with the signs of his totem in festive red and white ochre, is led to the hidden corroboree ground. His mother has made him a 'birthday cake' of lily-seeds, though he may not receive it from her hands. Far away in the camp, he can hear her howling, with all his sisters and his cousins and his aunts, in a shrill anguish of ecstasy for a piccaninny lost, much in the manner of the mid-Victorian mother, who wept over her little son's curls.

Through a long night of devil-dancing—a hullabaloo of demons in the hills it seems, and the slight black shadow of the boy in the thick of it all—through the whirling fire-sticks and showers of flaming spinifex, the child is dragged from dance to dance till dawn. Then, at the setting of a star, in a torpor of intense weariness, he is circumcised, reclining upon the backs of his mother's brothers—the swift, clean surgery of the savage with crude, sharp knife of stone.

Following circumcision, the great event of his life, the boy is well smoked over green leaves burning, and hidden away in the bush sometimes for two moons, visited only by the older men. To him now are given the spears of manhood, and on his back are carved the first of the tribal markings, livid weals made by a jagged stone or piece of quartz, and raised into glistening ridges by padding the healing wound with ashes. During all this time he lives only on vegetable tucker, the flower food, and to him is allotted the wife of the tribe's choice, of the right skin and totem, generally a piccaninny still in arms or a lubra yet unborn. Later, to all intents and purposes, he rejoins the tribe, but he is still alien. He must keep away from all women under pain of death.

A few years' wandering and hunting, and the youth comes to the second stage of initiation. Again he is segregated in the bush, this time to live for a period upon nothing but the blood of animals, brought to him by his mother's brothers and the brothers of his future wife. There follows the sub-incision, an operation performed very much in the manner of the first. In some tribes, the blood from these operations is carefully kept, saturated into paper-bark, and buried by a lily-pool to make the lilies grow, the lagoon lily of the Territory being one of the principal items of blackfellow food, stem, seed and bulb.

Now the boy is eligible to be shown the sacred boards of sex, with their symbols and concentric circles, the pronged sticks, the greased and ochred god-stones in many wrappings of paper-bark, the rain-stones and egg-stones of food and fertility, and he may join in the chants and dances of the 'dreamtime'—'before white man, before grandmother.'

Again he is an exile, this time under a ban of silence that has been known to extend for years, his sole communication with the tribe by means of 'finger-yabber,' a series of signs similar to those of the deaf and dumb with which the natives communicate at a distance. This silence can be broken only at the discretion of the old men, by the simple process of biting the ball of the hand.

With his hair in an elaborate chignon and the sacred small board of the insignia stuck in the back of it, the initiate is now a free man. Through the ensuing years follow the lesser ceremonials of achieved manhood, when he presents to the assembled fathers of his affianced wife the bees' nest 'tchugar-bag,' offering of humility and allegiance, and may take his wife to his own campfire, provided that she is sufficiently grown up. With a master-stroke of unconscious wisdom and humour, he is never allowed, on any pretext, to approach or address his mother-in-law.

There remain now but the final degrees of seniority, when he becomes eligible through fatherhood to take his place in tribal councils, and attains to the ultimate assumption of 'old man,' equivalent to the Grand Mastership of our Freemasonry, when he may lead the occult corroborees, take part in initiations and rainmakings, 'sing' the little girls to womanhood, and place the votive offerings to make their breasts grow.

There is no 'standing with reluctant feet' for the little lubra. In an initiation just as painful but without so much ceremony, she is subjected to what is more or less mutilation, and is possessed by every man of the tribe, who has a right to her in 'skin-ship,' in what must be for her a ghastly night in her very early teens.

Women of the Mejeelie tribes of the East Alligator have a quaint custom. From the moment that one of them knows she is to have her 'first-time piccaninny,' she carries everywhere with her what is meant for a doll, or effigy of the small expected.

I watched Murriba, one of the lubras of Gaden's buffalo camp, with a dilly-bag of fine banyan string, packed with corroboree fluff, human hair, scraps of bamboo and ochred bark, and any soft bright trifles from trees that had taken her fancy, strung round her shoulder by a fibre string. She cuddled the crude arrangement, sang to it, nursed it, and left it with her camp-sisters in the shade when she was called away.

She was bashful when I asked her about it, but the others told me it was *namur*, the Alligator name for baby. They would 'chuckim away' when the real baby made its appearance.

I was delighted. Here, among the primitives of the jungle, was an Ante-natal Care Society. But the aboriginal explodes the theory every time, as most human beings do.

A few months later I met Murriba again in Darwin, with no trace either of the bogus infant or the bona fide one.

'Where true-fella piccaninny?' I wanted to know. 'Him been come up long time.'

Murriba was casual. 'Been losim that one,' she told me cheerfully. 'Him been tchilleep too much close-up longa fire, been dead-fella.' For her own good and sufficient reasons at the moment of birth, Murriba had had no time to devote to that particular piccanniny, and so its career was a short one.

A weird ritual, in some of its phases lyrical in its beauty, in others almost blood-curdling in its horror—such is the saga of the Australian blackfellow, child of nature, who propitiates neither god nor devil, lives from day to day, and meets death, whenever it comes and however it comes, casually.

One more word of 'nigger-stuff' as the old bushmen contemptuously call it, and I am done with them. I went to the Australian wilderness to study the blacks. I found the whites in that vast and lonely country so much more interesting, so much more 'the story,' and the natives so palpably a lifetime's study—three lifetimes, rather—that I touched upon them only in passing, but under the coco-nut palms at Mendil Beach near Darwin, I found a little cemetery unique in Australia, the only aboriginal burying-ground on the continent, and I had to know all about it.

The aborigine has no vision of a heaven of pearly gates and twanging harps, no Mahommedan paradise of palms and lilies. For him the Dark Gateway leads back into the darkness, to the realm of all the malicious little devils of fear that howl in the wind and people the night.

When a man dies, victim of evil magic, his soul is evil, too. It haunts the place of his burial, waiting its chance to be avenged upon the guilty, and then to be re-born, as tree, or kangaroo, or human. Therefore, there is no attempt to preserve the memory of the dead, but rather to fly the thought of him, and never to repeat his name, lest it should be mistaken by the spirit for a call.

One tribe alone, of all those that I have come in contact with, is the exception, the natives of Bathurst and Melville Islands, 70 miles north of Darwin and at low tide close-linked. Splendid physical specimens, and far above the mainlander in mentality, probably because of their tincture of Malay blood, the Melville Islanders not only mark their burying-grounds with carved and brilliantly painted posts, but conclude their season of mourning with a funeral dance that re-enacts the whole drama of the dead man's life—Pukamini, the dance of death.

The burial of the dead varies considerably throughout Australia, as do the languages and tribal customs generally, and it provides many an interesting sidelight on the primitive reasoning of the native. In the very far North-west I have seen corpses interred in crannies and caves. Roaming the ironstone hills about Cossack and Roebourne, one frequently comes upon a vault of grinning skulls and skeletons whitened by the passing of the years, for the tribes of these places have now been civilised almost to extinction.

The Bing-his of Broome bury the deceased very decently, with the coffin and the professional undertaker, both provided by the Government, yet with a ceremonial that retains much of its pristine savagery. Patting the mounds all over with their boomerangs, they whisper loving words of assurance and cheer to the dead man that his murder—for even to these, after three generations of Christianity and white living, it is still murder—will be revenged, so that he need not return. Then the lubras and the chief mourners indulge in a wild orgy of grief, hitting themselves with nulla-nullas and gashing their heads with stones and tins to heighten the anguish, flinging themselves with abandon upon the new-made grave, until the signal fires are lighted to carry the news to tribes afar, when they make contentedly off to a corroboree or a turtle-feast.

In East Kimberley the bodies, wrapped in paper-bark, are laid, Parsee-fashion, on trestles of branches in a tree, about five feet from the ground, with stones ranged round beneath. Each stone is named for a tribesman or a possible enemy, and woe betide the namesake of that stone upon which the first drops of putrefaction chance to fall, for he is held to be the murderer who has been secretly 'singing' or boning the dead man.   In West Kimberley, corpses are often embedded in ant-hills, or hidden in the great hollow bole of a baobab tree, or carried in wrappings of paper-bark for weeks, and on the trail used as a pillow at night!

Throughout Central Australia, the dead are buried, the grave piled high with brushwood to keep the dingoes from digging it up.   In many tribes, the body is trussed, heels touching the thighs with the big toes fastened together to prevent it 'walking' with evil intent.   The face is turned in the direction from which the tribe has come, and the space about the mound cleared of tracks and fire-swept, so that the ghost cannot follow.   Uncivilised blacks of Arnhem Land and the Gulf Country invariably partake of some portion of the dead man, to absorb his strength and virtue.

But to the Melville Islanders alone belongs the death corroboree.   When a man dies on Melville Island, or on the mainland near it, for so frequently do the tribes ply backward and forward in their dug-out canoes that they have their own cemetery on Mendil Beach—the old man most closely related to the deceased 'goes *pukamini.*'   He must neither speak nor handle his food.   His share of the fish and dead lizard are conveniently hung upon a tree, so that he may reach it with his mouth, or else he is fed by the camp lubras.

The corpse is quietly buried as a matter of course, but in the wet season following the death the tribe makes ready for a grand memorial corroboree.   First the posts are cut, usually sturdy trunks of young saplings, and carefully painted with weird hieroglyphics, age-old fantastic signs that resemble Arabic and signify nothing at all.   As many as eight or twelve are put up to a grave, 'a blackfella business' of two or three weeks' duration.   When the posts are in place, by bush trail and native canoe, in come the Melville men and women for the dance.

Make-up occupies sometimes two days, and I have never seen better.   Their hair is decked with a patchwork of vivid colours.   Puff-balls of kangaroo fur and dingo-hair, powdered deep in red ochre, are suspended round the neck, with Elizabethan ruffs of birds' feathers, and the pink and grey and snow-white down of galah and cockatoo.   Bamboo and pandanus armlets are worn, of fantastic weave and dye. Magnificent figures are the chief mourners, generally the old men of Bathurst and Melville and the 'mother's brothers,' their fuzzy hair and beards stiff with paint, a polychromatic glory, and their gleaming black bodies speckled all over, a kaleidoscope of spots quickly dabbed on in these days of civilisation with the teeth of an old comb dipped in ochre.

The dance begins with a funeral procession of a mile and more through the bush, with the old men in the lead. There is no music save the dead march of drumming upon naked thighs, and a weird, unworldly chanting, a shrill tremolo that echoes in an eerie, continuous scream through the bush. As the dancers approach the grave, this chanting resolves itself into a litany, a recital of all the dead man's virtues and achievements, the woe of his fathers, the promises of vindication. Each invocation is followed by wild leaping into the air, the loud smacking of thighs, and a concerted shout.

Arrived at the cemetery with its old posts fallen and the new ones gaily conspicuous, the dancers form a mighty ring, in the manner of chorus, while the chief mourners take the centre one by one—the old group father, with the whites of his eyes turned up, and his black feet stamping and leaping, a lubra with a baby in her arms, wailing her grief for her husband in real tears, and the men who hunted with the departed crying the prowess of a dead comrade.

Every remembered action of the man's life is re-enacted in pantomime. Has he killed a python, the struggle and the strangulation, a Laocoön in living bronze; has he once been speared by an enemy in the false dawn, his starting from sleep, the creeping of the foe, the throwing and plucking-out of the weapon, and his dash for the safety of the jungle; or has he battled with a crocodile in the shallows, the thumb-nail drama of St. George and the Dragon over again in the black man's superb histrionic art. At the end of each episode, the chorus leaps madly, and shouts a shrill note, half-ecstasy, half-grief.

The *pukamini* generally goes on for two or three hours, often in tempestuous downpours of the monsoon, that sweep the elaborate make-up to a nasty mix-up and a muddy smear, and damp the feather plumes but not the ardour of the dancers. Finale is a medley of mad shouting, wherein spears, womerahs, bark baskets, and even milk from his own lubra's breasts, and the old men's whiskers, painfully torn in frenzy from their chins, are placed upon the grave as tribute. Then, with a shrieking pandemonium to scare the last lingering debil-debil, the tribes straggle away silently through the bush, with never a backward glance to those bright new posts in the graveyard.

No longer even a memory, the dead is left to forgetfulness, soon, in the tangle of creepers and the sodden soils of soaking rain, to make one with his native earth.

CHAPTER XXI

AUSTRALIA'S CROWN OF GOLD AND PEARLS

THE heat is fœtid and intense at Darwin at the end of
'the dry,' the day a bath of sweat, the night a fever
of mosquitoes. White men feel yellow and hate
their own bodies. Naked blacks glisten like bronze. The
Chinese noticeably thrive.

Tropic trees, with their flamboyant colour and exotic
scents, are no longer a dream but a nightmare, cloying the
senses, jarring the eyes, until, for sanity's sake, one longs
for them to go out of blossom. Legs and arms are heavy
with languor. Thought and action become delirium of
slow motion. The men drink beer and the women talk
criminal libel. Normally they are a merry and very good-
hearted crowd, but the social life is meagre, and the milk
of human kindness goes bad in humidity. For about four
months of the year, October and November, March and
April, the far north Territory is certainly not a country
for white men and women to live and labour in. The only
redemption is a constant activity.

Day after day I watched those pallid skies for aeroplanes,
or sat with my pencil in court, or trudged along the ramshackle Chinese lanes looking for headlines, and finding
them, too true to be good. Some day I intend to deal with
them in fiction, the maddest fiction ever written, and only
those who know will know that it is not fiction.

Darwin is hell and heaven and good copy. The amazing
natural beauty of the place contrasts so strangely with its
squalor and its scandals. Much government has spent
millions there in the wrong way and strangled progress,
because it was always pigeon-hole government from a
department thousands of miles away, by clerks and under-
secretaries who knew nothing of conditions.

There was no water system. In a country that is submerged for nearly half the year, there was not enough water
for a daily bath, except at the hotel, and a few of the
government houses with windmills. In one of the finest

cattle-breeding areas in the world there was no fresh milk. Dairy cows died in the drought or the rankness, goats were prohibited, so the babies were reared on powder. In all that teeming fertility there were no fruits and no vegetables. Long ago the Chinese were forbidden to grow them, in White Australia logic, and no one else had the patience and the energy.

When the monthly ship came in from the South, you made a bee-line for the only white store, and paid 3/6 a pound for grapes that were a penny a pound in Perth, 2/6 for four apples, and 6d. for a tomato. You took home 10/- worth in a little brown-paper bag tucked under your arm, and shared them surreptitiously with the best friend of the moment under the mosquito net, where you could enjoy them in peace. For the general health of the rest of the month, you pinned your faith to fruit salts.

There are flower-gardens, beautiful gardens, where some enthusiasts have succeeded, with the aid of olive oil and aspirin, in rearing roses and carnations, but all of the plants and flowering shrubs are set in oil drums, on the earth, not in it, so that they can be shifted round to the side of the house or the back when white ants threaten them or a flood breaks.

I spent all my spare time in a fury of personal washing, resultant on at least four showers and four compulsory changes a day. There are plenty of *dhobis*, but I was warned that quite a number of summer visitors have been arrested on the ship when leaving for a 'small debt' of £65 or so for washing. Besides, one day I watched Long Fat spraying the ironing by the mouthful.

For the rest, I sat typewriting far into the night, while the perspiration dripped rhythmically off the end of my nose into the little machine, and then lay stifling under the net, listening to the jungle growing, watching the restless flicker of lightning that lit sea and land to the colours of day. Darwin is not a good place for sleeping. There is menace in the taut silence of those steaming nights.

Suddenly came relief. It was on New Year's morning that we woke to the sound of rain galloping madly on the roofs. In from the sea rolled a milling tumult of black and blue, that broke above us in squalls. The monsoon was down. The rivers were down. The aeroplanes and the telegraph poles and the railway bridges were down, and all Darwin was up and doing in delight of the coolness. Chinese and whites paddled about under huge blue umbrellas, beaming blessings on each other and the rain.

The lagoons and the lily-pools and the creeks were brimming. It was impossible to travel ten miles in any direction for the next three months. Out in the Territory, every station homestead was an island. The buffalo camps and the pea-nut farms were deserted, and the mines where a few old prospectors scratch gold and tin, and the lubras dig out the tantalite with their yam-sticks. Where men and cattle had died of thirst a few weeks ago, they were now drowning.

At the height of a tropic summer, it was cold enough to wear overcoats. When I took my copy to the post office I waded to the bare knees through the rushing rivers in the main streets, always to find that the weekly train was held up by a washaway, the weekly air-mail stuck in the mud and coming on by pack-horse, and that the telegraph wires were broken down or water-logged anywhere on the 2,000 miles of them that stretched between us and the cities. There was nothing to do but wait. In any case, all the envelopes in town were hermetically sealed with damp, and tropic fungus had grown over the camera lenses. Shoes and hats and curtains and clothes were covered inches deep in bright blue mildew. Life was clammy, but deliciously cool.

Ninety inches fell by the end of March. Sometimes it fell on one side of the street and not the other, but mostly in a blind deluge, rising inch by inch in flood waters. Sometimes it stopped for an hour. Stopped dead. And the hot sun came out on smiling expanses of silver—and it was like living in a steam laundry. This country that knows no clemency of spring was idyllically green, greener than a coloured post card of Phœnix Park, with everywhere reflections of green, and an impenetrable tangle of trees and creepers and tall grasses. One day they brought me in a blade of grass 32 feet high!

Millions of flying things made in to the lights at night, and built their own funeral pyre of wings and wingless bodies, and still came, and filled our socks and our necks and our ears and the ink-bottles. I took the typewriter under the bed-net and carried on, but there was an enthusiastic young American entomologist from Harvard who had come to the Territory for two years' research. He landed in on a typical tropical February evening, spent ten minutes in the hotel vestibule, and announced that he was not going any farther. He said he had enough new bugs to last him for twenty years, right here in his beer.

There was an aviator named Matthews, who had flown north from Sydney to break the record to England. He changed his mind, but he could not change his clothes, and lived in the same khaki shirt and shorts for a month, while his plane fell to pieces out on the aerodrome. There was also a philologist from Philadelphia University, Gerard Laves, collecting blacks' languages on a gramophone, but the gramophone got badly water-logged, and the records curled up, and he lost heart, too.

Darwin is like one of those sinister South American flesh-eating flowers that close over one. Nearly all of the old pioneers I met there had come for three weeks, and missed the boat, and stayed sixty years.

Marooned on the hotel verandah, we watched the wet. We were all waiting for a chance to move on, and secretly a little afraid that it would never come. The sunsets and the fire-flies in the dusk were well worth waiting for, and the lily-pools covered with blue nymphæ and the rare pink lotus, and the beaches and the reefs with their submerged life, and the tin-and-cement streets with theirs. Now and again, when the weather permitted, we took our sticks out to the golf links, a couple of Larrakeah caddies, dressed in hair-belts and handkerchiefs, to scout our balls in the over-grown undergrowth, but it was better to practise on Mendil Beach in a bathing suit, as all golfing Darwin does in sum-mer, the crocodile in the salt creek a movable hazard.

I was bound for Borroloola, 'where the roads turn back,' the last, lost outpost of the Territory, away on the Gulf of Carpentaria, where there are five white men marooned for forty years among five thousand blacks. It was utterly impossible to get there. Norman Stacey was running the mail, which means that he ambled down the Roper and the Macarthur, 500 miles, with thirty or forty pack-horses, five times a year. Swimming the crossings, now a mile wide, and threading the flooded bush, he had not been heard of for seven weeks.

There was one other way, they told me. A little bit of a lugger made over across the Gulf from Burketown in Queensland, once a month except in hurricane weather. I could pick up a ship at Thursday Island to connect with her at the mouth of the Albert River, and come back a thousand miles to the Roper and Borroloola.

'But what do you want to go to B'r'loola for?' they wanted to know, with the accent on the 'loola.' 'There's nothing down there but blacks. Except for the policeman's wife, they haven't seen a white woman round there for six years, and then it was only a missionary.'

'That's why,' I said.

I waited another three weeks, and as Norman Stacey showed no signs of life in the sodden jungle, I bought a suit-case to pack the swag in, and a ticket for Thursday Island on the south-bound Singapore ship.

It was a happy respite, after a year of bush-whacking, to have a fleet of little Hainan men, with snow-white coats and leopard footsteps, to attend me. Eight hundred miles in four days across the polished glass of the Indian Ocean, and the *Marella* slipped one dawn into a labyrinth of lovely islands.

Not much more than a stone's throw from Australia in geographical fact, yet a world away in the colour and light of its setting, the polychrome of its peoples, and the glamour of daily living, lies this archipelago of the Torres Straits— a little Indies that the Spaniards missed.

Two hundred steep and deeply wooded islands, some of them not much more than a jumble of brown rocks with a rakish tiara of coco-nuts, lie between Cape York and New Guinea. Apart from the almost fabulous wealth of its pearls and pearl shell over a period of fifty years, the very stable industries of trochus and trepang, and the promise of its fisheries and plantations, gold has been found, and profitably mined, on many of these islands.

It is not generally known that the exact spot on Possession Island on which Cook declared the east coast of Australia British in 1770 is the shaft of a gold mine to-day.

Murray and Darnley, Moa, Mabuiag, Naghir, Badu, Prince of Wales, Hammond and Horn, Tuesday, Wednesday, Thursday and Friday, and fifty or sixty others of considerable area, rich volcanic soils and rare scenic beauty —for centuries they have been the home of a remarkably virile and intelligent race of Melanesians, a nation of some 6,000 people.

Utterly different from the shy and shiftless aborigines of the nearby mainland, the Torres Straits Islanders, with skins of burnished copper and magnificent depth of chest, in their native state built themselves houses and slept in beds. They cultivated their fields of taro, worshipped the coco-nut and the clam, sailed forth to conquest in their mighty war canoes, and passed down their properties from father to son.

For three hundred years, secure in the maze of reefs and shoals that baffled the navigator, they defied the white man. When he became too importunate, they ate him by the shipful, and hung his skull in triumph on the door-post. During the past half-century, thanks to the insistent activities of Christian missioners, pearlers and protectors of aborigines, the islands have been civilised and colonised, a crown of wealth to Queensland.

Thursday, one of the smallest, three miles across by two, is the hub of them all. A baby Venice of the tropics, with nine big islands within three miles of it, 'T.I.' is the Tom Thumb city of the Southern Hemisphere, very proud of its mayor and eight aldermen, a cathedral and an episcopal see. Perhaps the wealthiest fragment of Australia, for thirty-five years its annual revenue in pearls and pearl shell was £250,000. Now, the market at its lowest ebb, it tallies out at £150,000, and employs 1,500 men, nearly all coloured. Japs. and Papuans are the divers, generally naked, or in the helmet only.

It is surprising what they fit in on Thursday. Home port of a hundred little ships and three or four thousand islanders, it is one of the smallest dots on the map. Of its area of 845 acres, 280 are laid out in streets, with a permanent population of about 400 whites and 1,200 motley. Fifteen trucks, fourteen motor-cars, a couple of hundred bicycles and one horse constitute the traffic, and they all go thrashing round and round on less than five miles of made road. Four times round the island and twice through the main street, with a trip to the top of Garrison Hill to watch the sunset, is considered a pleasant Sunday afternoon's run.

There are six hotels, and, to offset them, six resident clergymen and a Bishop; three schools, one purely native; a nine-hole golf course, three tennis courts, twelve organised societies, a Royal Geographical Society that is one of the most active in Australia, a museum, a talkie show, social and sporting-clubs of all nationalities, a Japanese village—its flags flying for the Mikado's birthday—and the smallest daily newspaper in the world.

The island controls the approach to Australia from the East, and fourteen pilots are permanently stationed there to guide ships down through the perilous reefs and within the shoals of the Barrier to Sydney.

In the distilled sunlight of the streets, with their avenues of weeping fig and almond and light green coco-nut, are the shaded shops of Cingalese jewellers and Chinese merchants selling all that is quaint and delightful, from deftly carved trifles in pearl shell and tortoise shell to dugong steaks and long soup. Along the foreshore, where the dinghies are constantly unloading great heaps of mother-of-pearl and bags of trepang, is an unending procession of islanders and New Guinea boys, in blue dungarees or red lava-lavas as the case may be, their hair dyed startlingly scarlet with green mangrove juice. When 'the fleet's in' at lay-up, island dances of the old head-hunting days ring the welkin, to the swishing of the grass skirts and the pulsing of the wooden drums.

Waiting for the ship, I found a lot of interest and a lot of happy people packed in tiny T.I. The Islanders are always laughing, and the pearlers have nothing else to do. There was a marine florist's, the only one in Australia, its windows gay with delicate sprigs of coloured corals, and exquisite shell-petals of undersea bloom. One day there was a Manila funeral—tolling of bells in the trades, a priest in his robes, bare-headed, carrying the Cross, preceded by a troupe of frizzy-headed black acolytes swinging the perfume censers, and followed by a long procession of island girls carrying their fast-fading wreaths of tropic flowers.

From the crest of Garrison Hill I looked out upon a magnificent panorama of bays and islands, across the nine known channels of the Straits. I wandered among the old forts, where the bees were building in the gun-carriages and ferns sprouting in the powder magazines, and, across sparkling seas, my eyes turned south to the Land of the Holy Spirit, and the first pages of Australian history.

Out there drifted the high-pooped galleons of the Spaniards, making homeward with treasure of the Philippines, or to their doom on the rocks; the *Almirante* and the *San Pedro* of Torres; the little Dutch *Dove*, drifting down into the Gulf; Tasman just missing a continent, and James Cook finding it.

A few miles northward I could see Bligh's Boat Channel, where the grim old captain and seventeen men, in an open boat, fled for 4000 miles from mutiny and the *Bounty* in the South Seas, lighting fires on the beaches with their magnifying glasses, and living on oysters and cabbage palm, and here, too, sailed young Flinders in the *Investigator*, drawing the first map of Australia.

Fair names and famous. The sails of the pearling-luggers hold memory of them yet.

Eighteen miles to the eastward, a low mist in the distance, lies Cape York, where Kennedy and his party perished within sight and sound of the sea, and the abandoned settlement of Somerset, phantom streets in the bush. There the Jardines, historic pioneers of the North, once signalled through the barques and brigantines from England, or making south with Territory gold, and listened with horror, one moonlight night, to the pandemonium of the doomed in the drowned *Quetta*.

There is an ex-officer of the Black Watch camped over there to-day, minding the mobs of cattle that provide T.I.'s Sunday roasts—one 'Scotty' Mitchell, who proudly told me that he had been a soldier at sixteen and a wanderer ever since. There is also a remote telegraph station, on the peak of the peninsula, and a woman, Mrs. Holland, living with her five babies in a bough-shade home.

Directly beneath me lay Thursday Island, white roofs nestled under the coco-nuts, white sails upon the sea. On the wind came music from the little pearling-jetty, where the Thursday Island Town Band, polychromatic, but full of harmony, plays in the evening.

Under the baton of a Cingalese conductor, the strains of 'Dixie' are wafted across the Straits, none the less sweetly in that the ancestors of Solomon Salt, the big bass drummer, blew the conch and sounded the hide drums for the cannibal orgies of less than a century ago, and that the grandmothers of the smartly dressed audience were content with the green frilled skirt of a banana-palm and a necklace of shark's teeth.

CHAPTER XXII

ULYSSES OF THE GULF

FROM Thursday Island at sunset, on the tiny Queensland coastal ship *Wandana*, we dropped down into the infinite void of the Gulf.

Behind us the pearling-luggers were outlined on a road of gold. The dark shadowy bulk of Prince of Wales, Hammond and Friday disappeared in the sea-distance, and Waiweer, with its crown of coco-nuts a frieze against the blood-red tropic sunset. We passed a big ship down from the East, that is really north-west, waiting in the roads for the pilot. At one stride came the dark.

Through seas of milky twilight blue, we made due west to the winking Cyclops eye of Booby Island. A quarter of a mile long, white-capped as with porphyry, and undermined with caves like the aisles of a cathedral, Booby Island has collected more history than any speck of the Australian coast. Cook discovered it, Bligh named it. It was a world-famous marine post office in the eighteen-hundreds, when the trade route led down through the Straits, and a rock of salvation to a century of castaways. Casks of salt beef and biscuit were stored there by all the barques that passed, and letters left in the Post Office Cave to be honoured by ships passing to and from England. The log-book was souvenired some years ago by a steamer captain who realised that it was a valuable museum piece. He lost his ship in consequence, and so far that log-book has never dared to come to light.

In modern times there is a big attended light, with three families in residence, and the thrills of to-day are occasional unexplained sampans and raiders in wartime.

As we drew near, Booby blinked into conversational vein 'Good evening, and had we seen the lighthouse ship.'

Our signal flashed back. 'Passed lighthouse ship at Hicks Island. Should be on time. South-easter coming. All well.' And then, following the tracks of the *Duyfken*, the *Arnhem* and the *Investigator*, we turned south into the headwind and the night.

Following Flinders . . . here he wrote, the eager young lieutenant on his first command, that he 'had hoped to produce such charts that there would be nothing of further importance left for future discoverers, but with such a ship I know not how to accomplish the task.' A hundred and thirty years had passed, and in his cabin our skipper was bent above those charts—charts compiled in the sadness and imprisonment of the Ile de France—because no better have yet been made.

On the eastern shores of Carpentaria are a few solitary missions; on the west, Arnhem Land. It was just there that the *Douglas Mawson*, with her crew and passengers, seventeen all told, was swamped in a hurricane in 1925.

There were three other passengers aboard the *Wandana*, the doctor's wife at Normanton, going home after a holiday, and two Chinamen. On the second morning we passed Bountiful Island, where Flinders' men had a feast of turtle, and at dusk anchored at the mouth of the Albert River, where I was to pick up that 'little bit of a lugger,' the *Noosa*. There was no sign of her, but an ancient lighter named the *Porpoise* swayed out to meet us, from Burketown, thirty-five miles away. From the shouts and the curses and the sea-chanteys, I thought there were at least fifteen men aboard her, but it turned out there was really only one. He shrieked orders to himself at one end, flew to the other to carry them out, and then roared at himself properly for being all sorts of a fool.

When she was tied up: 'Where's the *Noosa?*' the captain bawled.

'God knows!' came the answer. 'Ten days late now. There's been a hurricane over the other side. She's gone down twice already, once in the Roper and once in the Macarthur. She only has to do it in the Gulf! We wouldn't know for weeks.

'You'd better get aboard the *Porpoise,*' advised the *Wandana*, 'and wait for her in Burketown.'

By a rope-ladder I swung down to the lighter, rolling violently, to find her in charge of a couple of 'mangrove mates,' Captain Jack Brand, an old sea-dog of the east coast of the Americas, and his silent partner, Eric, Malay-aboriginal, the engineer. Condemned long ago, the

Porpoise, 120 tons and 120 feet long, propelled by the engine of a truck thirty years old, is the ship that makes Burketown a port. Once a month it meets the *Wandana* for beer and petrol and potatoes. I had qualms, and an antidote for cockroaches. I found spotless cleanliness, a shower-bath, pretty d'oyleys in my cabin, home-make cakes, two more good companions, and many a stirring tale. For two days and two nights, held back by the tide, we drifted up the silver reaches of the flat, shallow river, picking our way between the crocodiles.

Every day the captain scrupulously holystoned the decks; every night he lit his 'port' and 'starboard,' though the *Porpois*e had never been known to pass anything, because there was nothing to pass. In the evening, by the wheel, with the fragrant smoke of wet mangrove to keep away the sandflies, there in the white tropic moonlight, the silence like a quivering gong, I listened to eerie old yarns of black baboons and the bucko mates and the glorious days of sail.

'When I was in the barque *Pinmore,* Calcutta to New York with jute,' the skipper would begin, or 'We put out of Baltimore in the 'nineties, bound for Santos and Port o' Spain . . .'—smoking his pipe into memories. With the constant attendance of these two quaint cavaliers, and a thousand kindnesses, I think there was never a happier journey in all my travelling.

Two or three days in the warm-hearted, little tin shack port of Burketown—once it had a population of 1600, but now there are thirty—watching the crocodiles dozing in the mud in front of the hospital, and the sharks coming up morning and evening to be fed, like chickens, and they posted the *Noosa* as missing. In desperation, I set out with a station owner of the border, to join his mustering-plant at Wollogorang, that, some day, somehow, he guaranteed would get to Borroloola. I had set my heart on that place, and now nothing would baulk me.

Two hundred and eighty miles through the beautiful cattle-country of the Gregory and Nicholson rivers, and we arrived at Wollogorang, to find that they were not sure if that mustering-plant would be in for six months. The rivers between were down. There was nothing to do but to hurry back to Burketown, hoping that the *Noosa* had not

come and gone. Joy of joys, she was at the wharf, and a
great story she had to tell. Three days fighting the hurricane, ten days fighting the first of the trades, her crew living
on sweet potatoes and cold water they found on Vanderlin
Island, and a baby born aboard her in the tumult, were only
part of it.

The mother was a missioner, who had been out on the
lonely shores crusading, with her husband and two little
children living in a bough hut—a cruel life for a woman.
Threatened, or blessed, with the coming of another child,
unable to return by land in the wet, she had sailed across
in a dinghy to Mornington Island, to catch the *Noosa* for
Burketown. The *Noosa* was three weeks late. The child
was born on a wild night at the entrance to the Albert Bar,
and in low tide the ship could not cross it. Happily, there
was another woman aboard, for the first time in seven years,
the captain's wife, who had never seen a birth, but did her
best. The child was still-born. The mother was now
hovering between life and death in the Burketown hospital
—and Borroloola was suddenly as far away as ever, for the
captain refused to take me.

'We've had a frightful time this trip,' his son informed
me, 'and Dad says to tell you he'll never take a woman
passenger again.'

This was a blow. I promptly interviewed the captain
personally. I intercepted him in the only street there was,
and brought all my innocence and naïve earnestness into
play, and crossed my heart on it that there would be no
trouble. He was normally a trustful man, and at last he
believed me, but he insisted on taking me over the ship
there and then to show me what I was up against. There
was no sleeping accommodation except in a little hole right
on top of those crude oil engines. There was no sanitary
accommodation, no exercise on those narrow, crowded
planks, meals on the hatch from a box of a galley on deck,
provided the wind was not too strong to light the fire, and
the *Noosa* was practically falling to pieces round him.

'You've asked for it,' he said. 'Now don't blame me.'

To book a passage on that ship was to take a chance with
wind and sea, and throw down the challenge to adventure.
A swag unrolled on deck under the wheeling pageant of

the night skies, a 'thumb-piece' of salt meat and bread a fortnight old, a bucket for the morning ablutions—because it is a juggler's job to hold water in a dish in the south-easter—these were my lot. I came back star-blind and sun-dazzled, and with some of Australia's best secrets in my keeping.

The *Noosa* is the bravest thing in Australian waters. Across windswept Carpentaria, groping her way by a chart that Matthew Flinders made from the masthead in 1802, swinging the lead by reef and sand-bank, battling against tides that have baffled the British Admiralty, and crawling through the snags and shallows of great tropic rivers in the darkness, she travels a thousand miles a month.

Her square of grey sail, year in, year out, is the only moving speck in those vast sea-horizons. A little black lugger of 26 tons, she carried only a few bales of loading. Blown up by the south-easter and forging her way back against it, for five weeks at a time she is completely out of touch. During seven years skipper and ship have been faithful to the trust of two isolated missions and a few lone settlers. To piece together the story of those seven years is to realise that the Australian coast has its heroes, the equivalent of anything in the Greek Archipelago in the good old days.

Through most of those years, Ruska has been alone with a half-caste. Day and night at the wheel, steering with his bare feet while his hands are hauling in the mainsail, wading up to the armpits in crocodile rivers to stake the changing channels, held up for days in the mangroves while the Gulf blows over to New Guinea and back, and living on raw food with the galley careering round the deck in the steady fury of the trades, he has never failed yet. If he did, the settlers of Borroloola and the Roper would be left to exist on pandanus tops and cabbage palm and lily roots, as they were once for nine months before he came.

The days of the skipper's loneliness are over. With her children grown up, Mrs. Ruska, mate in every sense of the word, joined the trip before I did. She had come up from Brisbane to share her husband's perils and privations, and with their eldest son apprenticed to his father, the *Noosa* has become a floating home from home. Monday's washing flying gaily from the rigging in that waste of windy waters, and the homely wheeze of an old concertina echoing in the ghostly mangroves of world's end, make it one of the queerest and most likeable tramps of the coast. The only other member of the crew is Sandy, the Torres Strait Islander cook. Sandy specialised in pumpkin fritters.

With a few bags and barrels labelled for Mornington, Borroloola and the Roper, caught in the upward swing of the trades, we made it a good day's journey of a hundred miles to Mornington, where the kindly missioners provided me with a bath, a turkey for dinner, and the last glimpse of white faces we would see for 300 miles. The captain went out of his way to show me Sweers Island, the site of the old township that came into being when Burketown was stricken with yellow fever in the 'eighties. There is nothing left but the fragments of a dinner set in the bush, two or three graves dating back to the 'sixties, some Chinese carvings in the barks of its trees, and a white-headed horse that has been monarch of all he surveys there for thirty years. At Bentinck, peopled by tribes of whom nothing is ever seen but their smokes, we did not land.

Between the Wellesley and the Pellew group lie 140 miles of open sea, a day's journey with the wind, anything from seven to ten against it. Across that waste of sea, the only pilgrims other than ourselves were the sun and moon. There is never a pearling-lugger in Carpentaria. Turtle and dugong go tumbling in the blue waters, with a ten-feet leap in the air skipjacks land on the *Noosa's* hatch ready to cook, and swarms of flying fish skim silver along the sea.

I slept always on deck. A goat also slept on deck. As I crawled along on hands and knees on windy nights, with the foam weltering over me from the low bulkheads, I realised that, if that goat suddenly stood up or became belligerent, I was lost. In the din of the trades, they would never notice a shriek more or less. Then Sandy killed the goat, and hung its head in the rigging and salted the rest of it, and the last stage of that goat was worse than the first.

At last the low sand dunes of the Pellews showed up on the horizon. The islands that so few have seen since Flinders are as empty as the sea. From Vanderlin to the mouth of the Macarthur is another twenty miles. Along the low shores of the mainland, native smokes were now sending news of our coming, and at the mouth of the river we were met by mobs of blacks. Propelling themselves out on crude rafts, consisting of a single log, or in paper-bark canoes, or swimming a mile through crocodile reaches and shoals of sharks, 'Tobacco!' they cried—tobacco, the corner-stone of Empire, the magic medicine of the white man, the stuff that dreams are made on.

For tobacco these myalls were ready to trade anything from wives to water-melons. White grins, and promises of fish, and upturned hands ready to catch, they swarmed about the ship, lubras and bucks and piccaninnies, clamorous for a single stick of black twist that would be divided between a tribe of forty, and then, ground with gum-leaves, do duty among the elders for a month.

We stopped dead at the Carrington crossing, while the tide of the river ran out for twelve hours, or eighteen, or twenty-three, at its own sweet will. You cannot gauge the tides of Carpentaria. Ruska and his son Fred went off in a boat and landed in a mangrove marsh to cut long poles, as fast as the mosquitoes would let them. Then they pulled back into mid-stream, and Ruska slipped over the side, chest-deep in muddy water, to hammer the poles in place, groping the depth with them in the perilous shallows, for the Macarthur is nothing but a ship-trap. Just then Sandy sighted the snout of a crocodile, down-river.

'Hoy!' we yelled, and pointed, with never a word. Although he can hear every quiver of his ship, Captain Ruska is as deaf as a post. At last he caught our meaning. 'He's all right!' he bellowed back. 'He's gone past!'

The amazing bravery of the man was bravado. I told him so, shouting it into his ear when he came on board. I was quickly put in my place.

'Don't you worry about me!' he said. 'I've been doing it for seven years, and if I don't do it, who will? They haven't got me yet, anyway.' I shall always remember the lilt of the little song he sang as he turned away:

> 'Lath, lather, lather me, Flo!
> Your little brush seems to tickle me so.'

That man had no sense in the world of his own heroism.

It was his job to get through, and he did it. Hanging like a monkey in the rigging watching for shoal water, sitting for hours at the wheel while young Fred nursed the out-of-date engines, battling bodily with the sails in a gale, and then throwing himself down in utter exhaustion for a few brief hours' sleep on the flour-bags in the hold, he had done this sort of thing for seven years! The ship had sunk twice, to be fished out by a tribe of blacks—luckily it had happened each time in a river. 'Third time proves it!' said Captain Fred Ruska. He loved a jest, he loved a tough spin when it was over, and he sang and he whistled most of the time, though he could not hear himself.

The tide turned late that night. Fred Junior took the dinghy and hung hurricane lamps on the mangrove stakes, and 'in and out the windows' we threaded the little yellow lights up-river. Then Sandy slipped back in the dinghy and collected the hurricane lamps, and away we went, dead slow, feeling for snags.

Forty-five miles up the Macarthur was Borroloola itself. Led by the music of its name, it had taken me a year to get there, and then I glimpsed its glories for a day. The *Noosa* could not approach within five miles. Young Fred Ruska and I rowed on in the darkness in a dinghy, to break the news of our coming. It was midnight, and there was nothing but the corroboree fires of the Yanyuella on the banks to light the way.

A couple of native canoes lashed to the paper-barks told us that we had arrived at the port. Up the steep bank on hands and knees we clambered, and by a half-mile track through the dense and dripping bush, phosphorescent with fire-flies and musical with many creeks and waterfalls, we came at last to a wan light in the jungle—the Hotel Macarthur, as it is facetiously known, kept by a bearded exile of Erin, and almost completely hidden by spreading tamarinds and tangled creepers.

Very, very, very few travellers come to the Hotel Macarthur. 'Bring your own blankets and sleep on the floor,' is the watch-word, and 'Goat or dugong?' Bunny, the lubra cook, shouted to me from the kitchen at morning-time.

There was scarcely any furniture in the dust-covered rooms, beyond a broken-winded bed or two, hung with cobwebs, a majestic chiffonier so genuinely antique that it would bring a record price at Christy's, and a couple of priceless Chinese screens left for a beer-bill by a sea-adventurer of long ago. But that shanty has seen its great days. Many a time three hundred men hobbled out their horses under the tamarinds and fought to enter its doors.

In 1873, when they were building the overland telegraph line, ships carrying poles and wires for the northern section put in to the Macarthur, and were met there by the teamsters. One of the most enterprising teamsters, with a couple of cases of gin aboard, set up a 'blind tiger' under a paper-bark tree, and called it B'r'loola. In 1886, the days of the Kimberley gold rush, and when they were stocking up the West from Queensland, the road led from Camooweal, through Anthony's Lagoons out to the Gulf, across the Limmen Bight, along the Roper, the Victoria and the Katherine to the Ord. That paper-bark tree became the Mecca of a thousand thirsty men, who 'sat down' on the banks of the pretty river for a while, and then went on.

Desperadoes who were wanted all over the world, and horses wanted all over Australia, were content to remain. Smuggling ships put in with contraband, to avoid paying duty at Darwin, and so wild and woolly were the times that it is a saying yet in the Territory, 'Brand and ear-mark your boots at Borroloola.'

To-day, with a population of four old men, the place is far off the new roads, and one of the most unget-at-able on the Continent. There is only one way out of it in the wet season, and that is to die. Two of the old hands did it just before I arrived, Fred Holt and Paddy Griffin, reducing the population in one fell swoop by 40 per cent. It was impossible to cross the creek to the tiny cemetery a mile away, so they wrapped them in their camp-sheets and buried them just where they were. 'Paddy ought to have known better,' they told me. 'Lived here forty years, and then he goes and dies in the wet season.'

For the rest, I found dear old Charlie Havey, with a tin shack 'store' near the blacks' camp, a few rusty hobble-chains hanging up outside, trading flour and tea and nigger twist for native canoes and old pack-saddles; Freddy Blittner, the 'Freshwater Admiral,' camped for twenty-five

years on a lily lagoon; Jack Moriarty, host of the inn, with
never a guest in years; and a North Australia trooper, to
keep order among infinite tribes of blacks.

A little corner of natural beauty unrivalled in the Territory, of singing creeks winding down to the river in
tropical ferns and flowers and forests, where you may see
the true native life unspoiled in its own sylvan setting, the
soils are so fertile that it will grow anything. 'But what's
the use?' they asked me. 'There's no one to eat it. The
blacks don't like vegetables, and cotton and sugar-cane only
run wild.' Now and again the place is mentioned in the
South as the terminus of a new trans-continental railway line
to open up the mighty Barkly Tablelands behind it, shipping
away unlimited sheep and cattle, but it never seems to
happen.

There was a surprise for me in store at Borroloola.
Closed in by the jungle and forgotten of men, I stumbled
upon a library of 3000 books, the finest and most comprehensive library in the North, that for thirty years has defied
the passing of time and the white ants. I peered through
the dusty windows of the old court-house, at myriads of
canvas-covered volumes, and could scarcely believe them
true. I hurried away to inquire.

It appears that a long time ago there was a policeman
there of bookish turn of mind. His name was Corporal
Power, and he wrote to Lord Hopetoun in Melbourne,
when he was Governor-General, asking for books—good
books, intellectual books, something to bite on, manna in
the wilderness. Lord Hopetoun responded immediately.
He sent up over a thousand volumes that were delivered by
horse-team, two years in transit, with contributions by
private persons to follow, and a Government subsidy for a
library of pound for pound.

The Macarthur River Institute became a kindly light
of sanity to men half-mad with loneliness. Drovers years
on the road, managers and stockmen, and bagmen who had
seen better days, would ride away gloating over a wealth
of poetry and prose in the pack-bags, and cooks and argu-
mentative swaggies would borrow bound copies of the
Parliamentary Debates, to lay down the law round the
camp-fires of a lawless country.

There is a complete set of Lytton, and another of Mark Twain, skewered through and through with the neatly drilled holes of the borer beetle; an eighteenth-century Shakespeare, yellowed with age and rain; a tome of a Gibbon of which the pages crumble as you turn. But most of the books are in good condition, carefully preserved, and though this part of the Territory has fallen upon evil days, and nobody comes to borrow them now, the trooper stationed there sends a young buck of the Yanyuella over fairly regularly to spray away the silverfish and keep the white ants at bay. He always gets the numbers mixed and the volumes wrong side up, but nobody minds that. There is no one to mind. With its forgotten library alone to tell of old fellowships and old years, the place is fading away.

I handled those old volumes very lovingly. I knew now what had called me to Borroloola.

CHAPTER XXIII

THE RIM OF ARNHEM LAND

WHARFIES who wore nothing but a *naga* carried the stores up the cliffs on their shining black shoulders, the old pioneers sat on the *Noosa's* deck to share a billy of tea and the news of the Gulf, and we were off again, down-river to catch the tide, and across the bar to breast wind and wave for the Roper.

With never a light aboard her in the night-time, and all the stars of the southern hemisphere a reeling geometry in the rigging, the *Noosa* slipped, a little black shadow between the islands, a hundred miles north to the mouth of the great river.

One of the most magnificent water highways in Australia, second in length only to the Murray, the Roper winds inland through 350 miles of densely tropical jungle. To the north of it lies Arnhem Land; to the south a glorious unexploited cattle-country, with a few far-flung stations, and scarcely a soul other than the blacks roam its banks. With never a shilling spent on it, the river is navigable for ninety miles, and the *Noosa* counts them all.

For two days our softly thudding engines carried us through the silver reaches where the pandanus struggles with the mangroves for supremacy. Month by month the rhythm of those engines is the only sound to stir wild nature there. The notched noses of the crocodiles disappear in the ripples, and at sunset clouds of geese bring darkness early. Once we were greeted by a solitary white man, out in a native canoe. He hailed us with a yell for tobacco, and as a quid was thrown to him, caught it with a leap, tore it with his teeth, tucked it into the top of the trousers that were the only garment he wore, and, chewing at the rest of it, gave us a grateful wave of the arm and paddled back to his camp. God knows what he was trying to grow— pea-nuts, perhaps.

Night by night we slipped our anchor into a riverful of stars, and sometimes we played bridge, by a hurricane lamp on the hatch, in a cloud of white moths.

'Sitting on the ace!' young Fred Ruska would shout delightedly. 'Sitting on the ace!' came the ghostly echoes from the mangroves recalling me to the sinister silence of the great river and the shadows of darkness beyond. We were now on the rim of Arnhem Land, the triangle of death.

Out of the zone of civilization lies this Arnhem Land, the only corner of Australia that has persistently baffled, and even frightened, the white pioneer. An isosceles triangle of broken coasts, dense swamp and river jungle in the far north-east of the Territory, its apex Cape Arnhem and its base a line drawn from the mouth of the King River to the mouth of the Roper, for a hundred years, by the sheer ferocity of its natives, it has defied colonisation. To-day the Commonwealth Government has written it down as a closed native reserve, and let it go at that.

From time to time, intrepid spirits have landed upon its shores and penetrated its fastnesses. A few have returned. A good cattle-country, believed to be rich in minerals, notably gold, in that 5000 square miles is no white settlement of any kind, no outflung station homestead, not a single camp of pilgrim prospector. The only station ever to be established there was Florida Downs, sixteen miles from the mouth of the Goyder River, a project of the South Africa Cold Storage Company in the early 'nineties. It was abandoned within two years, most of its cattle speared by the blacks.

Oriental crews of nine or ten pearling luggers that have put into its havens in the last twenty years have been swiftly despatched, and these are but sequels in a long tale of tragedy that dates back to 1800.

Alone among the Australian blacks, the Arnhem Landers throughout a century have refused the white man's rum and tobacco, defied the laws of his making, and, with a fierce patriotism, preserved their race intact. Tribes apart, feared and hated by the semi-civilised natives of mission and settlement farther south, they keep their country still.

The Air, and the Fire, and the Sun-blood people, Mara-mara and Yerracool, Nullakan and Woggiamana, descendants of Koonanbibba, the Great First Mother, who waded across the sea, scattering the nuts of the pandanus to spring up as her children, the Left-hand Boomerang Throwers;

they are a virile race of exceptional height and splendid physique, practically amphibious. Along the rivers and neighbouring islands of the Gulf of Carpentaria, they seek for turtle and dugong in their dug-out canoes, or swim through wind-swept and sharky seas, pushing a floating log in front of them, sometimes for thirty miles. Quick to signal the presence of the intruder, they are relentless and crafty in the offensive.

Malays and white men and Japanese have been despatched with a grim impartiality. From that dread triangle, no lone prospector has ever come back to tell the story. The helplessness of a shipwrecked crew has never strained their qualities of mercy. Whether it is that the atrocities of the trepanging Bugis or Chinese, in pre-Australian history, have left this legacy of hatred and hostility is not known, for little contact with their mentality has as yet been made.

Well-fed with a plenitude of fish and wallaby, geese and game, yams and lily-roots, numerous tribes inhabit the region—to the number of 4000 or more—but by the occasional luggers offshore, perhaps two in three years, nothing is ever seen but their smokes. Their women are never in evidence. They have made no approach to Christianity, and Christianity has not yet approached them. Strangers unwise enough to land upon these apparently uninhabited shores stand a hundred-to-one chance of being descended upon in an unwary moment, and speared and tomahawked to their deaths.

The written record of these native slayings, more numerous than in any other equivalent area in the history of Australia, began with the spearing of Morgan, the master's mate of the *Investigator*, in 1802. With the first attempt at colonisation of the Territory, seventy years later, two explorers, Permain and Borrodale, set out to reconnoitre the country between the Roper and Port Essington. At Tor Rock, a few days' journey north, they disappeared. A following search-party found the remains of their horses, which had been killed and eaten.

Old police records of the 'seventies and 'eighties and 'nineties are filled with particulars of similar tragedies in this sinister country. Sleeping on their luggers in haven, trepanging along the islands, and camped on the beaches and river-flats, white men and Chinese and Malays were frequently killed, sometimes at the rate of four or five in one year. Among them were Captain Thoms, speared through the porthole of his ship lying at anchor at Vanderlin Island, a prospector named Walker at Blue Mud Bay, Wingfield, a trepanger of Croker Island, Moore and Mackenzie, buffalo-shooters of the King River, Charles Gore, a pearler, a shipwrecked crew of six Malays at Cape Brogden, Chinese and white beach-combers of the Peron Islands and Bowen Straits, and Claude Spencer, found speared in his looted camp at Arnhem Bay.

By the end of the century, there were only a few tres-passers brave enough to take up the challenge of almost certain death, and most of them reaped it, between 1902, when a crew of ten Malays in a lugger blown south from Banda were massacred at Cape Wilberforce, and 1913, when Jim Campbell, an outlaw and trepanger of romantic history, was pinioned with seven spears in the mangrove mud at Guion Point, near Malay Bay.

Since 1915, the crews of pearling luggers have been slaughtered holus-bolus, among them, in recent years, the men of the *Avis*, the *Essington*, *Onyx*, *Iolanthe*, *Raff* and *Myrtle Olga*.

In 1925 was set in circulation the strange rumour, origi-nated by neighbouring tribes and elaborated by credulous settlers, and the Australian and international Press, that two white women were wandering with these savage tribes. The women were said to be Florence Willett and her mother, wife and daughter of the captain of the little Queensland ship, *Douglas Mawson*, wrecked a year pre-viously on the eastern shores of the Gulf. Many a search-party set out for Arnhem Land, but none of them penetrated deeply. Time and again, the rumour still crops up, and an occasional expedition sets out, and never arrives, but as there has never been either a glimpse or authentic tidings of the women, the rumour has been dismissed by authority as worthy of little notice.

To one who knows the type of country, the roving dis-position, the food and the habits of its blacks, it is scarcely within the bounds of credibility that white women could exist for one year, much less ten, under even the friendliest conditions, in such environment.

Nevertheless, there are white women living on the rim of Arnhem Land, hundreds of miles from each other, women who have faced the dangers and the loneliness for many years, unafraid and unmolested. For them the wild yelling of corroboree, the padding of black feet in the pandanus, or the sudden appearance of a naked, painted warrior with a handful of spears, holds no terrors whatever.

The painted warrior and his family are merely Billy and Charcoal and Topsy, as the case may be, all human and all friends, and corroboree a nightly entertainment of sorts, a little noisy and disturbing sometimes, like the party in the flat next door.

'You feel safer when the blacks are about,' these women told me. 'It is when they disappear on "walkabout" that the bush grows lonely and frightening.'

Among them is a sixteen-years-old girl who has known no playmates other than the piccaninnies, who has never been within hundreds of miles of a school, and who has never worn a hat other than a weird scrap of home-made millinery twisted out of pandanus leaf. She is Nell Hobley, daughter of a settler of the Roper, whose tiny wire-netting and paperbark humpy we passed, the sole habitation of that mighty river other than its police and mission station, perhaps the most pathetic homestead in Australia, that rejoices in the name of Riverview. A river view it is.

About fifteen years ago, J. N. Hobley and his wife came overland thousands of miles in a buggy through Queensland. It took them three years to do it. At Burketown they cut out westward across the Robinson and Wearyan rivers, through country never before and never since traversed by a white woman. In that buggy, they carried the whole of their worldly possessions, including a baby daughter and stores for twelve months, and the nucleus of a first-class stud of—Persian cats.

Hobley was an Englishman with no knowledge of things Australian. Hearing of Arnhem Land, remote, and as yet unexploited, he decided to settle there and make his fortune. The end of the trail was a cruel disappointment. Arrived at the boundary of the Roper, he was strongly advised, by both blacks and any whites he met, to go no farther, and that there was, as yet, no demand for Persian cats in Arnhem Land. He camped on the bank of the river, and built his wife and baby a shelter. In time, the Persian cats disappeared into a thousand miles of surrounding emptiness, to cross-breed with the spotted native variety, and propound another problem in Australian fauna for naturalists of the future.

For fourteen years the Hobleys have braved isolation, with many setbacks, supporting themselves by means of a tiny garden, growing cassava for flour, fruit and vegetables for their table, goats and game for their meat, reading by a slush-lamp in the evenings, and wearing boots of rawhide and pandanus weave. During those fourteen years neither father, mother, nor daughter left the Roper, save for one journey on foot for 300 miles to Mataranka, droving goats for sale.

Fifty miles away, at the head of the big river, where a bar of sandstone and shallow rapids prevented us from navigating it farther, at the farthest-flung police station of the Territory, I had lunch with Mr. and Mrs. Mounted-Constable Sheridan—'Sherry of Roper Bar.' Before her marriage, Mrs. Sheridan was an A.I.M. outback nursing sister, a city girl to whom the lure of the bush meant so much that she married a mounted constable and made her home in it. Three hundred miles from the nearest tele-graph station, Roper Bar depends upon a six-weekly pack-mail.

At that remote cottage, with its charming garden of paw-paws and brilliant vines and many vegetables, tending the blacks and the very few whites that come to her for attention, Mrs. Sheridan is hostess and chief medical officer. Quite recently she brought into the world the first white baby ever born on the Roper, there at the little police station, child of Mr. and Mrs. Buckley, the Roper missioners. The mother rode back to her home through virgin bush on a pack-horse, the blacks finding the track and a lubra walking behind to carry the baby.

So much for the tiny communities of the big river. A hundred miles north of Marranboy, twenty years out of civilisation, lives Mrs. John Reay of Meinoru. Each year 'after the wet,' with a blackboy and packs, Mrs. Reay travels in a hundred miles on a track that is known only to herself and her husband and the natives, bound for a spring shopping orgy in the deserted little tin-mining township of Marranboy. No roads lead to Meinoru, and that is the only occasion in the year on which she speaks to a white woman, if any happen to be there.

Another heroine who has lived and wandered with the blacks on the rim of Arnhem Land is Mrs. Hazel Gaden, wife of the best-known buffalo-shooter of the Territory. Mrs. Gaden has reared five children in bough shades on the trail.

Out on the Mary and Alligator rivers, sometimes so close to the haunts of buffalo that they will hear a fight or a stampede in the darkness, the big camp wanders, one white man, three or four half-castes, and twenty or thirty blacks, excellent shooters all. A bevy of lubras follows for the skinning of the hides, and, cooking for the camp, for many years Mrs. Gaden has gone too.

Three weeks here and three weeks there, moving across for the shooting, the native women carry the babies across the creeks on their shoulders, laughing at the risk of crocodiles, while the boys swim the horses. Once across, there are tents to put up, sometimes in heavy rain, beds to make out of fencing wire and plaited bamboo, and supper to think of. The blacks go out with a few cartridges and bring in a delicate meal—whistle-duck, hot roast yams, goose eggs, and wild fruits that they and the children love.

At dawn the hunters ride out, it may be one mile or twenty, to where the buffaloes are feeding on the flats, sometimes 500 together, to head the herds and cut out the young bulls. As the mob goes thundering by, the horse-shooters are ready, their ·303's and Martinis sawn off short for skilful one-handed control, shooting always backwards from the horse's tail so as not to frighten him.

On the outskirts of the mob, and in the paper-bark country where the cunning will run, the foot-shooters are ready, waiting to pick them off from behind the bushes. It is dangerous work. Sometimes a horse stumbles in pitted 'debil-debil' country just as the herd swings in. Sometimes a foot-shooter has a bad quarter of an hour with a wounded bull in a tangle of scrub. But they are excellent sportsmen, and a fatality is unknown in Gaden's camp, although one or two have come very near to it.

The herd passes, leaving twenty or thirty paralysed bulls, unerringly shot in the spine. It remains to finish them off. The skinners come up, the hides are thrown over the pack-horses, and the whole party comes back to camp to clean and dry them for carriage to Darwin.

The life has many thrills. Mrs. Gaden and the children have travelled miles along crocodile rivers in a native canoe. Once she was charged by a frantic buffalo. Her only possible hope was to lie down close behind a dead beast and trust in Providence. Happily the bull was headed off by a native rider in the nick of time.

The children are splendidly hale and sturdy, and, as soon as they were old enough, their mother, an active-minded woman with a vivid power of description, rigged up a table in the bough shade and taught them to read and write. 'We could have put them to school in Darwin,' she told me, 'but in emergency, from December to June, we could not have come to them, on account of the floods. It was better to keep them all under one roof, even though it was a grass one.'

Away in Mullingma, on the fringe of Arnhem Land, she was alone in camp one morning when a hiking party of twelve or fifteen myalls strolled in, great fierce-looking fellows with not one word of English among them, not even a pandanus leaf to wear, and carrying handfuls of spears. It was apparently a war party. There were no women.

'The camp was twelve miles away, shooting,' said Mrs. Gaden. 'I admit that I held my breath. They could understand nothing. Then, to my relief, they caught sight of the baby, and they laughed and laughed. I did, too. I laughed even more when, with amiable shouts and signs, the whole party wandered on.'

There is one touch of nature that makes the whole world kin. A woman with a baby, a lubra with a piccaninny, are always sure friends. For all their ferocity, the Arnhem Landers are just human, an unreasoning and ignorant fear the basis of their crimes. There is not a bush woman in the far outback of Australia who is ever afraid of the blacks, and it is not on record in this country that a white woman has ever been molested or intimidated.

Troubles arise through a conflict of misunderstanding. The Australian black is a gentleman at heart.

The Commonwealth Government has now sent a well-known practical anthropologist, Dr. Donald Thomson, out into Arnhem Land to make friends. So far he has been successful, and come back once alive. With his experience and bush-craft and sympathy, he will doubtless be first to bridge the gulf between the wild native's comprehension and the white. If not, well, a woman with a swagful of sweets, a bright pretty frock, a gentle voice, and an accordeon and a baby in her luggage, could easily pave the way.

CHAPTER XXIV

HALF-CASTE——A LIVING TRAGEDY

IT was in the Gulf of Carpentaria that I was approached by a beach-comber with a poignant little problem of his own. He was the father of four children. Their mother was a black woman.

According to Government decree, these children were now to be taken from him, and placed in an institution in Central Australia for their up-bringing and education. The protector had sent a policeman on a pack-horse. Must he let these children go, or could he claim the rights of fatherhood?

'They're well fed and happy enough,' he said. 'They have no clothes, but they don't want them out here. This is their country. They don't want to leave it, and I know they won't be happy. I don't suppose either I or their mother will see them again.

'They tell me you write for the papers, so you ought to know. Can I keep them with me? We've always been together, whatever else we've been, and the old woman will break her heart.'

Sadly enough, the answer was no. The father of a half-caste has no paternal rights in North Australia, and as for the half-castes themselves, they must learn to live white.

Is there a throw-back to the Australian black?

Dr. Cecil Cook, anthropologist, biologist, bacteriologist, Chief Medical Officer and Chief Protector of Aborigines in North Australia, after ten years' closest observance and research among the half-castes, quadroons and octoroons of the North, says no.

'The Mendelian theory does not apply,' Dr. Cook told me. 'There is no atavistic tendency as in the case of the Asiatic and the negro. Generally by the fifth and invariably by the sixth generation, all native characteristics of the Australian are eradicated. The problem of these half-castes can quickly be eliminated by the complete disappearance of the black race, and the swift submergence of its progeny in the white.'

Following a definite policy of concentrating the half-caste in the settlements, breeding him—or rather her, for the females predominate in numbers at the ratio of about three to one—with the whites to every possible extent, and, where that is not possible, establishing colonies of 'double half-castes' rather than let them revert to the black, the Commonwealth Government has aroused much contention in the north. On account of the lamentable scarcity of white women, settlers, fettlers and bushmen of the Territory are encouraged to marry half-castes and quadroons. These marriages are taking place at the rate of five of six in the year. Some of them have been happy and satisfactory. Some have not.

'The Australian is the most easily assimilated race on earth,' said Dr. Cook. 'A blending with the Asiatic, though tending to increased intelligence and virility, is not desirable. The quickest way out is to breed him white.'

Gathering in the half-castes of 500,000 square miles, by camel and packhorse from the farthest outposts, a pathetic little freight of misfit humans out of the blacks' camps from the Petermann Ranges to Point Pearce, and from the Gulf Islands to the south-western deserts, Dr. Cook is herding them all, regardless of circumstance, into an institution for vocational training at Alice Springs, with a number of girls kept at Darwin as a matrimonial depot and training school for their haphazard station in life. In a vitally interesting ethnological experiment, teaching these children to live white and think white, the Commonwealth Government is trying to prove Dr. Cook's theory. It will require the passing of some seven generations to write the end of the story.

The overwhelming problem of the North-west and North of Australia at the moment is the steadily-increasing propagation of half-breed races. The inevitable early history of every country where the white has made conquest of the black, it has been solved in many other instances by the swiftly-following influx of great populations, or by those countries rapidly taking their places as cosmopolitan stations upon the highways of international trade. In an isolated North Australia, there has been no such redemption.

Unrecognised by his father and unwanted by his mother.

yet a little human boy to whom the morning of life is just as fresh and sweet as to any other, the half-caste is the sad futureless figure of this lonely land. Child of a tragedy far too deep for glib preaching, half-way between the Stone Age and the twentieth century, his limited intellect and the dominant primitive instincts of his mother's race allow him to go thus far and no farther. Lost to him are the corroborees, the happy, careless wandering of an unclad, sylvan people, who pick up their food where they find it, and sleep beneath the trees.

He thinks, and is therefore accursed.

His only crime against society is that he exists, and exists in ever-increasing numbers. A prolific race, in contradistinction to the aboriginal, within the past fifteen years the half-caste population has trebled itself.

Particularly is this noticeable in the pearling-ports, where a half-century of sea adventure, isolation from the rest of the world, and the blending together of alien races with the aboriginal have produced a brindle race unique. Every town of the North and North-west has its 'rainbow' quarter, swarming with children, curly-headed little souls lovable as children all the world over, yet pitiable in that they are cursed with a dark skin in a white man's country, and all astray in life, menacing in that they alone are numerous where children of the white race are few. I met a hard-case pair in Shark Bay, Topsy and Bill, the progeny of a half-caste black and white woman and a Malay. Asked by the local school-teacher to find out their religion, 'Mother thinks we must be Roman Catholic, but Daddy says we're Mohammedan,' reported Bill on his return.

In all my experience in outback Australia, chary at first of a tremendous social problem where only fools rush in with superficial judgments, I found the half-castes always cleanly, helpful and trustworthy, only too anxious to realise the best of their white derivation, but, except in very isolated instances, prevented from doing so by the mighty marshalled forces of heredity and environment, that make playthings of us all. Travelling with the pack-teams through the Never-Never, born stockmen and excellent riders, forever anonymously and with no possible hope of reward save the daily necessities of life, they are playing a very considerable part in the colonisation of a country that is actually more closely theirs than our own.

White in all save colour, an outstanding few have won through. One of these is a station-overseer and master-drover of the Centre, Bennie Hughes, a reliable cattle man, a shrewd business head, and a generous employer of white men. Another was for many years manager of a station on the Roper. A third is the finest rider in Central Australia, accepted everywhere by the white people as friend and equal for his intelligence and integrity and grit. Yet another is a charming quadroon girl educated in Darwin Convent, an accomplished musician and an efficient clerk of some twenty years' standing in a Government department. At twenty-five years of age, engaged to be married to a white pearler, this girl is a striking example of the apparently complete triumph of environment over heredity in two generations.

These are exceptions.

As saddlers, stockmen, teamsters, sailormen, blacksmiths and overseers of camping and droving plants, well-trained half-caste boys can always be assured of a good living where they are known. The girls make excellent cooks and domestic helps and first-class needlewomen. But in all cases other than those of unremitting watchfulness and personal direction, education proves quite worthless. Early adolescence finds a practically complete and inevitable reversion to the black.

One of the most poignant of innumerable cases of this is a half-caste man of Darwin, whose life is a psychological treatise in itself. His name is Reuben Cooper. His father was one of the first buffalo-shooters of Melville Island. On two occasions this man was saved from death there at the hands of hostile tribes by the intervention and devotion of a young lubra. In his gratitude and honourable affection, he married her. The eldest son, a normal intelligent boy, almost white in complexion, was sent to one of the principal colleges in Adelaide to be educated. He returned at the age of eighteen, a splendid physical specimen, captain of his school, with innumerable cups and trophies for distinction in sports.

To-day, in his thirties, on the banks of a tropical river, he is living in primitive fashion, a camp of wild blacks his only associates. His defence, in answer to the reproach of a white resident of Darwin, devoid of all bitterness, is epic in its tragedy.

'I could never have hoped to marry a white girl,' he said quietly. 'Had I married a half-caste, my children would be outcast, as I have been. It is best that I go back to my mother's people.'

In the early days the half-castes were often acknowledged, reared and loved by their pioneer fathers, for the sheer humanness of their association in a cruelly lonely country. In later years, even to-day, they are very largely the children of derelict wanderers, left haphazard in the blacks' camps, to live, or, sometimes more happily, to die.

The attitude of the lubras to these children is problematic. In some instances they treasure the 'little yellafella' as they call him, with the utmost maternal love, trekking hundreds of barren miles with the baby in their arms to avoid its being taken, and weeping bitterly at giving it up. In others, they callously leave it at birth upon the track, or perhaps bury it in a snake-hole or rabbit burrow. As this uncertain fate is shared by the full-blooded black babies, it can scarcely be ascribed to racial prejudice.

So grave has the problem become in very recent years that the Commonwealth Government, in prudence and humanity, has been forced to decisive action. For the first time in the history of the Territory, an adequate home has been provided, at a cost of thousands of pounds, at Alice Springs, in the heart of the Continent, to which children of a thousand mile radius are being removed. There are 125, between the ages of two and thirteen, there in residence. Under the best conditions, these unfortunate little ones will be given every opportunity to outgrow their heredity—if they can.

The black woman in sexual contact with the white man is a tragedy that she herself never understands. The half-caste child of the union is a pariah, semi-sensitive. But the most poignant human misfit of the three is the white man. He alone suffers the curse of full comprehension. He has burned his bridges. He never comes back. The finer his character, the less he tries.

'Combo' they call him in the North, a word heard often

enough in Kimberley and the Territotry, but even those who in later days and a luckier fate have escaped living in glass houses never throw stones. Human nature is human nature, at its best and its worst, all the world over, and both together in the Territory. A man's life is his own up there, and these men have been the precursors of the pioneers. Without them, the country would never have been opened up. They paved the way, and paid the price.

With a city mind and a White Australia complex, I had hoped I would not meet them. I learned that it was difficult to avoid it. I also learned that many of them were the salt of Territory earth, and I was proud to shake hands with them. As I have said, their lives are their own.

Warned by the mulga wires of the approach of a white woman, and afraid of the tales she might have heard, and the reproach or repugnance in her eyes, there were some of them who 'went bush' rather than meet me, but the country had told me its stories in its own way. Before I had gone very far in that vast inimical silence, I realised that, in many, many instances, particularly in the old remote days, it had been a case of 'go native or go mad.'

The black woman understands only sex, and that she understands fairly well. She is easy for the taking. She demands nothing in return, neither house, nor home, nor protection, nor name, nor love, nor even food. Her mentality is such that she can neither give nor expect fidelity, and, until she is crudely enlightened, she does not know the father of her child.

Along the big rivers, eastward and westward through the jungle, and across the rugged hills, and southward over the deserts, she has been for fifty years and more the only woman. If there is any blame for Australia's present half-caste problem, it lies at the self-contained flat door of the white woman of the overcrowded cities, for men are only human.

The lubra has no moral ethics whatever. I heard a story that proves it at ——, no, I had better not say where. Polly straggled into the mission with her fifth half-caste in her arms. The missioner's wife looked upon her in hopelessness. She was weary of lecturing, and merely marvelled at the ways of the Unknown.

'Ah, Polly,' she said. 'And to think that I have been asking God all my life for a piccaninny, and He has never given me one.'

With quick intuition, Polly sensed the wistfulness, and was immediately sympathetic and helpful.

'You been catchum Billy Ryan, Missus,' she suggested. 'Him savvy quickfella!'

So far as the children of these unions are concerned, it is a mistaken idea that they 'inherit the vices of both.' Often enough, it is the virtues of both that are more in evidence, the common sense, the dogged tenacity of purpose, the desire to sow and reap, to labour and to build, of the white pioneer father, the lively instinct, the gentleness, the adaptability to circumstances of the black mother. There are occasional fathers who have defied convention and acknowledged paternity, and rear their coloured children in their own homes, teach them to read and write, lavish all their denied parental pride upon them, build up the station with their help—and can leave them nothing in the end. In the Northern Territory of Australia, an aboriginal is an aboriginal to the third generation, and may not inherit save indirectly through the Chief Protector. These men are the saddest of all, for, half-primitive, their sons are not their sons.

The half-caste girl, with her laughing eyes and sensuous lips, unmoral as her mother, is an easy prey for the un-scrupulous white wanderer, and her path in life is never secure, try as she will to be industrious and ambitious and faithful. The father of one such girl, well-educated and only too attractive, rode down through 750 miles of bush with the child beside him on her pony, to place her in charge of the sisters of a far-off mission, at an age when her waking to womanhood had become a menace. To stragglers passing the station, she was only a little nigger. He then rode back the 750 miles alone, robbed of the dearest love of his life, and thinking the long thoughts of what might have been.

How many times have I seen a now-prosperous holding and its successful owner, clever men, fine-looking men, worthy of any white woman's respect and devotion, but the fates had not written it so. 'This man spoke pidgin to his wife!' wistfully and whimsical reflection was mine, as I listened to political and literary discourses that would shame a University professor, there under the paper-bark trees. In imagination I could picture it:

'My word, Sundown, I think you catch piccaninny debil long that lily-hole!'

A ripple of half-embarrassed but quite innocent laughter.

'Yowi, Boss. I been catchum all right.'

The grinning gargoyle of comedy in the Territory!

Black-and-white, fifty-fifty, are, of course, only one of the blendings, and the North has rare vintages of its own. In many a strange acquaintanceship, I have wished to heaven that I were a Freudian psychologist, that I might draw charts of the mentalities and reactions of, say, a Greek-Chinese-aborigine—two of the oldest civilisations in diametric opposition, transfused through a minus—or a German-Afghan-black.

The trouble is that the aborigines themselves are problematic. Their origin has never been decided. Moreover, we know that the Malays and Bugis have been sailing south to these shores for centuries, poaching trepang, planting tamarinds, negotiating for the loan of women, or kidnapping them and landing them anywhere. Tribes of the Arafura islands and coasts all show distinct characteristics, mental and physical, of the Malays, and have Malayan weapons and words in their languages. Even the Darwin boys and lubras love to wear a sarong, though there is not a full-blooded Malay in Darwin that does. How deep does this influence extend?

The Asiatic strain takes a long, long time to breed out, its atavism is unmistakable, and, without the gift of clairvoyance, how can anyone know? Mendel gave his peas and butterflies nine generations to produce a bona fide throw-back, and seventeen for safety's sake. So far as the aborigine is concerned, Australia can count only six.

There are times when I fear, that for all the apparent watertightness of his theories, Dr. Cook may be propounding a domestic problem of the far future, with almond eyes and a coal-black complexion, that will be very difficult for highly respectable wives and mothers to explain away.

CHAPTER XXV

EVANGELISTS OF MANY NATIONS

GENESIS III, as transposed into blackfella lingo for me by Paddy Emu Foot:

'I been savvy that old man Cod. Him been lookemout that one boy Atom, been talk "Dis-one good place allabout, plenty water, plenty eberyting makem tucker along you. You been sit down dis place longa you missus."

'Been talk "You savvy dis-fella apple-y? No good. Cheeky-fella belong you guts. More better you no more been catchum."

'All right. Two moon, three moon, ole woman been come up, call him Eba. Been talk "What name that ole man been yabber long you? Dis-one apple-y goodfella all right." Atom been talk "Which way? Can't no more catchum. Belong topside fella." Ole woman been yabber-yabber talk-talk long time, finishim up that one apple-y. No more deadfella. All right. Atom been catchim.

'That ole man Cod go cranky, growl allabout, been chuckim fire-stick. Been talk "You two-fella proply cheeky-beggar, *Git Out!*" Them two gone walk-about, long way. I savvy that Cod all right. Ole man belong Hermansburg Mitchin.'

.   .   .   .

I take off my hat to the missioners of Australia, though I deplore their misdirected zeal.

At Drysdale River, 100 miles north-west of Wyndham, one of the most remote Roman Catholic missions in the world, three Spanish girls, all of them in the early twenties, have recently made voluntary sacrifice of their lives to the service of the aborigine. Senoritas sweet and vivacious, speaking little English, they are the first white women to be established in this country.

At Beagle Bay, 87 miles north across the pindan from Broome five Australian girls, gathered in from the five States, have been received as nuns for the same purpose, the youngest still in mid-teens. All from the cities of the

South, they have been specially trained to take the places of five Irish sisters who have lived in exile there for over thirty years.

Drysdale, a Spanish mission of the Benedictines, of which the semi-civilised natives attained fame a few years ago, when they rescued the German aviators, Bertram and Klauseman, from death, is an utterly unfrequented corner, inaccessible except by sea save to a foot-walker or a packhorse traveller crossing the rugged range 200 miles long. Twice a year the western ship *Koolinda* brings stores, turning 120 miles from her course to do it.

Beagle Bay, conducted by Pallottine monks and priests who have their headquarters along the Rhine, is one of the oldest missions in the North. Its blacks are fairly sophisticated now, and its altar of pearls and pearl-shell is an *objet d'art*. Even so, Beagle Bay sees as many as three passers-by in as many years.

With a remarkable—a superhuman—courage and devotion to their faith, these nuns, young and old, have laid the world aside for a life of deprivation, to tend lepers and to teach piccaninnies. Through days of heat and hardship they labour, and night by night they chant their litanies and Aves in tune to corroborees ringing round them in the bush.

They are not alone in their sacrifice. The story of the missions, of all denominations, in outback Australia is an epic of Christianity. Fired with the fearless zeal of Livingstone and Savonarola, many of them have been martyrs, and still they take their lives in their hands and go forth, as John the Baptist, to preach the gospel in the wilderness.

It was missionaries who first stumbled upon Australia, Torres and his six Spanish priests, Knights of the Holy Ghost, telling their beads in unknown seas, landing on the beaches carrying crosses of wood to redeem the heathen. Since then there have been Lutherans and Jesuits, Episcopalians and Nonconformists and Plymouth Brethren, from organised expeditions of the established churches with a bishop in the lead, to crank independents with a theology of their own, and even the Salvation Army, banging the big drum of salvation by a billabong.

As an outback pilgrim, I have stayed for a period at most of the missions of Australia, from Hermansburg in the

Centre to Roper River in the North, and Port George IV in the North-west, and either from observation of the natives on walkabout or contact with the missioners themselves, have been in touch with them all. I have never failed to marvel at the heroic self-sacrifice of the white man, and the equally remarkable amenability of the black, his gentle acceptance of this creed and that creed, for the term of his natural life or for the time being, according to the 'tucker' provided, his swift ability to learn, his amazing gift of tongues.

I have listened to those piccaninnies at Beagle Bay singing in seven languages—'The Watch on the Rhine' in German, an Italian barcarolle, a Latin Ave Maria, a Spanish serenade, a Gaelic folk-song, a Pindanawonga corroboree, and, as grand finale, with delightful unconscious irony, 'Advance Australia Fair'—while Australia Fair advances to wipe them off the map.

I have heard the old Lutheran hymns along Finke River. I have met witch-doctors of the Yerracool who spoke French and wore nothing whatever, a Berinkan along the Daly River who remembered a Gregorian chant from the old Jesuit mission there, and natives of the Dieri of Cooper's Creek, who could converse in the German language, write their own, string off yards of the New Testament, and still carried their own old stone mourra-gods about wrapped in blood-stained hair and emu feathers. I have attended the Easter festivities at the pretty little Quetta cathedral at Thursday Island, with its fuzzy-headed, white-surpliced choristers, whose grandfathers were head-hunters, singing 'For Those in Peril on the Sea.'

In so many instances the first to arrive in a howling wilderness, and to teach it to sing hymns, the missionaries in the remote places have played an incalculable part in the first colonisation of this country. So wide-flung is their influence, from Fowler's Bay on the Bight to Millingimbi in the Arafura Sea, from Beagle Bay in the west to Yarrabah in North Queensland, that with the exception of the coasts between Darwin and Wyndham, Darwin and Blue Mud Bay, and the wastes of the West, you cannot find a 'wild nigger' on the Continent, more's the pity. Battling along with a packhorse, or a camel, or a donkey, or a dinghy, these twentieth-century Crusaders have carried Christianity to Stone Age man, who accepts the white man's faith with the white man's tucker, and, provided there is enough tobacco to go round, is converted by the tribeful on the spot.

The most vividly picturesque of these outposts are Hermansburg, in the heart of the wonderland of Central Australia; Beagle Bay, where you can see blacks with corroboree paint on their faces, and lubras with a yam-stick and a piccaninny in the coolamon at early morning service; Melville Island, north of Darwin, where Father Gsell, a Frenchman, during twenty-seven years has bought the girl-babies for a few sticks of tobacco and some stores, saving them from the tribal iniquity of being married to the oldest men, and handed down in turn to their brothers; Sunday Island, mission of a man's remorse, in the lost North-west, and the solitary patrol of Ernest Kramer of Alice Springs, who hails from Switzerland, and travels the deserts on camel-back for thousands of miles.

Sunday Island, north of King Sound, has a curious history. Originally it was the 'black ivory' depot of a pearler who, in the old naked diving days, is said to have made a fortune there, beach-combing for tortoise-shell and pearls. In his later years, overcome by remorse at the injustice and cruelties he had witnessed, he gathered the natives of the coast about him, and devoted years of his life to their conversion and maintenance, teaching them the Moody and Sankey hymns and giving them many a 'tuck-out' as a sop to conscience. He has now retired to live in England, and the mission is carried on by a church society.

Another station of interest in the North-west is the Presbyterian mission of Port George IV, conducted by Rev. J. R. Love, M.A. Isolated with his wife and young family there for seven years, Mr. Love has devoted himself to the excellent practical work of agriculture and anthropology. With a keen interest in the natives, and a deference to their own laws and customs within certain limits, he has made a full translation of the Bible into Worrora. How he has achieved such words as 'ass' and 'ox' and 'manger' and the 'begats' of Matthew, I forgot to ask, and often when I have listened to an earnest preacher telling a helter-skelter little mob, eager for sweets and plum-pudding at Christmas, of the time when Herod Antipas was King of Judea, I have wondered, wondered. However, Mr. Love has interested and cared lovingly for the natives, as all missioners do, and no one can do more. He has even taught them to work, in reason. Concentrating their labours upon a few acres of tillable land, he has produced in that wild region some acres of yams and sweet potatoes and bananas and Kaffir corn, pineapples and pea-nuts and other produce, that maintain about 300 blacks in the dry season, and have been an invaluable experiment in tropical agriculture. His church is walled down the middle in deference to tribal tabus, so that those who must not look upon each other need not do so. His only touch with the world is the little mission lugger, which makes a monthly return trip of 700 miles to Broome.

Even more isolated and equally zealous are the Anglicans and Methodists and Roman Catholics of Oenpelli, Millingimbi, the Goulburn Islands, Fitzmaurice River, Roper River and Groote Eylandt on the north coasts, where there are no other whites established. They rear their families away from all kinship, gradually establish friendly intercourse with hostile natives, and each year penetrate deeper the Unknown.

At Mornington Island in the Gulf, Mr. Wilson and his wife and daughters, resident for fifteen years, are perhaps the only missioners who can claim to have made their holding self-supporting and a financial success, with many acres under cultivation and its own bêche-de-mer fleet. Practically all of the others in Australia are supported by subscription and contribution, for the aboriginal is not a paying proposition. Many of the Mornington Islanders are of Torres Straits derivation.

The Wilsons came to the island immediately after the murder by the blacks there of the former missioner, Robert Hall, in 1919, when the homestead was besieged for days by the rebels, the other white inhabitants narrowly escaping with their lives in a launch. Taking over the bullet-riddled house on the beach, and carrying on the work undaunted at a time when the island saw no passer-by in four years, they made it a prosperous haven of a population of five hundred. It now boasts an aeroplane landing-ground and wireless transmitting set in daily touch with Cloncurry.

The neighbouring island, Bentinck, is peopled by a wild shy tribe which defies all overtures of the white man, rejecting his flour and his friendliness, and flying from a camera as though it were a gun. After repeated efforts to establish contact, Mr. Wilson confesses himself beaten for the moment. But he knows the reason. Being no smoker himself, with a strong antipathy to the fragrant weed, he refuses to make friends with tobacco, so the natives of Bentinck remain pagan to this day.

Leading paleolithic man, whose justice is 'an eye for an eye,' into ways of loving kindness, teaching the godless to pray to an all-powerful and all-merciful God, and listless hands to labour, more or less, the missioners of the North and Centre certainly deserve to share—the honours of the explorers.

For it is to be regretted that the aborigine, the subject of all this care and kindness, and to some extent because of it, is fast fading out of existence. Swift to assimilate their teachings, to remodel their lives, to learn the prayers and hymns, and only too eager to live in amity and change the debil-debil for a God of love, he cannot survive the metamorphosis. A wild creature of the woodland, civilisation is his doom.

CHAPTER XXVI

LAST OF THE BEACH-COMBERS

BLACKENED by tropic suns, living one day at a time, and depending on 'God and the niggers' for to-morrow's tucker, a few white men that you could count upon the fingers of one hand are to-day the sole civilised population of the Territory shores of the Gulf.

Wearing nothing for most of the year but a hat of pandanus weave and a blackfellow's naga, these men fearlessly cruise hundreds of sea-miles in a native canoe, or a driftwood dinghy, with a rag of hessian sail, between islands of the Pellew Group and the Limmen Bight, and the low smoky shores of the mainland.

Nomads like the blacks, they leave but an upturned trepang pot or a fallen paper-bark shelter to mark their passing.

Roger Jose of the Wearyan River, doing his daily dozen in a suit of sun-tan out where a white woman has never yet been, Bill Harney of Arnhem Land; Harry Lake and Horace Foster, and old Alf Brown, seventy and half blind, who has spent forty years of his life between Cape Don and Cape Wilberforce—these names will perhaps never be written in history. As the last of the beach-combers, men who in a generation of clerks and salesmen can yet wrest their living from Nature in the raw, richly do they deserve to be.

Trepangers all, with a couple of dug-out canoes lashed together, they spend months in the lee of the islands, a few blacks enlisted to help them to gather the sea-slug in the shallows, to keep the fires alight for the boilers and the primitive smoke-houses, and to bag the prepared product for the meagre Chinese markets of Darwin and Thursday Island. It is only when the smashing hurricanes of summer have driven them across that they are to be seen upon the mainland.

The most extraordinary feature in the extraordinary lives of these men is that they have practically dispensed with civilisation. Some of them never buy a bag of flour in a twelve-month. None of them drink and few of them smoke —there are no cocktail bars or tobacco booths out along the Roper and the Robinson. A cherished chest of ration tea that, carefully guarded, lasts a year, and a pound or two of tobacco dust that, mixed with ashes, helps them to enlist the tribes in the great beginnings of colonisation, are the only item on the grocer's bill. Well-tutored by the blacks they live, and live well, on what the country offers.

Those shallow islands of blown sand and sea-grass that, to the uninitiated, seem scarcely capable of sustaining a gull, provide a richly epicurean diet that is the delight only of the wealthiest in cities. Here are crab and cray-fish and rock-oysters, daintiest hors d'œuvres ready to hand; turtle eggs and turtle soup; dugong, appetising and sustaining, cooked on the coals, to be eaten with the bread-pith of pandanus nut, the succulent inner leaves of the cabbage palm, and lily-roots, gathered at a water-hole, that boil tasty as young Spanish onions.

Recipes that will never be featured in any cookery book are part of the daily menu—of young shark and barra-mundi, baked whole in paper-bark, moistened with their own oils and kneaded between the hands into delicious fish-cakes; dampers of ground lily-seed, wrapped in a lily-leaf and browned in an oven of stones under the sand; of teal and turkey and quail and duck, and goanna and goat and wallaby; yams and tubers, sweet and savoury, melons and roots and Kaffir corn, and, over on the mainland, a frequent rib of wild beef or wild buffalo, with dessert of native plums and a custard of goose-eggs, garnished with innumerable fruits, berries and grass-seeds that, when you have the secret, are as palatable to the white man as to the black.

Life is by no means just sunshine and laziness to these beach-combers. Colonists all, they have taken up the white man's burden in black man's country, and are wide awake to possibilities, and undaunted by the bitterness of failure in that utter isolation.

In those crazy little skiffs that turn over in the first south-easter, and just as easily right themselves, they have taken sheep across to Bentinck and carried lime from Sweers— sheep that were promptly speared and eaten by the wild natives, lime that could find no market.

Clearing a patch for pea-nuts in the heart of Macarthur jungle, founding new stations with the wild cattle of the Goyder, planting coco-nuts on barren shores, 'sitting down' on copper mines of their own discovery, and dredging for gold in the little creeks, or shovelling salt into bags from the mirage flats of the lower Roper, and carting it by pack-horse to sell to the remote homesteads, they work from daylight till dark, forever on the move. When the pea-nuts are swept away by the river in flood, or sold for a song in the South, when the cattle are lost again in the dense bush, and the white ants and the wet have demolished the coco-nut suckers, and there is a stock of salt on the stations sufficient for the stews of fifty years, they make back to the islands again—the islands that few have seen since Flinders—a curl of smoke on the loneliest beaches in the world to tell their coming.

Most of them are well-educated men, tossed up by the tides of destiny far from each other. No longer do they need the companionship of their fellows.

It was out there that I met Bill Harney, who had salvaged his lugger in Blue Mud Bay, where she drifted with blood-stained decks, from a Japanese slaughter in Caledon country, a hundred empty miles north of him— Bill Harney, who could quote Shakespeare act by act and word by word, and had written a remarkable book with Horace Foster, based upon the myths and sagas of the Mara-mara of Arnhem Land.

It was there that I came across Jack Johnson, stricken with malaria, and ranged about his camp, preserved in the whisky and gin bottles that spoke the ancient history of Borroloola, a collection of North Australian reptilia that would set museum directors of the world agape; and Tom Kerin, whom the same Bill Harney had taught to read, and who longed to win a lottery that he might 'sit down by a big library for ever.'

Out there, where the days are a timeless blur of blue and gold, far from the stress of cities and the dolefulness of the dole these men are living adventure in an age when adventure is a fairy story. Their books are the tracks of the bush, the living dramas of revenge and jealousy and love and hate of the primitive people about them, their talkies the phantasmagoria of corroboree in the starlit theatre of the jungle.

And if there are moments when they bend to a tattered scrap of newspaper in the flicker of a camp-fire, harking back through those measured lines of print to the world they have forgotten—with all that the years have given them wrapped in an old grey camp-sheet, and home the shadow of a milkwood tree—they count the world well lost.

It is a different story on the western coast. The beach-combers of the North-west now have their wives and children with them, Tarzans of the ferny forests living in houses of pandanus trunks that actually put down their roots and grow. This is quite a new departure in popular romance.

Two families are already established on the 'undiscovered islands' of the Buccaneers and the Admiralty Groups between Broome and Wyndham, Mr. and Mrs. Bill Haldane and their five children at Bigge Island, Mr. and Mrs. Drysdale in Yampi Sound, with three babies. Haldane is a returned soldier with a war-service pension. His wife has had no respite from the tropics in her life. They went off to the islands, where generous Nature pays the rent and the butcher's bills, to let the pension accumulate to provide a holiday in the South. The Drysdales have tried everything else in Kimberley, from dogging to donkey-teaming, and failed. They succeed in the simple life.

The time-honoured beach-comber of South Sea fiction, the broken-down cynic who ekes out his life under a coco-nut tree with one arm round a cask of rum and the other round a dusky beauty, certainly does not exist in the Australian north. The beaches provide no treasure of copra or ambergris—only tucker.

The procedure is simple. Taking out a beach-comber's licence and a permit to employ native labour, you hire an old lugger at Broome for £1 a month. You stock it up with stores for six months, and set out for where you fancy 'up east.' The native labour does the rest.

Pearl-shell, trochus, trepang, tortoise shell and sandal-wood, these are your quest, and trochus is the main source of income, plentiful and profitable at £70 a ton. Trepang, the dark variety that the Chinese delight in, brings $40 a picol in Singapore and the Dutch Islands, sold through shipping agents. It works out at about £10 a cwt. Tortoise shell is marketed in London, at from 4/- a lb. to 32/-, according to its clarity and quality. An occasional patch of good arable land brings in a fair little cheque in a few months from pea-nuts, and the income can be well supplemented by a trail of the nearby ranges for dingo scalps, for which the West Australian Government pays 30/- apiece—until recently £2. A few baits spread about in a blacks' camp out there will earn a miniature fortune overnight—and the undying hostility of the tribe. Many a man has lost his life by shooting a nigger's dog, and, in any case, it is a poor-spirited white man that will do it.

For the blacks are his Elijah's ravens in the wilderness. A pound or two of tobacco at 13/6 a pound, a few gay rags and cast-off trousers, and a reasonable supply of flour, tea and sugar, and the tribes are yours to command. They will man the ship, feed the family, track up the dingoes, plant the pea-nuts, pick up the pearl shell, smoke the trepang, look after the vegetable garden, build the house, do the housework and mind the baby with a smile that never comes off if you treat them properly. In these unsurveyed seas, their eyes and their local knowledge are the only sailing directions. On their mangrove rafts or in dug-out canoes, some of which hold a dozen of them, they sail out to the reefs at low water, dry-shelling for trochus and pearl-shell, walking and wading miles in the day and enjoying it. They dive for the sea-slug in the shallows, unafraid of the sharks, cut it and gut it, run up a smoke-house of saplings on the nearest beach, stretch it on sticks for the sun-drying, and bag it ready for export. They follow the hawksbill to his feeding grounds, or waylay the mother turtle on the sands at night-time, eat the inside and the eggs she has just carefully buried, and bring back the shell, ready cut and crudely preserved and polished—and there is always the chance that one of them, in his naïve simplicity, will hand over a £1,000 pearl for an extra stick of tobacco. It has happened more than once in the great North-west.

Not only do they so cheerfully provide the white man's profit, but with a regal hospitality, that always offers the best to the guest, they will feed him as long as he likes to stay.

Barefooted winter and summer, in a single garment or without it, and brown as the piccaninnies, the children roam the beaches, take their freshwater baths in the rushy creeks and their salt in the rock-pools, speak three or four black languages before they know their own, swimming and sun-baking childhood through. Their mothers are perfectly happy. They never hanker for the little social round of the outback town, and they never suffer from the nostalgia of the bargain counter. What do clothes matter in Eden?

By this time, I, too, rolling my little swag beneath the stars, and waking to the call of the first bird, had learned the rapture of the lonely shore. Not for me the twopenny tram section yet awhile. I would go round, and come back.

Book III
THE LIVING HEART

CHAPTER XXVII

MYSTERIOUS NULLARBOR

ACROSS the interior of the Continent, in the maps of our childhood, damnation was written in four words —'The Great Australian Desert.' By train and truck and car and camel and packhorse, east and west as far as civilisation goes, and further, I was to travel 10,000 miles of it within the year, to prove those words untrue. The allegedly 'dead heart of Australia' is vitally alive.

Two thousand miles across, wide as the moon and nearly as empty, an age-old country of hills fretted away in the slow alchemy of time, of burnt-out craters, brown stony deserts, and rivers of sand that run into the sand, yet a country of great mineral and pastoral wealth when all its secrets of water and rare metals are known—such is the immensity of the centre of Australia, from the 30th parallel north to the 15th.

To leave the rim of coastal colonisation is to enter a weird prehistoric world where the bones of the diprotodon are still found, bleached white in the salt lakes; where opalised shells and fossilised fish 600 miles from the coast denote the bed of that great inland sea that once divided the Continent into two islands, and where the dazzled earth shines like a moonlit sea with gypsum and mica. Boiling bores of the artesian basin, from hell's kitchens 4,000 feet below, send a white drift of vapour into the air. Rolling dust-storms and whirls of sand, like genii of the Arabian Nights, come striding across the land, a land without horizons, where the vacant earth merges into the vacant sky.

Dawn in the desert—the livid crimson and grey of a galah's wings—and a wind across the salt-bush, keen as a wind of the sea. Eastward across the Nullarbor, on the first 1,000-mile lap of the great right-angle, the transcontinental express carried me on to its swinging rhythm, the big train that links the capitals of East and West. The only thing that ever moves in that mighty circle of monotony it is a blackfellow's devil come true.

Four hundred miles by four hundred and fifty of withered saltbush, from the Western Australian border to Ooldea, across four parallels of longitude, the Nullarbor Plain is one of the most melancholy patches in Australia. Never a foot-traveller dares to challenge its sun-dazzled wastes, never the wing of a crow stirs the pale blue above it. For a thousand years before the coming of the white man, Oondiri the Waterless was shunned by the tribes as the domain of Dijarra, an immense legendary serpent. That legend of its ghostly voices and its evil god kept them in abject fear. Should a hunter more daring than the rest venture too far, he never came back. Probably he died of thirst, or, more probably, of terror. The natives believed him devoured. Until the surveyors of the East-West line drove their pegs across a thousand miles of uninhabited country in 1912, Nullarbor knew not human life, and humans knew not the Nullarbor.

When the first engine puffed its way across in 1917, madly the blacks fled. Belching smoke and sparks by day, a winding dragon of lights at night, Dijarra had left his haunt at last, to ravage the earth with death in his breath.

From the sand and the mulga ridges away to the north-west, from the Musgraves and the Hann and the Warburton Ranges, hundreds of miles on bare feet still they come, the most primitive blacks of the Continent, to gaze on the phenomenon with panic and awe. A few weeks, and they have learned that the big train is a fairy godmother and not an ogre, in dirty and inadequate rags to follow its trail of chocolates and sixpences, and whine and beg in its wake. Commercial travellers and Yankee tourists lean out of the windows in amusement to see a cannibal scramble for a pink-topped biscuit.

Eyre skirted the edge of the Nullarbor in 1841, facing death by thirst every mile of the way, a week at a time without water, killing his horses for food, waking morning after morning 'weary and unrefreshed,' and brushing the salt-bush before sunrise with his blistered lips for the dew.

A South Australian surveyor named Delisser discovered the Plain in 1866, and because he could not find a single tree to break that grey horizon, gave the place the Latin name that is strangely aboriginal. Giles followed him in

1875, and many years later Tietkens, who found there the bones of a diprotodon, low inland cliffs, wave marks and fossil shells, showing that it had been the bed of a sea. Not one of these explorers could ever induce a native guide to accompany him, and as the plain has never yet been crossed from north to south, the exact extent of it is unknown. It was one Alfred Mason who, with his camels lost, walked 160 miles to Eucla, first told of the blow-holes with which the Nullarbor is pitted, the dank smell, the unhealthy fœtid breath of earth, and the screeching of the winds at night.

With the building of the railway, a chain of tiny settlements has sprung up in the desolation, a unique community of railway fettlers and gangers constantly working to keep the line from creeping and crippling in the heat. Linked by 330 straight miles of railway—dead east and west, the longest straight line of railway in the world—these villages in blankness are all named in questionable honour of Australia's notable statesmen—Forrest, Deakin, Cook, Hughes, Fisher, Reid and Watson. They depend upon the passing trains for wood and water, and all of the necessities of life.

In twenty years, the population has doubled and trebled. Cook, in the centre of them, has become a street of big comfortable bungalows in the very heart of Nullarbor, with never a blade of grass to its credit, but a school, a church, a cemetery, a slaughter-yard, a locomotive workshop and a store. The 'Trans' and its people are a little world sufficient for themselves, a remarkable colony of government servants living in progress and contentment in the desert. From A to Z—Augusta to Zanthus—1,000 miles with scarcely a tree and never a permanent water, they have their community interests and 'camp romance.' Fettlers make friends with fettlers, the fireman marries the engine-driver's daughter. With wireless to broadcast city concerts and the results of the races, week-end dances at Cook, and a weekly shopping orgy on the 'Tea and Sugar' train that brings their water and supplies, and with generous holiday trips provided by the Commonwealth Railways, cheerfully they weather it out.

To these people has been unfolded the extraordinary physiography of the plain, its stark horror in the drought years, and its remarkable beauty after a downfall of rain, when the wastes are swept with a snowstorm of immortelle daisies, and every donga is a vivid patch of the scarlet of Sturt's desert pea. It has just been discovered, moreover, that the Nullarbor is not a sand desert, but the roof of a mighty honeycomb of mysterious caves of crystalline limestone and subterranean rivers, icy cold, flowing 50 miles southward to the sea, where the plain undulates to a level of 600 feet, and terminates abruptly in the spectacular cliffs of the Bight.

These caves explained away the hollow rumbling and the haunted voices. Further, it was found that water could be obtained almost anywhere below the surface, saltish and bitter to taste, unsuitable for locomotive purposes, but plentiful and palatable to stock. Pastoralists have secured a lease of the country, two or three sheep stations are already established with their flocks steadily increasing. Bores are being put down with success, and as soon as they can provide sufficient drinking water for increased stock, the frightening Nullarbor will become a fine sheep country.

The caves are a curious formation, caused evidently by the washaway of soluble limestone. Some of them are 40 and 80 feet underground, approached through the blowholes and by a dark descent over step and slippery rocks. Several on the rim of the plain were sacred hiding places of the blacks, and one of them, the Murrawidginie, Cave of the Bloody Hand, presents a fearsome spectacle, with many red hands imprinted on its walls. Others are filled with ghostly stalactites, and even on the hottest days there is a deathly cool draught, due to barometric pressure, that, emerging at the blow-hole entrance, will lift and hold a man's felt hat in the air for minutes at a time.

Two graves are to be found out on the waste of the Nullarbor, in a crude walled bush cemetery, one stone bearing the name of 'Annie. 1874.' What was the strange life drama that led to the presence of a woman there in those early years, and her death, and the preservation of her memory?

There is little wild life—a few snakes, a few turkeys,

never a rabbit in rabbit-infested country, never a wallaby or wombat. Bird and insect life, except in good seasons, is practically nil. Even the lizards, those hardy little denizens of the desert, are rarely seen. Nothing stirs in that low smouldering smoke of the saltbush. The eastern terminal is Ooldea, a siding in the sand-hills. Ooldea was once famous for its magic gift of clear fresh waters, the Mecca of the desert blacks for generations.

Ooldea Soak is just a sandy depression some hundreds of yards wide, like countless others nearby, yet here in the worst drought years a blackfellow or a kangaroo could scratch with its foot and find water in plenty. The natives tracked there from thousands of miles away in a bad season —in all of the sand-hills about it you can find the chipped stones they brought with them to fashion into spear-heads, and the deserted wurlies and the crude wells fashioned of laced sticks made by the tribes long dead. Ooldea Water has saved the life of several of the explorers, and for years the engineers and locomotives of the railway drained it to the tune of 70,000 gallons a day, by means of pumping stations and a pipe-line. But in an attempt to locate the source of its waters, the blue clay bottom of the soak was irremediably ruined. Ooldea Water to-day is but a name.

Nobody knows where the miraculous waters came from, nor where they went to, but Mrs. Daisy Bates has translated a charming, typically aboriginal legend, as told her by Jinjabulla, last of the Ooldea tribe, who died in her arms.

It was in the days of the dreamtime that Karrbiji, the little marsupial hopping-man, with his skin bag full of water, set out from the ranges in the far North-west, and in the first night of his travelling sat down in Ooldilbinna, a swamp. There he heard the whistle of Ngabbula, the spiked-backed lizard. It was a grim drought, and Ngabbula, perceiving the water-bag, followed Karrbiji ever south-ward, into the domain of Kalaaia the emu, totem of the Ooldea people, and there killed him in a fight of teeth and claws. Kalaaia, from the sand-hills, watched the battle. In the last throes of Karrbiji, he saw him hide the skin water-bag beneath him, deep in the sand. Karrbiji called Ginnega, the native cat, and together they routed Ngabbula and killed him, thus keeping the water for their people for all time.

Since that moment, the totems of emu and native cat have ever been friends.

My first quest in the Centre was Daisy Bates—a name that will certainly be written in Australia's history.

As the woman who has wandered the wilderness for thirty-five years with the most primitive of earth's races, already she is known to three continents. Correspondents to Ooldea from all over the world included American and English scientists, publishers and authors of note, and Mrs. Bates has been hailed by certain ethnologists as the most reliable living authority on the life and customs of the Australian aborigine.

Living unafraid in the great loneliness, chanting in those corroborees that it is death for a woman to see, she had become a legend, to her own kind, long lost, 'the woman who lives with the blacks.' To the natives, she is an age-old, sexless being who knows his secrets and guesses his thoughts—Dhoogoor of the dream-time. Voluntarily she gave up thirty-five years of her life to wandering with the nomad tribes of half a continent, speaking their languages, tending their sick, accepted as tribeswoman and guardian spirit of this occult, shy people.

On the rim of the Nullarbor Plain, sleeping in a bough shade under the stars that are to her an open book of aboriginal mythology, I spent five days with Daisy Bates, to learn her strange life history, and to glean a remarkable mind. A daughter of the old sporting gentry of Ireland, a rider to hounds and a fluent linguist, here was a woman who could tell time by the passing of the sun, followed tracks like a native, and cooked her food in the ashes. Achieving the impossible, for the scientific work that is her life's mission, she learned to 'think black.'

To her little camp in the sand-hills neither white man nor black ever penetrated. No native could be enticed inside it for a bag of flour. It was 'maamu'—magic. A tent for reading and sleeping, a tin tank that was a library, and a high breakwind of dead mulga and mallee to keep out the wild dogs howling about it—since 1917 that had been her only home. Around her in the sand-hills were the graves of eleven of the aboriginal dead, whom she had buried with her own hands.

For a thousand miles round came primitives of the desert
—women unclad, with red berries in their hair, timid
shadows among the trees and great bearded men in the
coloured headdress of the savage. Frantic at first at the
passing of the train they flew to her for refuge. To her
keeping they brought the sacred boards and wanningis made
of human hair that no woman must look upon. Guileless
they stood, to be buttoned into the shirt and trousers of
civilization.

Of her own means, unbiassed by creeds and unsubsidized
by governments, Mrs. Bates fed them and clothed them
and cared for them in illness, her only reward the casual
confidences of a race whose traditions and thoughts are
swiftly passing into oblivion. This was her 'field work.'

In 1899 Daisy Bates, a journalist from the London staff
of *The Review of Reviews*, came to Australia and took
up a station property at Nullagine, in the North-west. She
was one of the first white women to travel Kimberley, riding
for months behind eight drovers and 800 of her own cattle.
It was then that her quick sympathies brought her in touch
with the aborigine in all his native simplicity. On uncharted
northern coasts, in the empty sand-wastes of the West,
among the extinct Bibbulmun nation of the South-west,
where she was given the freedom of the totem and made
'blood-brother' of the tribe, she travelled across the Great
Australian Bight from Eucla in a camel-buggy, and at the
'orphan water' of Ooldea Soak, she has been faithful to
the age of seventy-six years.

A fluent linguist, she has added 115 black languages to
her accomplishments, and for that human understanding,
intuition, and sympathy of which only a woman is capable,
her work has been of outstanding value to ethnologists.

To travellers of the East-West Line her name was a
byword, yet Mrs. Bates rarely visited the train. With an
abhorrence of cheap publicity, she dreaded the prying eye
and the pointing finger. A quaint little figure in the chin-
veils and shirt-waists of Edwardian days, her hands were
always elegantly gloved—those hands that were ceaseless
in their service for the derelicts about her.

For many years, save for the natives, she elected to live
in utter loneliness. To the fettlers' wives of the distant

siding, her life and thoughts were a mystery. Tracks of those little high-heeled shoes could be found in the sand-hills for many miles round. A keen naturalist and botanist, she has contributed much of value to the book-data of South Australian fauna and bird-lore.

About her tent in the mornings the wild birds were tame, daily visitors that she greeted always by their musical aboriginal names, and the rare little marsupial mouse, with Jagal the bicycle lizard, would eat from her hand. But the aborigine is her life's study and her life's care.

I found her labouring in the intense heat, carrying the sick upon her back, trudging for two miles each day with water in tins over the sand-hills, looking to the needs of poor human objects repulsive in their degeneration, and using all her influences against the propagation of half-castes and a frightful and incorrigible cannibalism. She was, in fact, tracking up a woman whom she suspected of being about to give birth to a child, and eat it. We found the girl in time together, and before I left I was reassured at seeing a proud mother, beyond reproach, sitting up in her wurlie with her baby in her arms. Her grisly hunger for human meat—'meeri-cooga'—had been staved off for the time. Even so, I could not help thinking, purely as a journalist, that God and Daisy Bates had robbed me of a thundering front-page story.

Distantly, quietly and courteously, Mrs. Bates spoke to the natives always in their own languages, never in pidgin. Never did they perform the slightest service for which they were not promptly repaid. They call her Kabbarli—Grandmother. An undemonstrative and unthinking people, there was little response on their part. Her own serious illnesses she faced alone, and, in a scorching drought a few years ago, a fire carelessly lighted by a blackboy swept the camp. It seemed that her valuable manuscripts of thirty years' compiling would be burnt to ashes. Great holes in the earth were quickly dug by those nervous little gloved hands, and the situation saved.

'I have no illusions,' said Daisy Bates to me, very sadly. 'They are a lost people. Already they are but the remnants of the old tribes and totems, poor hopeless derelicts, wan-derers with no comprehension. I shall not see the last of them, but this century will. In living among them here, all that I can do is to make the passing easy. There is no hope for to-morrow, but I can help each one of them for to-day.'

So it is that in that little tent at night, when no black-fellow would venture out for fear of the debil-debil, a white woman, voluntarily exiled from her own kind for thirty-five years, has found all her joy in writing the legends and the songs of the vanished tribes, and in reading the old Latin poets for the music of the words.

CHAPTER XXVIII

WITH THE CAVE MEN OF COOBER PEDY

NIGHT in a cave, deep down in a maze of grave-holes. . . .

Walls of pink and white sandstone closed in on me, ghostly in the fire-light, gleaming with snake-trails of gypsum, and scraps of jewel that shone like cat's eyes in the glim. Now and again I could hear the muffled coughs and dragging footsteps of men that moved about me in the hill, unseen and unknown, and I was alone in the desert, 2000 miles from home.

It was not a dream, for I crouched over the fire with a coat round my shoulders, unable to sleep in that dank cold, till dawn had streaked the skies to harlequin opal, and made things sane again. It was my first night at Coober Pedy.

For a week, the typewriter rattled like a skeleton's teeth in that cave.

Six hundred miles from the sea and eight feet below its level, in the Stuart Ranges, South Australia, lies Coober Pedy, where the opal gougers live in caverns of the hills, like the robbers in Gil Blas.

One of the most remarkable communities of white men in the world, you will find it only on the most comprehensive of maps, and you could pass right through it in a motor-car, daytime or night-time, and not know it existed. To believe it true, you must travel out across 200 miles of mostly saltbush, and sleep in a cave as I did.

Coober Pedy. Coober = man. Pedy = hole in the ground. Deep in the hills, away from the blinding glare and a torment of flies, I found a hundred men and eight women, Slaves of the Ring, condemned to eternal digging. Never a gleam of sunshine penetrated their dug-outs. Hardly a straggler was seen by day, threading the track of its thousand graves, graves of lost hope, or a fortune. There is no geological logic of opal, no reef to follow, as in gold. You dig and dig, and give up digging in despair, and the next man takes on the hole and digs two feet further and finds £1000 worth.

One of the richest of Australia's opal fields for a season, twenty years ago the Stuart Ranges were a patch of desert. In 1916 a prospector named Hutchinson .wandered out across them with camels, bound for Western Australia. With him travelled a mate and his young son. The boy was cook and camel driver, the men sought water and gold.

Night after night a camp-fire in the empty dark, and the same maddening question: 'Any luck, Dad?' One evening the boy brought out a scrap of sandstone from inside his rag of a shirt. 'Well, I found something,' he said hopefully, 'but I don't know what it is.'

Curiously the two men bent over the thing in the fire-light, the humps of the camels shadowy behind them. It was sun-shot and raddled with heat, but it glittered like the eyes of a snake. Opal? they wondered.

The desert beat them. The horrible sores of scurvy rot came out on the boy's arms. The water-bags hung limp. The camels were perishing, one by one. They turned back.

The stone was sent to Adelaide, to T. C. Wollaston, Australia's best-known authority on opals. It was a 'floater,' quite worthless, but an indication of the jewel in the country. An expedition was sent up, of six men with camels and provisions for six months—one of the men is still at Coober Pedy. Fifty miles from the nearest water, with not even the shade of a mulga, these men worked and thirsted among the gibbers. For shelter from sun and flies, they dug themselves a hole in the hill, as everybody has done since. They searched for months with no luck. Then they lost their camels.

On the last hundred gallons they decided to walk back to Port Augusta. It was a mad project, but with death due in a week or two it was the only thing to do. On the last night they were awakened by two brothers, Jim and Dick O'Neill, who had come out from Anna Creek Station in a dray, and followed camel tracks to the cave.

Jim and Dick wanted to join them, but the expedition had had enough. As one man, it bartered the hundred gallons, the lost camels and the desert *in toto* for the dray, and set out in the morning for Anna Creek.

The brothers stayed. They found the camels and they found the opal. They found £17,000 worth of it in one hole in nine months. Their fortune was made for life, it seemed. Dick is dead. Jim, with his fortune and one or two others a thing of the past, is out on the trail of gold.

In two years Coober Pedy had a population of 400 men. They came from the world-famed fields of White Cliffs and Lightning Ridge, now played out. They came from the cities, and they came from England, and from little 'shows' across the Queensland border, men who knew all there is to know about opal and men who had never seen it. They burrowed themselves into the hills as the first had done. They honeycombed the desert for forty square miles with shafts 70 feet deep, so close that you cannot find foothold between them. They lived on rabbits and saltbush in hard times, and carried their water for fifty miles on bicycles, or bought it from camel-teamsters at £5 a hundred gallons.

They dug for a day and found 1000 ounces— 'luck from the grass down'—or they dug for years and found nothing. For such is the fortune of opal, jewel of luck that knows no law, crystallized light of the sea.

A jagged scrap of the mineral magic lies on my table as I write—white fire of the diamond, living red of the ruby, peacock wings of emerald and turquoise and the 'heaven-hued' sapphire, misted over with the roseate nacre of a pearl, a jewel of sea-change and distilled sunlights. A sedimentary silica of pure crystal, it is yet non-crystalline. That prism of shattered radiance is nothing but an optical illusion, the splitting of the spectrum by microscopic veins into the most brilliant colours of earth and fire and water. The only gem that cannot be produced synthetically by chemical science, it burns away to a little pure limestone. The blacks of Australia associated it with their evil serpent-gods. You will never find a blackfellow within miles of Coober Pedy. They think the white man mad.

There is no opal in the world like Australian opal, in quantity and quality and living fire. The barren sands and buried bones of the oldest continent are alight with its dazzling beauty. It belongs almost exclusively to the low levels of south-west Queensland, western New South Wales and the north of South Australia, where wave-washed gibbers and dazzled flats of brine and salt lakes thousands of miles across denote the bed of that inland sea of the

cretaceous ages.   Before the Australian discoveries, there
was a slight scattering on the face of the globe, in Mexico
and in Hungary, where it was mined thousands of feet
below earth's surface. I have seen Hungarian opal, and
compared with that of Australia it is as inspiring as tapioca
with an opalescent gleam.

Coober Pedy, the last of the big fields, provides little
more than 'tucker' for its miners just at the moment, but
the price of the stone is rising rapidly and there is great
hope for the future. The old gougers will pin their faith
to it whether or not. Once they have seen the fire of it,
down there in the dark, their eyes are held spell-bound.
Victims of its uncanny mesmerism, they will follow the
gleam of it all their lives.

It was a Sunday afternoon when I swung down from the
plain of mirage into the Stuart Ranges. Two hundred miles
from Kingoonya, a siding of the East-West line, through
the ever hospitable stations twenty and thirty miles apart,
I had come upon a truck with Jacob Santing, the old Dutch
mailman.   Jacob is Coober Pedy's only friend from the
world outside. Apart from the mails he brings the meat,
and vegetables that are freighted 800 miles from Adelaide.

On the road he has a bad time—we ourselves were
bogged all night—and to leave the road is to lose it. Once
Jacob turned up at the opal fields a week late, with a case
of condensed milk missing from the stores.   Thrashing
round in the bush for five days, he had had to live on it.

'We've just got to make the best of life, aindt it?' he
told me. Even so, it is not safe to dwell on the subject of
condensed milk too long in his presence. On another occasion he forgot the meat, or was unable to obtain sheep from
the stations. Rather than let the little community go meat-
less for a fortnight, that valiant old Dutchman, after a 200-
mile journey, set off immediately for William Creek, 100
miles there and back in the scorching day, and then made
straight in again to Kingoonya to catch the express with the
mail—three days' incessant travelling, with never a wink of
sleep. Coober Pedy has never forgotten Jacob for that. He
is the darling of their hearts.

The population was *non est* when we arrived. There was
nothing to mark the habitation of man save the little cocked

hats of chimney pots here and there in the hills. The rumble of the truck brought a few heads above ground, a hail from the nether regions.

There was no accommodation, as such. The only thing visible was the little tin store. But although I was an unexpected stranger, they made me welcome, and offered the best little dug-out on the field, a miniature palace of pink and white desert sandstone in Crowder's Gully, with eight men burrowed into the hill about me. The nearest woman was somewhere in the recesses of earth three-quarters of a mile away.

There, when my eyes had become accustomed to the darkness and my mind to subterranean living, buying my tinned goods from Jacob's store and borrowing daily bread, for I cannot make yeast bread, I made my home for a week of many friendships in the realm of the Arabian Nights.

About me, in the white dazzle of day, shone the harlequin hills of opal ore, no six feet of ground alike, a patchwork of terra-cotta and milky white, amethyst, sulphur yellow and bright gold, red ochre and rose and silver and slate-colour and black, spangled over with the tinsel of gypsum and the steel-white of alinite. Through those quaint streets where a false step means a fall of sixty feet—through Bolshevik Gully and Poverty Terrace and Peaceful Valley and Gibber Hill, the Deep Sinking, Black Flag and The Willows, names of rich humour and glamorous history, each day I took my way to learn the stories of a hundred holes.

There were holes that had yielded a tenner or £10,000— or nothing but rheumatism; the hole where Wainewright, Clarke and Fabian unearthed £20,000 in a few months; where two men had been blown to pieces in an argument over a plug of dynamite, and where another had fallen to his death.

Each day I was a welcomed visitor at the queerest little homes in Australia, some of them made comfortable by a woman in residence, some of them merely holes in the ground with dug-in fire-places and beds and an air-chute, fantastic with the gleam of potch and angel-stone and fragments of opal itself. Each day, swinging down to the bottom of the shafts, I watched the opal miners at their work, peering with keen eyes through a candle held on a piece of twisted iron called a 'spider,' for a glint of the lovely jewel in the seams of desert sandstone.

At night we played bridge in the dug-outs, our shadows grotesque in the lamplight on the rough stony walls, our laughter echoing uncannily in the bowels of the earth.

With a journalist's nose for news, I discovered a fact of which Coober Pedy had been totally ignorant. A baby had been born there, the first white baby. The mother was a stranger who, with her husband and five children, had recently come in on a truck. She had scarcely been seen above ground in a month. When the time for her delivery came, her husband dug a little annex into the cave for her privacy, and she and he attended to the matter together. A child was sent the round of the camps to inquire for 'a little brandy and a doctor's book,' but nobody asked questions. A new little son came into the world by candlelight in a cavern. In three weeks, the child had not been seen by the other inhabitants of the hidden village, and the mother requested that I should sign the application for the baby bonus as the only one who could testify to its existence. I did.

The most successful of all these troglodytes is an English girl, mining opal alone, Minnie Berrington. Seven years ago, a London typist, she came out to join an adventurous brother in Australia, and these two came to the fields with a travelling hawker to find that she was the only woman there. Cheerfully she set up housekeeping in a cave, and accompanied her brother to the shaft, 'pulling dirt' in buckets while he excavated down below.

One trip down by a swinging rope, one glimpse of opal sparkling in the gloom, and the fascination was complete. Her brother, fired by other ambitions, has moved on, but Minnie works her claim alone, digs her own shafts, classes and polishes and sells her own opal, and save for an occasional holiday, has never left the field.

'Sure-footed as a goat, and so independent that she wouldn't let you pull a bucketful for her,' said the old miners. 'Only a slip of a girl, and you should see her throw out the stones at seven and eight feet! Why, she's found a good deal more than most of the men.'

'Oh, but I like hard work and fresh air, and this is a good life,' she told me. 'You have no idea how thrilling it is suddenly to find £60 on the shovel when you have only gone down four feet. Among these men, typical of the Australian bush, I couldn't be nervous. My best friends in the world are among them. London is the only city I want to see again, and, with opal at its present prices, London's far away.'

Minnie Berrington is always cheery, in good luck and bad, and her hands are not the least bit horny. She is a well-educated girl, with a musical speaking voice and a charming reserve.

'Ah, but did you notice her eyes?' an old miner asked me. 'Ain't they fine? Beautiful eyes for gouging! Wish I could see as well, through the candlelight down there. Minnie's a great little girl, and what a worker! I would like to see her strike a patch!'

Three hundred miles from the nearest police and telegraph office, for all their fantastic habitations and their subterranean lives, here is one of the finest and friendliest little communities you could find. In a night of formless darkness, a conspirator's den of holes and drives and getaways, the miners, splendid characters all, are a law unto themselves. No police proceedings have ever been known on the field, no opal robberies, no drink.

Their lives the 'potch and colour' of romance, there in the painted deserts, from daylight till dark they dig, the men that handle the playthings of wealth and live in poverty, content to be chained forever to the slavery of a precious stone.

CHAPTER XXIX

FROM Port Augusta at piccaninny daylight, the jagged heights of the Flinders Ranges cut purple against the sunrise, the waters of Spencer's Gulf paling to amethyst beneath a paling sky, on the meandering little train they call the 'Marree Mixed,' I faced the 2000 miles to the North, across the 'steel-clad desert.'

Up through the Pichi Richi Pass, a thousand feet in an hour we climbed to the very crests of the mountains lost in mist. About our track the little hills were mustered, brushed silver with morning dew; below us the lower slopes of a rich pasture country, with here and there a jewel of English landscape set in the sylvan glory of Australian bushland. It was at Woolshed Flat, just such an old-world corner for all its colonial name, that we reached the summit, and from the peaks of majesty looked down upon far fields of ripening wheat, and then with an easy rhythm dipped down into the valley, where the little hills skip like sheep above the clustered roofs of Quorn.

The 'Marree Mixed' is the little sister of 'the Afghan express,' which outdistances it by 700 miles, from Marree to Alice Springs. Twice a week since the early 'eighties, it has threaded the Flinders Ranges to the last of their foot-hills in the North. It brings mails and newspapers and supplies to all the far-out southern stations, and loads thousands of bales of wool brought in by donkey-teams. Mixed, indeed, its passengers range from turbaned sheiks to shearers shouting a wool-shed chantey.

Out of Quorn, across the far pastures and the wheat-fields, where the teams are valiantly ploughing eight abreast, we passed the quaint old townships of Gordon and Wilson and Canniga Creek. At the Gillick Arms at Wilson, they showed me a genuine Australian mosaic of hundreds of bottle-necks and bottle-tops, cup-handles and broken dinner-sets and teapot-lids, embedded in Moorish colour design in the cement of its walls by an old-timer with the thirst of a Silenus and the hand of a Michael Angelo. At Hawker the mountains crowded in again.

The Flinders Ranges! Could there be a more fitting monument to the man who named Australia than these leonine peaks that, running 300 miles due north and south, 'stand up like the thrones of kings'?

Here are the hills that Hans Heysen painted, parched with the fierce colours of drought, jagged knives of earth serrating the pale skies; hills of ineffable and tenderest blue, gracious against the clouds and spattered with pools of sunlight and depths of grape-bloom shade; a harlequin patchwork of light and colour, red sand and rock and purple scrub; hills hunch-backed and sinister, stubbled with a black beard of pine-trees; hills in the distance like a camel-string that travels to infinity.

Precipitous heights fenced perpendicularly and diagonally in the most amazing fashion, the ranges are a maze of sheep stations, jewelled here and there with little settlements that link them to the railway line and Adelaide. As yet untamed and unexploited, the time must come when they will challenge the Blue Mountains as a tourist resort. To-day there are just a few pilgrims—donkey-teamsters bringing in the wool, naturalists listening to the songs of the birds, and men and women threatened with death in the cities who find health and hope on the heights.

With definite evidence of nearly all the known metals, the potential mineral wealth of the Flinders Ranges to South Australia is inestimable. Hills of copper and silver-lead, diorite and dolemite and iron pyrites, hills of quartz and rock-crystal, and, incidentally, the only radium as yet unearthed in the British Empire, provide a lifetime's prospecting for multitudes of men.

But those white gum gullies and whispering gorges hold secrets stranger still. Eighty miles east of Copley, I found a hole in the mountain-top with a curious history. About eight miles from the Mount Painter radium mine, it was disclosed some years ago to a prospector by an aborigine, as the abode of a devil in the middle of the earth.

Shrouded in bushes, and scarcely large enough to admit a human body, the prospector dropped a stone into it. The stone reached bottom in eight seconds. Always curious, always hopeful, one day he descended by a rope. Swinging down in the darkness, he fell 238 feet before he found a foothold. When his eyes had become accustomed to the gloom, he found himself in a cavern 120 feet square, lofty and spacious, lined with silver-white and filled with silver-glittering stalactites. 'Pretty as a picture show,' he told me, 'and you could drive a donkey-team round inside it.' He broke off one of the shining brittle projections and tasted it. It was acrid and bitter—ammonia.

At first he thought he had discovered an ammoniam spring, and tried to float a company. But the ammonia proved superficial. Beneath it were layers of fluffy dark guano, which the Adelaide Museum classified for him as the excrement of a vampire bat long extinct, a formula of potash and nitrogen with big possibilities as a fertilizer. The stuff was put on the market and is now one of the most popular fertilizers of orchardists on the Murray River. It is sold at from £7 10s. to £11 15s. a ton, and the men employed in its excavation—the 'bat-manure miners' they call them, wear gas-masks to deal with it, and frequently unearth a little furry corpse old as the hills themselves.

Gold and guano, galena and bismuth, coal and copper and silver-lead, asbestos and mica and the kingfisher ores of torbernite, mother of radium—they are there among the peaks and gullies for the finding. But because the pioneer prospector is so sadly a figure of the past, because Young Australia prefers its thrills in celluloid to the tang of real adventure, the Flinders Ranges, an impressionist artist's heaven and a poet's dream, toss their defiant heads to the skies, and keep their secrets still.

Between the Flinders and the MacDonnell Ranges stretches a mighty sunken valley 700 miles long and westward to the infinite that is one of the most inhospitable to the eye in all the world. The wide blue lakes and the branching rivers of the map are a cruel delusion. The hills are below sea-level, the water-courses of sand, and the lakes, Torrens and Eyre and Frome and Amadeus, seas of the beguiling blue of mirage hundreds of miles across, are dry as a bone and white with a crust of bitterest brine.

I was now in the realm of the dust-storms, that rage sometimes for days and nights on the Willochra Plain, and all the plains north of it. The windows were shut in stifling, gritted heat. Above the peaks towered chimerical alps of sand, red and yellow and violet and grey, enshrouding form and colour of earth. Smaller than the moon, the sun was a bright balloon bouncing about the sky, this way, that way, in seething clouds of sulphur.

At Parachilna, there is a little tin hostelry where refugees fly for shelter when 'the land goes walking' in suffocating hurricanes. They dust the dining-tables with brooms there, and make up the beds before you get into them.

North of Quorn, the farmers dare not plough their fields, or those fields would blow away. Nothing grows but the saltbush, stunted and sparse, yet sweeter than clover to hundreds of thousands of sheep, an unfailing fodder of the drought country that produces Australia's lightest and finest wools. Only those that have seen it, veiled in the colours of dawn and twilight, or eaten it boiled with young rabbit, can testify to its delicacy both ways.

One shower, and the surface of this grey earth is covered with gayest green and the glamour of wildflowers.

Fish and frogs are to be found in the very heart of these sandy wildernesses—frogs that bloat themselves with a year's supply of water when the precious stuff is to be found, burrow into the earth, and can actually be tapped, like miniature tanks, by blacks and desperately thirsting whites. Black swans and pelicans sail serenely along the little rivers of the bore-drains, snavelling the minnows that, soused but lively, are swimming to within a few feet of the boiling boreheads, where with a match you can light to flame the gas that gushes out with the water.

How the early explorers traversed this country, limping along over the blistering sands and the gibbers rounded and polished with centuries of hot wind and blowing grit, their blankets their only shade, their men and horses dying, baffles the imagination. Through days of delirium and sleepless nights of thirst, each morning climbing the little rises to watch for a wisp of smoke and follow the wild blacks to water, each evening sitting silent by the camp-fire, shadows of men, their bloodshot eyes grateful to the darkness and day's ending, they battled on—to death or God knows what.

Leichhardt and his whole expedition vanished into thin air. Four times and for four years McDouall Stuart tried the crossing before he won through to the sea. 'Other deserts there are on the earth's surface,' wrote Stuart in the magnificent phrases of his frenzy, 'but they present not the steel-shod surface of this. The deathlike stillness of these solitudes is frightful and oppressive. We have not seen a living creature, either beast or bird, only the mirage, bright and continuous.'

I can never look out from the windows of the Alice Springs train on that land without horizons, but that grey company of heroes is there.

Yet even at its worst, Australia is a land of strange beauty and many surprises. Thousands of sheep and cattle are pastured upon those apparently inclement plains to-day. Many a homestead with a garden incredibly green is hidden in the sand-hills. Water, even in these luckless regions with five inches and less of rainfall in the year, is to be found everywhere, in shallow well or deep bore, in sandy creek and rock-hole, could governments and the individual but afford the money to obtain it.

Some of the withered hills are natural basins, unfailing, bottomless pools that are a redemption to the stock in the driest seasons, natural phenomenon in that a man might perish on their very slopes within a few yards of water, never dreaming it was there. Permanent springs and soaks are known to whites and blacks in the heart of desolation. An inch of rain, and so swift is the response of thirsting earth that all the creeks and rivers are running torrents, and the hard-baked flats of mirage a marsh impassable.

The first thousand miles are the worst thousand. When Stuart, in 1862, rode through the Heavitree Gap, the narrow gateway into the MacDonnells at the very threshold of Alice Springs, his agony was over. There one comes to the salvation of green valleys and blowing grasses, a fine spinifex and prairie country which, north of the Tropic, shares the monsoonal rains and gradually deepens to jungle.

From Marree, a few tin roofs in flatness, where dawn and sunset are vivid as the Oriental scarves that its Mohammedans wrap so reverently about their Koran, to Alice Springs among the smouldering hills, the Afghan express, or 'the 'Ghan' as it is familiarly known, takes up the running every second Thursday. The route lies another 700 miles due north, along a railway that when, or rather if, it is completed will be the mid-rib of the Continent. A long, long line of covered trucks extending for a quarter of a mile like a camel caravan, it has taken the place of the 'Ghan teamsters, six days to the Alice and back where they took months and sometimes years. Through the blinding dust-storms and the flood washaways, now buried in sand and now wrecked in a foaming creek, with scoop-gangs to clear the hills off the line one month, and a 'flying-fox,' a trolley hitched to a wire, to carry passengers across the rivers the next, 'the 'Ghan' brings Sunday dinner and takes back cattle and gold.

Beneath the grey desert and its melancholy mist of mulga and saltbush, earth goes in motley, colours gayer than the rainbow and a tinselled glitter of gems.

Practically every known jewel is found in this country, even including the diamond, admittedly of poor quality in that none has yet been found with the blue-water gleam of those of Peru. Amethysts and an occasional weak emerald are picked up anywhere from Western Queensland to the Buccaneer Islands. The sapphires of Anakie are famous, and the black opal of Lightning Ridge world-famous. Tourmalines and beryl and garnet and quartz crystal are so plentiful that they are scarcely reckoned of worth.

Broken Hill, when it was first discovered, was an Ali Baba's cave, a mineralogist's paradise of sparkling specimens weighing anything from a carat to a ton.

Calcite crystals and quartz crystals, chalcedony and chrysolite and jasper, sequined pyrites stained with iron and faintly pink, enamelled felspar, the prismatic flash of tourmaline, steely ores of antimony and kingfisher ores of radium, azurite, blue as the night and as starry, olivines like limpid drops of pond water, and ribbon-striped malachite—these are the flowers that blossom under that barren earth. The old miners keep them all as specimens in a tobacco tin, and in an idle moment con them over, explaining away their beauty in a bushman's geology, and tell you where you can get them by the hundredweight.

They can sell copper and gold and mica, but for all the

romance of its name and the liquid green gleam of it, who will buy an olivine? A passing tourist maybe, one in three years.

A camel-load of rubies sounds like the finale of an Oriental fairy tale, yet east of Alice Springs the hills and plains are sparkling with the red glitter of 'MacDonnell Range rubies,' not quite rubies unqualified, but more richly red and of deeper fire than the garnet, the true Burmese corundum. So plentiful are they that they can not be precious. For some years the miners, finding chosen stones, made profit from them until an unwise prospector loaded up a camel with the gems, and freighted them south to Melbourne, where they sold at a couple of shillings a dozen! Central Australian rubies have been left to lie in the spinifex since then. For a stick of tobacco a lubra will find you a pannikin full in an afternoon, with some beryl and crystal thrown in for good measure.

But the most luminous and illuminating sermons in stones are the cockle-shells and mussel-shells petrified in glowing opal in the barren heart of Australia. When the ichthyosaurus and pterodactyl dragged their slow lizard length across a half-baked world, these iridescent shell-fish were live things in the shallows of that vast warm sea lazing south from the Gulf of Carpentaria to Spencer's Gulf. Now stranded high and dry above the receding tides of the ages, they live immortal in the colours of sun and sea that shone before the dawn of a human day.

At White Cliffs, about twenty years ago, were unearthed an opalized fish 3 feet long, found at 41 feet below earth-level, and the almost perfect skeleton of a dinosaur, $3\frac{1}{2}$ feet long, excavated at 8 feet, and now in the British Museum, to say nothing of pipe opal, the jewel-claws of prehistoric crayfish, mulga sticks, thick as a man's arm, with bark grooves and notches visible, 'pineapples' of aggregated crystals, and the bones of birds extinct.

Another phenomenon of absorbing interest that has intrigued and to some extent baffled men of science is that of the tektites, or Australites, or obsidianites, or meteorites, call them what you will, and each name is more or less correct—the little round Nubians of iron and nickel alloy, said to be infinitesimal bits of other worlds pelleted on to this, or bubbles and blebs of lava that have travelled perhaps for millions of light years, tiny vague missiles through inter-planetary space.

The blacks know them as 'warragetti milki'—emu-eyes —and from the fact that they are frequently found, brand new as it were, on well-worn tracks, after a windstorm or a shower of rain, believe them sky stones of magic power. These little obsidian bombs take a dazzling polish, and are then practically indistinguishable from black onyx. They make striking pendants, and, set with small diamonds, flash-ing and distinctive ear-rings, but they, too, are unexploited.

Not long ago a station lubra of the Centre brought a handful of the stones to her employer, and told him they were 'medicine stone belong blackfella, spose him cold-sick, spose him leg-sick, all right, rub him longa that one, quick time better.' When he demurred at robbing the camp of its panacea for all ills, 'No more,' she assured him. 'Black-fella catchim aspirin now.'

CHAPTER XXX

STRANGE CASE OF MRS. WITCHETTY

IT was out in the Flinders Ranges that I stumbled upon the most amazing document in the annals of the Australian outback, the life history of Mrs. Jackie Forbes, otherwise Witchetty, the only authentic case to date of a white woman 'living black' with the tribes. Mrs. Daisy Bates, c.b.e., is a writer and scientist. She could not exist in a blacks' camp, although constantly among the natives on errands of mercy, and in the celebration of their occult ceremonies.

Mrs. Witchetty was for eighteen years the wife of a full-blooded native, the mother of his half-caste sons, who have recently been 'initiated.' To gain the story from her own lips, I travelled by car and truck, eighty miles to a little village of wurlies at Nepabunna.

I found her living on blacks' rations in the centre of the camp, in a ramshackle low-roofed hut of kerosene tins and flapping bags, a cheerful and active-minded little soul, with twinkling brown eyes and very white teeth. In a welter of dogs and billy-pots, with a skinned rabbit hanging to the tree above, she welcomed me pleasantly, and there in the tin humpy, with her swarthy little son as witness, recounted the life story here told.

'Mrs. Forbes,' as she prefers to be called is an Englishwoman. 'My name before my marriage was Becky Castledine. I am fifty-five years old. I come from Greenwich, where they tell the time,' she told me, laughing. 'Although I was born within the sound of Bow Bells, the whole of my early life was spent in the shadow of the big Observatory.'

With her uncanny blending of vivid phrase and 'blackfella lingo,' let her tell her story herself.

'Life's a lottery,' she said. 'It was my fate to marry an Australian aborigine, and to spend my life in a blacks' camp. I have never regretted it. They are a free, good-hearted people, and in all my eighteen years among them I have made no enemies. Sometimes they get annoyed, and I have to stand the racket.

'My old man died last year. He was always a good husband. I had never married before, and I shall never marry again.

'He was a New South Wales boy from the banks of the Darling, a fencer and horse-breaker out along the stations, and no horse could chuck him when he was a young-fella. He was about the last of his tribe, the Billidapa I think it was, but of their tribes and totems I have never taken much notice. Although my two sons speak mostly the aboriginal languages, I have never learned them—there are too many. Why, my old man used to speak four lingoes.

'I came to Australia twenty-one years ago on the liner *Oruba*, on her last trip. After seven months in Brisbane, I went to Sydney and was employed as cook at the Blind, Deaf and Dumb Asylum, and after that at Sydney Grammar School for another eighteen months. Always a wanderer at heart, and anxious to see the country, my next position was at Wynbar Station, then owned by the Hopes, a big sheep-run with a ninety-one-mile frontage to the Western Darling.

'It was there that I met my husband. A splendid worker, honest as the day and well-spoken of by all the station people in the district, when he proposed I could see no reason for rejecting him.'

'How did he propose?' I asked, indelicately, but, knowing the social limitations of the aborigines, amused and curious.

'He asked me to be his wife,' said Mrs. Witchetty with dignity. 'He had knocked about with white men since he was seven or eight years old, and knew the lingo all right.

'We were married at Bourke just eighteen years ago, by the local magistrate, with two policemen as witnesses, and then by the fire-stick ceremony of the New South Wales tribes at night. You know the blackfella wedding? A burning fire-stick is placed between you, and an uncle or godfather—generally an old man of the tribe—comes along and tells you that you must cook meat for yourselves now, that the man must not give his woman too many hidings, and that if you have any quarrel or argument you must keep it in your own camp, and not bring other people into the fight.

By the way, they've pushed a wedding for to-night. If you hear a big noise, don't be frightened. It will be a wedding, not a row.

'At first I was worried lest the blacks should object to a white woman in camp, but the policeman promised that if there was any trouble, he would make them see reason. But they were quite pleased about it. They held a big kooloo-mookoo in our honour, an all-night corroboree that lasted till daylight. We pitched our tent and a wilpie there in Green Gully, and I have lived in camps ever since, for nine years at Yandama, near Broken Hill, and for the last seven years at the Ram Paddock Gate.

'My two sons were born in camp—it's quite true that the old women are wonderful midwives—Jack on the home-stead camp at Tilcha Station, and Raymond at Yandama. They speak good English, but better blackfella, and belong to their father's totem, and I mustn't tell you anything about that without first asking Albert, the head man here.

'I am sorry I cannot show you a photograph of my old man,' said Mrs. Forbes. 'We never keep the belongings of the dead, and always shift camp, away from the haunt of their spirit.

'Since he died, the policeman at Beltana and the Chief Protector of Aborigines in Adelaide have written to me, asking if I would leave the camp and live white again. That would mean rent to pay, and the children to educate, and with living so dear I prefer to stay here. The natives are very kind to me. All have their share, and the widows come first.

'I get the blacks' rations, a little tea, sugar and flour from the Government every week, with a gin's frock of blue galatea and a blackfella's blanket once a year. With my four goats and five fowls, I can manage along. Of course the meat is wild—they go out rabbiting and hunting kanga-roos—but someone kills a goat occasionally, and I always get a bit of it.

'The policeman said that if I would come out of the camp and put my name on the electoral roll, he could get me the regular white rations for the indigent, but I would sooner sit down here where my boys are among their own kind. Besides, the neighbours might get jealous if I were on white-fella tucker, and I don't like to make bad friends after all these years. I do their little bit of writing now and then, about donkeys and jobs and supplies; my mustard-plasters are very popular when they're cold-sick, and at baby time I'm the head serang.'

Mrs. Forbes and her husband, better known as Jackie Witchetty, have always been respected out on the border stations as an estimable couple of the highest moral rectitude. The black man is intensely moral, a broken ankle or a hit on the head with a waddy—among the wild ones a death-dealing spear—being the inevitable punishment of infidelity. But all through the outback the colour line is a social bar sinister.

Mentally above the average, writer of very interesting letters, Mrs. Forbes, since her unique marriage, has had practically no association with women of her own race. Even now that a mission is established at Nepabunna, she remains in the camp and of it, rarely seen, never approaching the missioners spontaneously, and, like the blacks, speaking only when spoken to. On the other hand, she knows no inferiority complex. With no housework to do, she spends all her days in reading hair-raising thrillers, blissfully unconscious that she is the most hair-raising thriller of the lot.

'It has been an experience,' she smiled, 'and I am alive to tell the tale. Often I have thought of writing a book of my life with the blacks, of our wandering from station to station with the New South Wales tribes, of life in a wilpie by a campfire, and the nights I lay awake listening to corroboree. Nowadays they are a dull people, what are left of them in the South. They never sing their own songs, all about the hills and trees and animals.

'My husband had a special corroboree of an Afghan killing a sheep according to his religious rites—the squealing of the sheep mixed up with Mahommedan prayers and curses. He was a good mimic, as they all are, and always used to be the hit of the evening.

'I love to think of those nights, out along the Darling, when the music of the boomerangs would seem to me to echo right through the world, and then stop suddenly with the stillness of death. But the corroboree and I belong to the old days now—we shall go out together. I am afraid

my book will never be written. I have become lazy and
contented like my husband's people.

'No. I never think about the old life in England. That
seems too long ago to bother about. I have three brothers
and three sisters somewhere there. I get a chance to see
the London papers occasionally, when a station manager
sends them over to the missioner that is here now, but I
never see anybody advertising for me.

'I don't worry. The path has led me into strange places,
but I have no regrets. If, as they say, a wife always takes
her husband's nationality, I am an Australian, actually the
only real white Australian there is.'

As I said good-bye to Mrs. Forbes, she began to rake the
fire outside the mia for the evening meal with her little
son—that hanging rabbit, skinned only because of its pelt,
and destined to be cooked whole under the ashes, as is all
'blackfella tucker.'

A bedlam of dogs and screeches broke out again as I left
her there in the camp, amazed at the incongruity of a white
face among so many black ones. But it was no case for
sympathy. Completely inured to her weird life in a weird
environment, she 'thinks black' with the rest.

Those who know have told me that when the sacred bull-
roarer whizzes its warning at the beginning of those initiation mysteries that it is death for a woman to see, with
a quiver of fear and excitement, and in company with all
the other scuttling lubras, Mrs. Forbes makes rapidly for
the door of her wurlie, and shuts it tight against the prowling
of the debil-debil.

CHAPTER XXXI

A FRIEZE of date-palms against a painted sky, the tinkling of a camel-bell, and the high clear call of the *muezzin* at sunset. . . .

It is a far cry from 'Baghdad's shrines of fretted gold' to a colonial sheep station, but South Australia bridges the gulf. In the sand-hill and salt-lake country that lies between the Flinders Ranges and the MacDonnells lives a strange alien community—old Sheikhs, dark-skinned, that gallop away to the sundown with flying turbans, white men who spread their prayer-mats and salaam to Allah with the best, Australian women who have made the pilgrimage to Mecca.

Every station of the line north of Copley has its "Ghan's Camp,' with a population equal to that of the rest of the town, picturesque with camels and a little tin mosque. Here are Australians, with a vote, that wear the balloon pantaloons and the curved slippers of the good Haroun al Raschid, and treasure the Koran of the Prophet wrapped in the silken shawls of the East.

Arab and Turk and Afghan and Hindu, over a period of fifty years they were brought to this country to track with camels in the sandy wilderness. Many of them, by a lifetime's residence and loyal service, have earned the right to share our nationality. Their own women prohibited, they have intermarried with ours. Their children are Australians.

Impoverished by lean years and the ubiquitous motor-truck, a few are still scattered on the trails of Wyndham and Meekatharra in the West, and Cloncurry and Wave Hill, but most of them have settled in the little cattle and sheep towns of the Centre, ekeing out a living as teamsters of stores and wool at much cheaper rates and much longer time limit.

For a few shillings a week in this country you can hire a camel, his shadow by day and his warmth by night, a peg in his nose and a pack on his back, to carry you over the rim of beyond, and on the way he will feed himself and never ask for water. Should you be an appraiser of true worth, valuing not appearances but the unfailing fidelity of every day, the patient co-operation of years, for £5 you can buy him outright.

To watch the unending camel-strings that, in the height of a good season, are bringing in South Australia's wool to the railway sidings is to realize the tremendous part this grotesque yet graceful beast has played in the history of out-back Australia. With two 150 lb. bales balanced on each side of his hump, 600 lb. in all, uncomplainingly he does the work of a small truck, plodding along day after day for 2,000 miles and more. Returning with stores for the out-posts, he carries an even more awkward burden of petrol cases and sawn timber and 20 ft. water pipes, strung by the nose to the tail of his comrades in misery, ever gentle and amenable.

In sands that baffle the aeroplane and the motor-car, those silent splay feet still lead the way. As a turbaned philoso-pher remarked to me at Marree: 'God puttim camel all right!'

Once upon a time—so runs the story as told me by the mullah Assim Khan, in the shadow of the old tin mosque— there lived in the Arabian desert one Sali Allahi Salaam, true precursor of the Prophet. By precept, prayer and fasting, this holy man had led the nomads of his country to righteousness, long before the writing of the Koran. But there came a time, in a grim season of famine, when he was doubted by his people. With taunts and jeers they perse-cuted him, even as centuries later they persecuted Iasu Allahi Salaam that the Christians worship to-day.

Following to his hermit's cell in the desert, they mocked and spat at him, reviling his faith and his teachings, and when he cried upon their unbelief, they challenged him to show that he was indeed the chosen of God.

'If thou art truly a prophet,' they said, 'call down the power of Allah thy Father upon this rock, that it give milk to our starving children, and bear our burdens in the desert.'

Goaded at last beyond human endurance, the Prophet Sali spread his prayer-mat, and raised his arms to Heaven, crying 'Bismillah!' And from the skies came the white fire of

Gabriel, the messenger of God, splitting the rock to fragments, whence arose the Sacred Cow, mother of all camels,
and her suckling calf.

That is not quite as Assim told it to me. He threw out
his dirty old sleeves in gesticulation, and said 'Damn' quite
a lot. 'Rock bust, camel come up!' he shouted at the
climax. But there it is, and that is why, in all Mahommedan
countries, the camel is always regarded as the special gift and
blessing of Allah the Merciful.

I have a lot of time for the camel. In endurance and grit,
he stares the horse out of countenance. It is futile to goad a
spent horse, but a camel will go till he dies. In South
Australia, his record is 140 miles in the day, won by a brag-
gart Englishman on the road between Boolgardie Station
and Kingoonya. He killed a valuable riding camel in
making it. Ahmin Khan, at election time some years ago,
brought down the ballot box from Innamincka to Farina,
280 miles, in two and three-quarter days. Karrum Bux of
Alice Springs ran that record a close second for a bet when,
on a cow-camel, he covered the 340 miles south to Oodnadatta, and was in to answer the Azan to prayer at the fourth
sunset. I saw the camel alive and well thirty years after.
One of the 'Ghan teamsters of the Cloncurry trail travelled
a loaded wagon, drawn by a team of twenty, 318 miles in
seven days, from Pandi-Pandi Station to Marree, and then
beat his own record back by eighteen hours.

In enduring the pangs of thirst, Winnecke's record of
fourteen days in hottest summer still stands, but in the
cool weather, a fat young bull-camel, tied up in a deserted
station yard, was forgotten for twenty-seven days. He was
in fair condition when they found him, although he had
had nothing to eat or drink.

As for spirit, a bucking camel can keep it up for half an
hour at a time. When he does waft you off, with a thirty-
foot loft and a gentle ballooning motion, he has time to
kick you hard three times on the way down.

Like his master, he is a trusty friend but a vindictive
enemy. I met several Afghans at Marree with their arms
bitten off by camels, and there was one, whipped with a
thong at Kopperamanna Bore, that watched its chance and,
a week later, as the teamster bent to draw water, embedded

its teeth in his head. White men's camels are always better cared for and better tempered than the Orientals'. The supercilious and lofty creature is never friendly. He appreciates kindness without familiarity, and, well-handled, gives less trouble and more service than any beast of burden on earth. Remarkably he has adapted himself to his environment. Where the camels of India and Africa travel well only in the sand country, the Australian-born sets off across the rocky ranges and rivers and through the scrub with the swing of a kangaroo, and never minds a paddle in the surf out to meet a ship.

It was at Farina—Far in A. as they write it up there—that I had my first experience of Afghans and camels. My little stocks were at a low ebb after a long and trying train journey, all day long dust and heat and tedium and weak tea. We pulled in late at night. There was a solitary light in the distance and a ramshackle old truck to take me to it. I sat in the front of that truck with my typewriter bruising my shins and the camera sticking into my ribs, wondering what sort of a fool a woman was to go trudging round the Saharas of Australia when she could have a staff job and write delicately cool things about *crêpe de Chine* and sweet peas. I was dirty and disheartened, and about to weep for home and the bath-heater, when somebody switched on the headlights.

Eight feet away from me was the Sheikh of Araby! Mounted on a magnificent charger with a swarthy young henchman holding the reins, a superb profile beneath the turban, a fair complexion, blue eyes and a little moustache of brushed gold—flappers delight! he was too good to be true. My tiredness was gone in a flash. I scented a story. The truck-driver threw the mails in the back, mounted beside me and hauled back the brakes.

'Just a moment,' I said. 'Do I see what I see, or is there a fancy dress ball on?'

He laughed at my interest. 'It's only Sher Ali Mahomet,' he said. 'One of the boys round here. His mother's a Frenchwoman. They live in that shack over there, see?— the one with the dome roof.'

In the miserable little shanty bedroom I blew out the candle and fell asleep rejoicing, hearing the bulbul in my dreams. Early next morning, manfully shouldering the camera, I made for the dome roof.

I found my story in Adrienne Lesire, a woman of Paris with hair the colour of white gold, and noble old Gool Mahomet. As his wife, she had travelled the deserts of Australia for nearly thirty years. It appears that in the hey-day of Coolgardie gold, she came out as travelling companion to a French family, and married this Afghan of high caste according to the rites of his faith and the laws of this country. With him, she immediately set out on the thousand miles of sand that few had crossed between Kalgoorlie and Port Augusta. There was no railway then, no signs of life. It was a two-years' journey, as they travelled it, and in the course of it the eldest son, Sher Ali, the boy I had seen, was born. Once the woman and her child travelled for five days without water.

Since then there have been five other children, sons that the grave and bearded father has deemed the blessings of Allah, daughters that combine the veiled duskiness of Eastern women with the vivacity of their mother's people. Known as the beauties of the line, these girls speak three languages and are accomplished needlewomen and musicians.

Far above the rabble of the camel-camps, a contractor in fencing and well-sinking, old Gool Mahomet is looked upon as a wise man and leader of the Afghans, and for his ungiving integrity and high moral standards is much respected by the whites. The eldest daughter is betrothed to a handsome young Afghan half-caste who will work for the father two years to win her, as Jacob worked for Rachel.

In all of those walled settlements that dot the railway-line for 600 miles north to Alice Springs, with their camel-yards and date-palms and minarets of tin, I met swarthy men who have stood face to face with death with the explorers, who have been in at the finding of gold at Coolgardie and Hall's Creek, and silver at Broken Hill, and copper at Cloncurry, and have scattered the dates of their beloved date-palms on all the sand deserts between.

There is Moussha Khan of Marree, stooped now with age, who has travelled his camel-caravans for half a century, and once billowed on and on for three years in the vast uninhabited without seeing a white face. A pretty daughter of his has just given birth to twins, the quaintest little humans of the line.

Next door lives Bejah of Baghdad. In '96 Bejah tended the camels for the explorer-surveyor Larry Wells in the Calvert Exploration that made north 1,000 miles in Western Australia that no one has crossed since then. At one stage the party travelled for twenty-seven days without finding water, the camels dying from poison weed, and the men rationing the last thirty gallons when they reached the Joanna Spring. Two of those men died of thirst on the next stage. It was Bejah that found them, and their unfinished journals and broken compass.

Mullah in the 'Ghan camp at Marree, a fat and jolly old scamp who delights to tell of the seven hells that await the wrong-doer and the paradise of palms and lilies that rewards the faithful, is Assim Khan, who well remembers when he made north from Tarcoola with Winnecke on the successful search for gold. On that trip the camels were for fourteen days of summer torture without a drop of water, their packs weighted down with a precious freight of nuggets—a race between death and fortune in which fortune won.

Within the high tin walls of these 'Ghan camps, white women are living, the only ones in Australia who have blended with the Asiatic to any extent. One, who is known to the camps of the line as Bibi Zatoum, has attained a high place among the free-lance journalists of South Australia. She has made several voyages to India, speaks Hindustani like a native, and a few years ago, following a pilgrimage to Mecca, was sent for by King Amanullah to become the English governess to his children. Following his deposition, she returned to Australia, and is supporting her three Afghan-caste children largely by her writings.

Some homes are elegant in the Eastern fashion, with daises and divans and silken brightness. Some are wholly European, with pianos and wireless. The visitor receives the utmost hospitality—but there is a border-line. Children attend the public schools, but are watched by the eagle eye of authority against too close an association with the Infidel. Never are they allowed to inter-marry with the Christian, being usually sold to ancient Afghans or betrothed to half-castes like themselves.

But the most extraordinary characters I found there are certain young white men who live among them, turbans incongruous above their typically Australian faces, bearing such names as Roy Khan and Bertie Shah. The explanation was simple. These are mostly step-sons who have been brought up from babyhood according to Afghan traditions, working a lifetime with the camels—Australians who bow their heads at the setting of the sun, and cry in a strange tongue that 'There is no god but Allah, and Mahomet is his Prophet.'

CHAPTER XXXII

THE GHOSTS OF COOPER'S CREEK

SUN-BLIND through sandstorms of summer on a two-ton truck with its engine-fittings held together by safety-pins and bits of string, I set out from Marree on a Sunday morning with young Ken Crombie—bound 400 miles north to Birdsville—Birdsville, where the birds fly backwards to keep the sand out of their eyes.

Two of the big rivers of the Centre lie between, if they were only there, Cooper's Creek and the Diamantina, and 370 straight miles of ribbed sand-hills, an infinite sea of crested waves of sand to 200 feet high, that change their geography in every dust-storm, among them the ruins of a score of stations telling the horror of drought. If you would turn to the saddest chapter in the pioneering history of Australia, travel the back way to Queensland. The abandoned homesteads and the fallen yards, the bones of many thousands of cattle, and even the whitened and shrunken skeletons of humans, swept bare of covering earth, will tell you the story, and the few old hands that are left there, remembering the days when the Cooper was a river.

Cooper's Creek! The name rings out like the crack of a stock-whip, waking memories of the old Australia, when men were centaurs. Just south of it lies Mount Hopeless, where Burke and Wills turned back to die.

Once the greatest river of the inland, famed in song and story for its horses and its horsemen, it is twenty years since the Cooper has come down across the bar of the Strzelecki, good seasons following its regular floods in a country that is desolation without them. An eerie country, this, rich in fertility and beauty in good seasons, with salt lakes and clay-pans, and boiling bores fuming in the landscape like the white smoke of a bushfire, that cool as they run into miniature rivers, and polygonum swamps and stony deserts, and the barren bed of the Cooper and the milk-white waters of the Diamantina to cut it in three.

Since days when this was the great southern stock route

from Queensland to Adelaide and Melbourne, men and cattle and sheep and horses in their thousands have travelled these sandy wastes that cover a thousand square miles about Lake Eyre, but 'sanded out' is the cry you will hear to-day, sanded out the stations, two little settlements that were almost towns, the roofs and the fences covered thirty feet deep and the stock all dead. Sanded out the lakes and pools that were salvation. Sanded out the pioneer men and women who fought drought and flood there for half a century.

The Cooper trail, when I passed along it, was a wilderness of wild flowers, a wide, wide carpet of herbage, a drover's paradise. It was too late. Not even the splendid courage and endurance of those pioneers could withstand 1929. In that year, the ninth with not a drop of rain, the last starving remnants of the 'big mobs' died at the wells and bores, bloated with water but with not a shred to eat, five hundred cattle in one mob down on their knees and smothered in the dust-storms, or bogged in the salt lakes. In that year horses and camels were shot in hundreds to save a few withered weeds for the doomed cattle. In that year men and women gave way to a terrible despair, and walked out of their homes, leaving the furniture in the houses. Now the sand has swept across the verandahs, seeped through the doors and broken window-panes, piled deep in the rooms, and risen to the roofs. It was blown away from the graveyards, and in drift-sand the dead lie, unburied by the wind, with quizzically tilted chins and hollow eye-sockets, twisted, it seems, in a horrible silent laughter at the joke that went against them, the irony of this year's wild flowers.

Medical students that want skeletons will find them in hundreds, black and white, along the Birdsville track.

Ken Crombie, the mailman who wafted me across the Cooper and through the Fence to Queensland, had just attained his twenty-first birthday. He is the son of one of the bravest of those pioneers, a man who staked his whole life, and lost—tracked out into the desert with the woman that was his, made his home where a wheel came off the bullock-dray, built a little town there, and watched it fade away into the sand. Last of eleven children, lovingly known as 'Young Ken' to the length and breadth of 2,000 square miles, each trip the boy makes a new road of his own, and travels undaunted a mighty silence where nothing stirs but the shadow of the brown hawks wheeling.

Mostly he travels alone. A broken gear-box or a broken leg in the last 180 miles of desolation, and the world would know him no more. On one occasion he shattered a piston rod on a stump. He walked eighteen miles to a bore-drain. He found there a couple of old crocks of horses. Making a bridle with strips of his camp-sheet and bits of wire, he rode one of them eighty miles to the nearest habitation, living on flour he carried and one 'pinky cocky' he made into a stew. Other people tell that story; Ken sees nothing in it. He has done that sort of thing since childhood. It could not even teach him a lesson. Next trip he had to walk back twenty miles for the starting handle he had absent-mindedly left by the roadside. Blessed with the splendid carelessness of youth, he whistled all the way.

The Birdsville mail rarely carries passengers, and when it does they are mostly hoboes, from one State into another. There is a local saying that the truck provides for three classes. First class sits in front and minds the water. Second class sits on the back among the mail-bags and lends a hand in necessity. Third class pushes all the way.

I was all three, and I did a good bit of digging on that trip, scooping out a six-foot groove for the front wheels while Ken jacked up the back on to strips of tin and drove a truck-length at a time.

Out from Marree we passed the ruin of a mosque and the old date plantation of Lake Harry. There are still many healthy palms there, which have borne in their time half a ton of dates to the tree, but the industry was not a success. Australian dates are of just as fine quality as the Arabian, but with white labour, at 1/- a pound, they could not cope with coolie wages at a penny a day, so Lake Harry was abandoned to sheep. It was the last stocked station we were to see.

At twenty-five mile intervals, we rattled by the silent ruins of the Clayton, on a bore-drain that runs for sixteen miles, a little synthetic river with birds and waterfowl nesting in myriads in the sedges; Blazes Well, an eating-house of the stage-coach days, and a great meeting-place of stockmen and drovers when the cry of 'Cooper coming!' brought them riding miles to meet it with song and revelry; Dulcaninna, Etudinna, Booltarkaninna, Kopperamanna and Killalpaninna, for sixty years headquarters of a great Lutheran mission to the Dieri blacks, where a street of sixteen houses, a £1,000 homestead, and a church are buried to the roofs. To the east, towards Innamincka, lie Carra-weena, Tinga Tingana, and Merta-Merta, nothing now but names.

The ghosts of the ruined homesteads never worry Ken. Sometimes he borrows the tin roofs to mat through. Some-times he leaves a bundle of mail on a fallen doorstep for an Afghan teamster passing. Knowing the houses to be the abode of owls and vermin, he never camps there. On the first night, and 120 miles out, he lights his fire and unrolls his swag in the Matarannie Sand-hills, and, like all the Australian bushmen, sleeps best under the stars.

It was at Canuwaukaninna that we came to the first of the boiling bores. From black jacks 4000 feet down are bubbling millions of gallons a day of seething soda water, within half a mile cooling off to charming little creeks with clemency of trees and rushes and birds. I did a spot of washing in Nature's own laundry at the borehead, and found that Canuwaukaninna has a history. In the pre-white-man days when the Dieri roamed up and down the Cooper trading pituri and ochre, it was a native sanctuary. A Dieri legend tells that it was here each night that Ditchamincka the Sun, with a cockatoo crest of red feathers, crept into the cave that led right through earth to morning.

In the little shack cottage there, a few years ago, an Englishwoman lived alone, one Betsey Moore Broadbent, descendant of Tom Moore and friend of Sir Thomas Lipton, an eccentric who, though she loved the Australian bush, could never lose her fear of it. Each silent night for four years, Betsey bent to her crochet by lamplight with a loaded revolver on the table. A white man, with a half-caste wife and two extraordinarily fair children, made me very com-fortable for the night. I remember my amused amazement at the youngest, a baby of three who was a chain smoker, toddling round and piping away at one cigarette after the other from a smart little holder of her daddy's. It was much more efficacious than a comforter.

We crossed the dry bed of the Cooper, three miles wide of dead coolibah trees filled with the nests of eaglehawks, and set out over a panorama of almond-scented stock to deliver our mail to the sole survivors of the drought. In 370 miles there were three of them left.

The first was George Aiston at Mulkanundracooracoora-tarraninna. He painted it in white letters on a suitcase once, and was the joke of the railway porters of the Continent. George Aiston is the man who realized his life's ambition by running away from it, and there in the southern Sahara he keeps it to himself, a private armorial museum unique in the world. Aiston was born with a passion for weapons. He collected them in childhood, and was a member of the permanent artillery in Adelaide. Then he enlisted as an outback trooper, was transferred to the desert, and put his hobby out of mind.

Registering cattle-brands and tracking up perished men, he was continually picking up quartzite spear-heads and pointing bones and chipped stone chisels of the vanished native population, learned to tell t'other from which, and after thirty years' study is recognized as the leading authority on tools and weapons of paleolithic man. More, he exchanged his treasures for those of the other four continents. The armorial museum he had in mind at twenty is an accomplished fact, notwithstanding that there is no one to admire but drovers and turbaned teamsters.

Touareg swords, Japanese kazukos, Burmese dahs, Somali spears, Persian casques, pikes and cutlasses and Damascene swords, mail chain gauntlets of the twelfth century, with worm-eaten leather cuffs embroidered by ladye fayre for gallant Crusader, a Sepoy's knife found in the covered way of the Burn Bastion at the Siege of Delhi, a French cavalry bugle that rang Reveille at Waterloo, the armour of a Japanese daimyu, and the whole evolution of guns from the arquebus onward—these are a few of the curios that hang upon his walls side by side with a medal of the Legion d'Honneur found in the swag of a perish on Cooper's Creek, notatherium teeth from the Diamantina, and hundreds of varieties of spear-heads and spears and wooden weapons and fighting hats and cursing bones—all the equipment of Stone Age Man right down to the emu-horn trifle on a minderee string on which black babies cut their first incisors.

Keeping in touch with scientific progress, the author of several works on the subject and innumerable brochures for the Royal Geographical Society, and now and again invited to Canberra to decide a knotty problem in skulls, Mr. Aiston is content to remain in his pretty adobe home in the Never-Never, with the patient and lovable wife who has been the companion in all his sojourning. Happy and full of interest was my visit.

The next two settlers were 'good stories' too—Mr. Alex. Scobie of Ooriwilanie, who, with his stock depleted, has earned a living during five years for a family of seven by plaiting excellent stock-whips of kangaroo hide valued by the drovers everywhere, and Mrs. Morley, one of the most unusual women on earth. Keeping a little store for the drovers in the old police station of Mungeranie, she has never a soul to speak to for months and months on end. Her nearest neighbours are 18 miles south and 180 north, and in twenty-five years of residence along the lonely track, she never noticed the silence. The last camp of the Cooper Dieri has built its wurlies on the sand-hills near her, and put on a corroboree to entertain her now and then.

Over the rise from her dwelling is the old Mungeranie homestead, walled with cane-brakes, where Ken's mother and father were vanquished at last. Fifteen years ago Mungeranie was another little town, with post and police, a church and a dance-hall. To-day it is a ruin. After the disasters of the nine-year drought, the pioneer was stricken to his death out in the last sad muster; the children, the finest riders of the Cooper, were scattered far, and the brave little woman who had been all her life a battler died alone with the blacks at the homestead she had helped to build. With all the furniture still intact, and a forgotten player-piano in the dance-hall, Mungeranie was steadily becoming engulfed. Two of the blacks went over each day to sweep the sand out of its rooms.

With eyes on the desert ahead, Ken always hurries by.

What human interest I found buried in those Cooper sands! I spent some days with each of these heroic settlers, learning the stories of their lives. The bitterness of failure had not robbed them of their courage and kindness. The glad old cry of 'Cooper coming!" and the haunted desert will ring again.

When the Birdsville mail picked me up in a fortnight's time, there were two other passengers, a drover travelling north to join his plant, and a man with strange, vacant blue eyes who was not sure where he was going, except that it was 'out bush.' In any case, he was stone deaf, and would not answer when they wrote him questions.

We camped for the night at Mount Gason, a picturesque and rat-riddled ruin 80 miles north of Mungeranie, where you could make tea with the bore water bubbling and boiling from a tap in the wall. Three hundred cattle were grouped about the borehead, in horribly lifelike attitudes, except that the eye-sockets were empty. They had been dead for three years. Many had died standing and sitting, and sunk down only a little deeper in the sand. Hides and horns were mummified in that dry air. They were denied the mercy of decay.

So hurried had been the evacuation of Mount Gason, that the furniture and effects were all there, falling to pieces. A brand-new porcelain bath had been forgotten, there were clothes in the wardrobes, pictures on the walls, letters and books open in the dust. It seemed that the men and women who lived there had fled the place in panic at the end.

We were squatting round the fire in the tumble-down kitchen when it transpired that the deaf man had lost his tucker-box, all the food he had for the trail. Somewhere back in the wilderness it had fallen from the truck. He was obviously agitated, muttering to himself—a typical Australian Digger, except that his eyes were so blank.

'I would not be surprised if this man were deafened at the War,' I remarked. He could not possibly have heard me, but he answered my thought. 'It was the same at Gallipoli,' he said. 'Three shells out of four hit the cookhouse!'—and he left us to prowl aimlessly about outside.

'It's Aiston's fault,' said one of the men. 'He shouldn't have let him handle all those guns and bayonets last night.

He's looking bad again,' and when I asked for an explanation, 'He's just out of the Parkside Lunatic Asylum down in Adelaide,' they informed me. 'Been there since 1919, but he's quite all right now. Must be, or they wouldn't let him out.'

I hoped so—you can never show the white feather in front of the bushmen—but I shall never forget that night, the endless bickering of the bore, like garrulous women whispering, the uncanny white light of the moon shining in on a litter of broken furniture and cracked mirrors, the scuffling and the gnawing of the rats, and those restless, restless footsteps, padding round in the sand hour after hour.

Dawn came at last. A fire lit and a can of tea, and we set off into it, across an immense 30-mile plain of polygonum, a low grey claw-like scrub. In its waste were two or three letter-boxes, belonging to Pandi-Pandi and Clifton Hills far off the road, and Muttaburra, where for some extraordinary reason a man and woman are living out in the sand-hills that sweep down to Lake Eyre. Once a blackfellow met the mail, and carefully tied the letters with horse-hair to a stick. Once a white man. His reins thrown over his arm, he ripped out the bundle, and with hands quivering his eagerness, selected one with the obvious English postage stamps. Without a word to us, he dived in, page after page, in rapt silence, while the mailman unpacked some papers and a package of patent medicine. Once he threw back his head and laughed heartily. The Great Australian Loneliness sobered him up for a moment, but he answered us absently. His heart was in England.

Beyond the bleak awfulness of that plain, the sand-hills menaced again. Winding his way, Ken dug the wheels through the sand. Sometimes he picked up the truck from behind and shook the sand out of it. So we got through Cooncheri, the Potato Tin, and even the Dead Man's Sandhill. This is the place where once they found the gruesome relics of four men together, rags of their shirts on the bushes, the throats of the horses cut, a billy-can of dried blood . . . but that was before Ken's time. What worries him is that in wet weather you have to go round the Dead Men, eight miles down and eight miles back, because a ravine 200 yards straight across it is impassable, and generally he is alone.

If seeing is scarcely believing in the bright light of day, night-driving is an experience stranger far. Then, indeed, one travels in a world of goblins.

Everything is dyed in the unnatural inky green of the headlights. Little islands of spinifex swim away from the car. The spectre fingers of polygonum clutch for it. The bush is a phantasmagoria of eyes—eyes of a mob of cattle, burning like live coals; the eyes of sheep, small and bright, like glow-worms; eyes of a stray dingo, a baleful glare, glassy-yellow; or of a native cat, magnified to the power of a lighthouse reflector; or of a fox, a vicious flash of green.

Through haunted aisles of skeleton mulga the road is alight with a million shining pin-points of tinsel brightness, like dewdrops, or perhaps rich deposits of mica, that on investigation prove to be eyes again—the eyes of a little grey bush spider that weaves its webs in the ruts.

A shower of rain, and the mallee-leaves, wet and brilliant in the lights, flash about the car as though it were winding through a Hall of Mirrors, amid shadowy shapes and witch-crafts that belong to the brush of a Goya or the pen of an Edgar Allan Poe.

Nearing Birdsville now, we came up with an Afghan's camel string, the mangy beasts turning slowly to look at us, and making, down deep in their throats, the curious sound that is like the appogiatura of a harp—and then, glorious sight! a flock of 11,000 sheep, bound south from Queensland. It was quite impossible to take a picture, they were nothing but a sea of wool. Eight men and many dogs travelled with them, and a dray carrying stores. They were months on the road, and every night a yard was built to fold them in from danger. 'Wool-blind' the drovers said they were.

Dinner-camp by the milky white waters of the Elinor River, a tributary of the Diamantina, and past two more deserted stations, Goyder's Lagoon and Karratunka, we neared our journey's end in a glory of birds' wings, parrots and cockatoos wheeling, flashes of scarlet and dove-grey and green and gold in the sunlight. After a final joyous dash through the broken netting fence that is the State border, one more problem faced us, the big pool of the Diamantina right at Birdsville's threshold. When the river is down,

Ken has to leave the truck there and row the mail across in a boat, and then make a signal for a car.

Until recently that signal was a pair of white trousers on a post, but the drover who owned the trousers came back last year and claimed them, so now Ken makes a smoke.

Nothing but a few roofs blazing among the gibbers, virtually a Queenslander in that it is seven miles above the boundary, this little town is South Australia's stepchild. Five hundred miles from a railhead in its own State, all of its mails and supplies come up through South Australia, the way I had come. Blistering in the summer heat, back o' beyond and unbeautiful, it is a friendly and happy little settlement even so. Ken is always sure of a rousing welcome there, and nobody minds if he is three days late. Why should they?

While the townsfolk answered their letters, the boy started vigorously in tying the truck together again for the journey back. Next morning with the return mail, a hunk of freshly-cooked beef from one of the cattle-stations, and two precious loaves of yeast wrapped in a tucker-bag, with a farewell from the whole population of fourteen, light-heartedly we started back for Marree.

CHAPTER XXXIII

'SUNSET' OF OODNADATTA

'SUNSET' of Oodnadatta, as the bushmen say, lies some of the most impressive country, from an artistic standpoint, in Central Australia—and that is saying much. Land of fierce lights and desolate distances, this hard-baked desert glows like a rose, hills change like rainbows the whole day long, evening shadows burn and fade across the bluebush, slate blue and winey-red and the wind-blown gold of sand. When Australian artists have finished with Sydney Harbour and Prince's Bridge, some Cortez with a palette in his swag will find a new world.

A hundred miles across the gibber plains, that glitter with gypsum like moonlit seas, I found orange groves and vineyards, rich sheep lands and far winding creeks, and hills that flame with red and yellow, so arresting in their beauty that even the station blacks try to paint them with corroboree ochre on the tin tanks.

A hundred and fifty miles farther lie the ranges, the Musgraves, the Everhards, the Mann and the Petermann, their gigantic peaks touching 5,500 feet, their water-polished slopes and balanced marbles weighing thousands of tons, a throw-back to the glacier age, with virgin mulga forests, and millions of acres of Mitchell grass never yet eaten down, and buck spinifex 20 feet high.

These ranges have been crossed only by a few intrepid explorers and one or two prospectors seemingly mad. In serried ranks of colour, visible for 80 miles, they overlook the borders of three States, and are the hunting-grounds of many tribes of natives. A scattering of white men is out there, camped on the hidden soaks and springs, but they rarely see one another. These men are conquering the wilderness with flour and tobacco, writing the first faltering sentences in the age-old history of nation-building.

One is an old prospector, washing gold in the bed of the mountain creeks, living mainly on blacks' tucker. The others, business partners over an illimitable distance separately followed the trail of the tribes in the puppy-season to barter for dingo-scalps, and museum specimens, and rare birds, with as many as 300 agents of the Pitchentara tribe snaring by the waterholes, or tracking the wild dog to his lair. The fourth is one Stan Ferguson, who found an excellent spring called Ernabella, and had made the nucleus of a station there. Once a year a camel-string comes in with thousands of dog-scalps, a crate or two of birds, and a few tobacco tins of rough gold.

Among the world's best sellers are the birds of this region, rare and colourful finches, the dainty Burk parrakeet, the Princess Alexandra, her wings an iridescence of opal tints, and a unique scarlet-chested parrot that is now practically extinct elsewhere. Two pairs of this variety sent by rail from Oodnadatta attracted much attention on the way down, and reckless offers were made, but they were not for sale. One pair was a gift to the King, the other brought £100 in Adelaide.

To the camp of the white man in the night-time, the wild blacks bring their catch—a fluttering captive held in the hands, a dead dog thrown over the shoulder, or a stone shot with gold. Lithe bodies and white eyes shine in the firelight, they will haggle for hours for another pitchi of flour, a precious spoonful of tea, another lump of sugar. The lubras are their interpreters, quick to find out what the white stranger wants exactly and what he will give for it. One false step—an obvious avarice, the excitement of suspicion or jealousy, or a weak generosity, and the trader is doomed. Dead men of the Musgraves tell no tales.

Thanks to the invincible spirit of these few men, the conquest of the Musgraves is in sight. By a South Australian colonization scheme, should a prospector or settler discover a permanent supply of water to the extent of 4,000 gallons a day, he receives a grant of 100 square miles with an advance of £200 to stock it up and commence activities. The water grant was claimed for the first time by Ferguson at Ernabella—8,000 gallons a day from one spring. Now he has taken out sheep and cattle into the ranges, and trucks have thrashed their way to him through the spinifex, bringing supplies. On a tableland 1,200 feet above sea-level, with a temperate climate of stimulating winter frosts,

Stan Ferguson has planted wheat beside his water-hole, and reports that it is thriving.

Sydney Harbour a thousand miles deep in the heart of Australia!—majestic heads enclosing a sparkling expanse of blue water, a little flotilla of white-sailed yachts just off the headland, and the masts of tall ships close inshore, proudly they showed it to me from the veranda at Oodnadatta, a magic of mirage. The Heads in actuality are hills about thirty miles away. The masts are telegraph poles, marching off to Macumba Station, and the sails of the yachts, magnified to five times their normal size in the dazzled crystal air, are tombstones of the little graveyard out on the gidyea flat. So Oodnadatta, in the spiritless heat of its summer, dreams of Mosman's Bay.

A few tin roofs beneath the gum-trees, an A.I.M. Hospital, and an occasional corroboree are all that is left of the town, famed in song and story. Head of the line fifty years ago, it was the 'cattle and 'Ghan' city of the centre, depot of the drovers of the Continent. There were 500 teams out on the road to Cloncurry, and sometimes as many as seven stock specials in the day. But the continuation of the railway to Alice Springs has meant the passing of Oodnadatta. Soon it will be nothing but a whistling-post. A station-master, a store-keeper, a mounted policeman and two A.I.M. nurses greeted me there on the banks of the mirage, and a few others who remain just because they belong to it. North and south for 600 miles are the gibbers and the sand-hills and the little villages of ruined cottages that were once the abode of railway fettlers. Eastward there is nothing whatever out to the Queensland border, but 'out sunset' a country that, when it is truly discovered, will put the place back on the map.

Two mail routes swung out westward, and I chose the southern one. The first stopping-place was a hundred miles away across nothing but stones, the station of Welborne Hill, an oasis of comfort and culture, where Mrs. Ernest Giles is growing larkspurs and lemons, cedars and figs, oranges and mandarins, on the banks of Henrietta Creek, and nasturtiums and grape vines and poppies and sweet peas, just to show what the desert can do. The afternoon that I arrived, Mrs. Giles was wool-classing, with Secretary, one of the blackboys, to do the shearing, and Turtie, her favourite lubra, bent over a tub at the scour. She has a little flock that she 'puts through' herself for pin money.

Fifty miles south-west of the homestead is 'Paddy O'Toole's,' a brand new opal field where repeated discoveries of black potch promise the priceless black opal. One of the men rode in to meet us for the mail, three days with three camels. Alas! there was not a letter for him, not even a bill.

Past the old deserted ruin of Wintinna, and with a night at the bright little homestead of Mount Willoughby, we came upon the startling beauty of the creeks and ranges of Arkeringa. Here are parklands and pastures deep in grass for hundreds of miles, creeks that wind and double across far landscapes, under hills of chalk white and terra cotta and striped yellow smudged with outcrops of scarlet and amethyst and deep blue, hills of extraordinary form and gipsy colouring—The Monkey's Knob, the Bullock's Hoof, the Afghan's Turban, a wasteful splurge of pigment in one of Nature's maddest impressionistic fancies, where never an artist has set up an easel or opened a box of paints.

In a small white homestead in the heart of all this glory lives a wonder-woman of the West, Mrs. Macleod. Wife and daughter of the pioneers, she has been blind since childhood, yet she has managed and worked in her station home for over thirty years. Mrs. Macleod reads in Braille, rides by a leading line, swims in the billabongs, finds her way about with quick confidence, plays the piano, does all her own mending and sewing, and knows the step and voice of every white and black she has ever met. A presence is instinctively felt, and the comings and goings of everyone on the station are uncannily known to her, she is always first to report the illness of any of the pet lambs or a visit of a strange bird, or the blossoming of a shrub, and with much delight she points out the beauty spots to the traveller.

'Well, I've read a great deal about you and your pilgrimages round Australia,' she said, as she hurried in and out bringing me hot water and towels and an enjoyable tea, and flowers from the garden, 'and Heavens above, there's not much of you.' A mere handshake and my light step had told the story. All the events and interest of the country are known to her, and now the news of the world, from a wireless recently installed. Her husband and her sons she has never seen, yet when they put a new grandson into her arms, those quick loving fingers flew over the little sleeping face. 'He's the image of Alec,' she said gleefully. It is scarcely possible to credit the tragedy hidden behind those dark glasses, and for a bright smile that never fades and the indomitable spirit that refuses to realize one of life's saddest disabilities, Mrs. Alec Macleod is known and loved through the whole of the Centre.

There is a lot of desert 'out sunset,' for all its beauty and its possibilities. Sometimes the drought years take a lot of winning through, but so long as the people who live there show the splendid courage of to-day, the promise of the future must come true.

Oodnadatta nowadays is facetiously known as the 'dog capital' of Australia. A price on his head and his scalp a coin of currency, the Australian wild dog, *canis dingo*, is providing a living far surer than gold for scores of men in the very far outback. Out on the borders of the Centre and the Territory and the West, this strange quest is the beginning of colonizing. There are also increasing numbers of white men 'out dogging' over the Ranges in Kimberley, from the head of the Ord and the Fitzroy to the King Leopold Ranges. These wanderers are not often seen in the settlements, and they subsist solely on the revenue from dingo-scalps. So indefatigable are the Governments of four States to eradicate a ruthless killer of sheep that they make it worth while. Queensland, South Australia, and the Commonwealth Government of the Territory pay from 7/6 to 30/- and £2 for each scalp.

With the blacks and like the blacks, the doggers travel from soak to spring and from spring to waterhole, euro for their meat, flour and tea their only rations. Two or three times a year the spoils are sent in, to Hall's Creek, the Katherine, or Alice Springs or Oodnadatta, as the case may be, to be counted at the police station or store, a credit balance against flour and trade tobacco. The dog-catcher gets a good living, and the dingo is not noticeably becoming extinct. It pays that he should not, and the natives have the sense to save the mother-dingo and the daughters for next year's revenue. The Never-Never is bristling with dog-farms.

They were preparing for the A.I.M. Bazaar at Oodnadatta. 'You can't have it next month because they're all away at the shearing,' said one of the organizers, 'and you can't have it in August on account of the mustering.' 'No, and you can't have it in September,' said a voice on the outskirts, 'because that's the puppy season!' Oodnadatta sent down 4,000 scalps last 'puppy season.'

In the little known desert regions north-west and west of it are between 15 and 20 men, all pilgrims, trading with the tribes of Luritja and Pitchentara and Pintubi, who scour the sand-wastes for them, sometimes covering 400 miles and securing 30 dogs in a week. Most of these white men are old hands who have lived out there for years, used to hard living and lack of companionship, and able to track almost as well as the natives. Packed in bags of about 100 each, the scalps are freighted south on the 'Ghan for official check and verification, surely the most unfragrant of railway freights. This year, one man tallied 790 scalps—nearly £300. His only regret was that many of the dogs were Western Australians, from just across the border, for which he should receive at least £1 a head, but the nearest western outpost, Hall's Creek, was 1,000 miles north, and his camels were 'done out.'

In his wild state, the tawny dog of the tawny deserts is a splendid specimen, sometimes five feet from nose-tip to tail-tip, and two feet high. He is the only true wild dog in the world, and the highest intelligence and animal development in Australia's antique fauna. There has been endless controversy as to whether he is, strictly speaking, Australian, or an importation from Asia. If the latter, he roamed across from Malaya before the continents divided, and pre-dates the aborigine, for his bones have been found with those of the Pliocene saurians.

Most of the early explorers found him in possession, and Dampier writes of 'two or three beasts, like hungry wolves, and lean like so many skeletons.' He hunts in pairs and he hunts in packs, but mostly alone, living upon the smaller marsupials and rabbits, active as a cat in leaping upon birds, with a snap of jaws like a steel trap. He is clean-limbed, built for speed, splendidly proportioned, and of good hair and fine colour.

A silent hunter, he never barks, but calls to his mate with that eerie wail that is one of the terror-haunted voices of the wilderness. He never makes friends with the human for long, even in the blacks' camp, but, like the aborigine, when apparently tame, affectionate and contented, suddenly answers the call of the wild.

In Kimberley and the Musgraves the white man carries traps, which he finds it necessary to smear with jam and strychnine, otherwise the dog, with its remarkable sagacity and strength, will either valiantly free himself by gnawing his very foot away if need be, or drag the trap for miles. The blacks prefer to follow their own primeval methods, spearing him at a waterhole or tracking him to his lair, watching to catch him asleep—and it takes some doing.

Where a white man will laboriously secure two or three in a week, the tribe comes in with twenty slung across its shoulders. Scalp, strip and tail are duly handed over for a pound of flour or a stick of tobacco, and then there is a communal feast of trussed dog, singed of its hair and baked in the coals, a grisly naked-looking dish, horribly like a small cooked horse, but a pleasant change from lizards.

The pursuit of the wild dog, farther into the desert and the ranges, is certainly colonizing the country and opening our eyes to the geography of the unknown, but there is no doubt that in the process of this strange new industry, dependent on a Government policy of protection to sheep a thousand miles farther in, two ancient Australians, the black-fellow and the dingo, are coming in for a good deal of unnecessary exploitation.

CHAPTER XXXIV

A WEEK ON A CAMEL

HIGH and dry in the heart of the oldest continent, it rises in ranges stark as the craters of the moon—the oldest river in the world, the Finke.

Two hundred and fifty miles of glittering white sand, from fluted hills of Egyptian red smouldering away to the ashes of hills, across the ribbed desert it winds—to nothingness. Gone are the prehistoric days when it was a river, flowing into that inland sea swiftly drying to lizard slime. The ripple of its running waters, the glory of its billabongs and palm-groves are but fleeting memories, the majesty of its floods an Indian summer. In Central Australia, thirsting sun and thirsting earth drink deep.

The Finke is a mystery.

Where does it rise and where does it flow to? Somewhere in the Western MacDonnells, beyond Glen Helen, out where the hump of the Razorback rises against the paler blue of the skies, the source is a scarcely-discernible creek-course, threading down through the rocks. Somewhere in the leprous brine-flats of Eyre, the mouth is sifted over with centuries of wind-blown sand.

Five big tributaries and a sparkling expanse of water miles across empty themselves into Lake Eyre on the rare occasions when the Finke is in flood, yet Lake Eyre is ever waterless—the finite lost in the infinite. Perhaps these waters, from 4,000 feet below, bubble up in the boiling bores of the vast artesian basin. Perhaps they flow on forever, a Lethe underground.

For scenic magnificence and sunburnt colour, there is nothing in Australia to approach Finke River. If you would, at one and the same time, glimpse the wakening of the world, and gasp at the age written in the wrinkles of the face of earth, follow the Finke.

But there is only one way to surprise it. Follow it on camel-back, as I did, otherwise you might cross it and re-cross it, and never know that it was there.

There is a camel-mail follows the bed of the river for 160 miles, from the Horseshoe Bend to the Hermansburg Mission—the only camel-mail left in Australia, but I was still in time to catch it.

The Finke appealed. I sent a telegram to Horseshoe Bend from Oodnadatta. It was an inn and station 150 miles north and 15 miles west.

'Will give you our best camel,' they wired back.

I travelled on by the 'Ghan for a night and a day, and first crossed the river, a serpentine depression in the sands, at Finke Siding, where a little railway village has conjured up a brief memory of parklands, white gum, and native myrtle, with rock gardens of the scarlet desert pea. There I found an old man of seventy-three years who had never seen a city in his life, treasured up his story for the next telegraph station, if ever I should reach it, and rejoined the train as far as Rumbelara.

Rumbelara is a one-man town, its only population being the station-master, who depends on the fortnightly train for his conversation. Eastward of the siding is the curious polychromatic hill that, from both shape and colour, gives the place its name, Mbalara, meaning 'woman's breast' in the Arundta tribal language, 'rainbow' in Myaladharra. Twenty miles away is the quaintest mine in Australia, a yellow ochre mine owned by a man named Harvey. He employs a bevy of lubras to dig out the greasy, sulphur-coloured clay, 99 per cent. pure pigment, and freights it in by camel for carriage to a Sydney firm of paint manufacturers at £2/10/- a ton.

The way to the river lies westward, 15 miles by car across a paradise of purple parakelia, a rambling ground-weed that provides both water and food for stock even in the cruellest droughts. For all the world like a Mexican ranch, its roofs and corrals shining in the sun among the hills of angry bull-red, I looked down on the Horseshoe Bend.

Horseshoe Bend was a far-famed hostelry of the over-land in the days when, before the railway went through, camels carried the stores for Alice Springs 340 miles north from Oodnadatta. Exploratory expeditions made it their depot, cheered on the blank trail westward by Mr. Augustus

Elliott, one of the first pioneers of the Finke, and his kindly and hospitable wife.

Don't ask where the Finke is at the Bend, because it is right beside you, covered with blacks' camps and camel yards, but they have seen the phenomenon of its floods, when travellers cross by a tied wire and a raft.

Drowse of afternoon wakened into a music of pack-bells and hobble-chains as the horses and cattle and sheep and goats came in to the whip-spring wells, urged on by a half-caste stockman and lubra shepherds, a piccaninny turning the waterwheel. Donkeys brayed like steamboats. A long string of camels came billowing along the river-bed, the mail-team among them. Blue smoke rose from the blacks' fires. The profile of Pretta Arrakoodja—Stone Woman—and the pied red-and-white strata of Mount Engoordina towered above the sands, outlined in living gold. Sunset, smouldering, along the ranges, swung back the scene a thousand years to Egypt, timeless and magnificent.

The Hermansburg mail is in the hands of a white man with a black off-sider. A woman passenger was an unknown occurrence in its forty-five years of history. Duly impressed, Okey of the Arundta, the camel-boy, had bought the first pair of socks in his life in my honour.

But the mailman was weighed down with responsibility. A camper-out under the wide sky, content to drink out of the top of a quartpot, he began a fevered hunt for an axe-handle to cut the nightly tent-poles, and for a little brown teapot he had seen knocking round the men's kitchen some years ago. When he continued the search further for a cup and saucer, the stockmen at the Bend became openly facetious.

'Take a butter-dish and a toast-rack, take an extra string of camels, and a —— dining marquee!' they advised him, and the fun at his expense became fast and furious.

Lean as a lath, and therefore known from Marree to Alice Springs as 'Bony Bream,' Mr. Harry Tilmouth is one of the senior members of a big pioneering family, and he has run the Hermansburg mail ever since it started. With every true bushman I have met in the length and breadth of Australia, he was the soul of chivalry and courtesy to a woman. It was his forethought and kindness, and the merry tales he told, ambling along behind me in the string, that transformed an arduous, an almost impossible journey, into one of the pleasantest excursions of life.

'I hope y'r in good health,' was all he said before we set out.

We loaded up next morning, with the help of a bevy of fat, smiling lubras, like American mammies in their bright frocks and kerchiefs, and went billowing away across the sandy bed of the river. First came Rudolph, the leader, with a rifle strapped to his side, and Okey on his back; then King Solomon, with the tucker-boxes; the Royal Mail, weighed down with canvas bags; my own mount Midgeree, and behind him Sweet Marie, carrying the mailman, her lanky little calf a straggler.

Misery—his name had been converted by the blacks at the Bend—was an excellent steed with an inimitable graceful swing, but he wept a good deal for his native Arabia, and his sad heart tired in a mile. Keep his nose well up to the preceding tail, and there were no complaints. Let him hang back, and he progressed in dreamy absentmindedness, then caught up with a devastating gallop. A galloping camel is murder. I found that out myself. Once I stopped him to take pictures of a spectacular ravine, from this angle and that angle, and the string disappeared over the rise. Suddenly Misery saw them half a mile away, climbing another one. He was off. I just hung on to the saddle and said a prayer or two while the seven-pound camera flew out in the wind, and belted its angles down on my starboard hip every time we touched bottom. That bruise was a futurist thunderstorm for months.

Riding a camel is one of the best new experiences in life. You begin by feeling like the Queen of Sheba, and end up looking like a lubra. An alien after three generations of acclimatisation, he still refuses to speak the King's English, and your 'Hoosh-ta!' has to be couched in Amanullah's purest Afghan before he will deign to obey.

When he stands up, it's an aeroplane in a tail-spin. When he sits down, with three changes of gear and his knee-joints sticking out the wrong way behind like a deck-chair, it's an earthquake To mount him is to abandon yourself utterly to rhythm. If he is a good camel, you go to sleep and fall off. If he is a bad camel, you jump eight feet to be seasick.

A week seems a long time on board the ship of the desert. A compatriot of Omar Khayyam, he cannot see the force of hurrying. Across vast plains of buck-bush, through a Mohammedan paradise of Billy Button daisies, yellow and white, where the hungry beasts snatch a mouthful in passing, and by groves of the desert oak, dusky and willowy, we took our way at a steady three miles an hour, three days to the first sandy little pool of water. The steeds had had none, but they carried our drums ungrudgingly.

Our shadows shortened to the noontide, then swung over to the eastward, the age-old camel shadows of the sands of Egypt. Day after day the caravan moved to a lullaby rhythm, the recurrent ring of hobble-chains, the pad of soft feet in the dust. Night after night we boiled our quartpots at a camp-fire in the lonely dark, and Okey, child of the most self-effacing race on earth, would sit with his back turned to us in the firelight, eating his thumb-piece of bread and goat.

Supper over, the mailman, arms white to the elbow in an old tin dish, would make to-morrow's damper and bury it under the glowing coals, while I crawled into my little white wurlie, a camp-sheet strung over the camel-saddles, to fall asleep to the diminuendo of camel bells. The beasts wandered far, seeking parakelia, but Okey was out on their trail before dawn. One morning we discovered the track of a ten-feet snake that had wound about us as we slept.

'Might him carpet,' said Okey, studying the track philosophically. Carpet snakes are not venomous, and Okey was an authority. Why worry?

Twice we delivered mail in this wilderness to half-clad blacks, letters for Erldunda, and Middleton Ponds and Tempe Downs, stations out on the edge of nothing.

Thirty-five miles on the third day, a very long stage with a camel-string, brought us to the only human habitation we passed, the log homestead of Henbury, in the blood-red sandhills 80 miles from the Bend, with its big permanent waterhole, the hospitality of a lone white man, and a large family of the Arundta camped on the hill beyond. There is a post-and-plate at Henbury to commemorate the discovery of Finke River by Warburton sixty years ago, and the pioneers that followed him. The place claims a geological interest unique in the world. A few miles from the homestead is a gash in the landscape ten miles across, with thirteen distinct craters and a great scattering of smashed nickel iron, marking the spot of a terrific bombardment by a meteorite of the Tertiary age, a falling star of 50,000 years ago.

From Henbury north, Finke River is a doubling serpentine, a trail of glory, a pageant of colour, a paradise of birds. Next morning we climbed into its majestic gorges, to camp for the night at Lalgra—a lovely, liquid word as the blacks say it—a secret billabong of the ranges, streak of quicksilver in the dusk, with the first stars reflected. I asked Okey what the word meant. He told me 'Blackfellow puttim bone through nose, call him Lalgra,' and with its out-jutting rocks in the centre and the lightly-rippled waters reflecting the evening sky, I could see the symbolism.

The mountains closed in round us, the James, the Gosse, the Waterhouse and the Western MacDonnells, falling sheer to the dazzling sands in precipitous cliffs, pierced by steel shafts of Central Australian sunlight and scimitars of shadow. Eight miles from Lalgra the river is a flowing stream, Park's Running Waters, bordered with rushes and white-limbed gums, sweet with reedy whistles, the 'burn-burn-boolaloo' of the Central Australian bell-bird, and the insistent cooing of a little ventriloquial dove. Wild brumby horses thunder in to drink there at morning and evening. All through the drowsy day still reflections are broken by the feet of myriads of wild duck and waterfowl. It is for this reason that the mailman carries a rifle and fish-hooks, and that Okey occasionally darts off into the scrub to find him witchetty-grubs for bait.

Mooning along with tales of gold and cattle, we threaded the river-valley beneath towering ledged and patterned hills of Tutankhamen red, the camels showing themselves sure-footed as goats over the slimy rocks where a false step meant a fall of twenty feet. Twenty-seven times we crossed the white sandy bed of the river beneath the Arizona grandeur of its mountains, a rich country, a glamorous country—slopes of Ida, and not one of the dryads left. Not a camp-smoke in the daytime, not a corroboree fire at night. Many a cave of old witchcrafts we ambled by, many a little brush snare at a spring, where once stealth lay in wait for the euro, and many a shrouded rock standing out in the range that had known weird, inarticulate worship. An age-old mysticism brooded over the hills.

'Used to be mobs and mobs of blacks in this gully,' said the mailman, 'but they've all gone in to the mission. Once they learn about tucker and tea, they'll never come back to hunt. Pity they have to make 'em Christians. It leaves the place darned lonely.'

He had scarcely finished speaking when there came an echo of haunted laughter from the rocks, lubra voices, piccaninnies crying, and the shouts and the high sustained tremolo of the men on the trail. 'Did you hear that?' said 'Bony' in amazement, and his eyes lit up under his old felt hat 'By golly, they must have come back!'

'There's a camp of blacks down in the W.W. Gully,' he announced to our guide, philosopher and friend at the dinner-camp. 'Missus and I been hearem.'

Okey was vastly amused at our innocence. 'No more!' he contradicted, with the flash of a grin. 'Bowerbird makim yaki all-same blackfella.' To me it was a poignant little incident, ineffably sad. The birds of the country remember when its people are gone.

At one of the waterholes we delivered mail to a drover, riding round 500 cattle from the far North—a year-old *Bulletin*, a wire about the stock, a pastoral review, nothing hand-written. He looked disappointed, and then, as an afterthought, asked me if I had any ink in the pack. I unstrapped the camel-boxes, and found him a bottle with a patent stopper that interested him keenly. I left it with him as encouragement.

At Boggy Hole, Irramungera the natives call it more musically, a glory of slashed terra-cotta cliff reflected in a mighty waterhole, with pelicans and blacks duplicated in the silver, we heard a whisper of Kurdaitcha. Prenty was about, Prenty the 'bad nigger,' terror of the West Country. Only a moon ago he and his gang had nulla-nulla-ed a camp of seven, lubras and piccaninnies among them, at this billabong. 'He not friends longa we,' Okey told us mildly.

'Might him come up to-night longa Boggy Hole?' I asked, hoping for a thrill and a story. Okey thought not, and we turned in early, while he took the gun and went off up the billabong to get a duck. With my nose in the little swag pillow, I chuckled at the adventure of it, and wondered what friends at home would say—in wild nigger country, and the only man in camp with a gun a black one. A little later I heard the boy's quiet footsteps in the dust. He put the gun beside him, and sat down in the firelight to pluck the duck. Now and again he looked up to the big black shadow of the hill, and listened, but nothing happened. I was to meet Prenty later, in at the Alice Springs, handcuffed with his razor-gang of seven for a brutal murder out west at Mount Liebig. They were sent off by motor car a thousand miles to Darwin, after they had walked nearly a thousand through the desert, to stand their trial in the Supreme Court. Prenty and Punna, his henchman, escaped on the way up.

'Well, Okey,' said the mailman in the morning, as they hoosh-ta-ed down the camels for loading, not knowing I was awake, 'it's just as well it's the last day. If a mouse fell into the tucker-box, he'd break his bloody neck.' Provisions were running short. Even so, it was with a little sadness of leaving a trail of sheer wonder, that we swung on down into Hermansburg, through the smoky magnificence of the James Range, past the old homestead at Ellery's Creek, first station of the Finke, with its river-soak and its stockyard long abandoned, a kingdom of the ants.

Six miles from the mission, the natives saw us coming. Six miles away they descried the unfamiliar figure of 'white lubra' and passed on the word. Heaven knows how they knew, for I was like a black one. A big mob of piccaninnies ran beside the camels for a mile, shrieking welcome, though they scarcely expected mail, and there were three hundred smiling black faces and three white ones to greet us at the mission gates.

Our Arabian days and quartpot nights were over.

A bath and afternoon tea, and I went to say good-bye to Midgeree. He had carried me well and faithfully, and I thought a few well-chosen words would not be amiss.

A horse will show affection after the long trail, and rub his nose and ask for sugar, but a camel is an ungracious

brute.   With the peg in his nose and the string attached
exactly like the lorgnette of a supercilious dowager, he cut
me dead.   When I tried to make overtures with an apple—

    'Bah!' said Midgeree, and showed his yellow teeth.

    He had done his job.   No thanks to me.   Imshi!

CHAPTER XXXV

REALMS OF GOLD

IN a glorious valley flanked by four ranges lies the big Lutheran mission of Hermansburg, famous throughout Australia. A white-towered church, streets of whitened stone and grass-roofed Kaffir huts, with schoolhouse, community kitchens and dormitories make a picturesque village where the Arundta and Loritja tribes, under the guidance of earnest teachers and preachers, are trying their best to live white. Established for seventy years, this was once the farthest outpost in Central Australia.

Eighty-seven miles west of Alice Springs, with more or less regular truck communication and a daily wireless connection with far-away Cloncurry, Hermansburg is now a thoroughfare. Chars-à-bancs of overland tourists, University parties studying the aborigine or anything else that occurs to them, painters and novelists seeking copy, prospectors for gold in aeroplanes, all pay it a special visit—a visit that is well worth while.

I stayed a week there, waiting for transport to Alice Springs. There was a gold rush in progress. I knew it was good copy, and I wanted to be there. At last a truck came out from Wallis Fogarty's store, and thankfully I threw my swag aboard it.

I arrived in 'the Alice,' as they call it, on a Saturday evening, to find it seething with excitement, and there I saw my first rough gold. Joe Kilgariff of the Stuart Arms came up the dark passage by the bar with glittering ounces in his hands, payment of a beer bill. Outside there was a loud hum of emotion. Bushmen were gathered together in little knots in the dusty gum-shaded streets. Men and women alike were showing each other stones that they carried in their pockets and handbags, and pointing to the ranges. For years they had been looking for it. One glimpse of the precious stuff in ounces had set them crazy. There is no mob madness so infectious as the madness of gold.

Four hundred miles to the north-west, by a low ridge of

rocks called 'The Granites,' four or five old prospectors digging away at the Never-Never, and living on bush rats and cornflour when the camels failed to arrive, had unearthed over 300 ounces in three months. Unemotional in their good luck, as they had been in bad, they sent it to the Alice to pay their debts at the store, and kept on digging. Upon them, one sunset, happened the trucks of an expedition of some twenty or thirty city men, with great expectations and wireless. It was the first raw gold that most of them had seen. They bought the claim. News of a new discovery rang throughout Australia. I had heard it two months before on the wireless at Marree, I had heard it by 'mulga wire,' while I was meandering round on camels in the ultimate bush.

The excitement was now intensified. By the time I arrived at Alice Springs, three £250,000 companies had been floated over friendly whiskies and Granites specimens in the stock exchanges of the cities. The 'Ghan had become the Gold Express, the population had quadrupled. Men, and women among them, from the four corners of the Continent were flocking in, by anything that would carry them, from specially-chartered aeroplanes to broken sandshoes, having done 1000 miles in the day, or the month. Old prospectors and young adventurers were all making out to that patch. Neither fear of the blacks in an uncivilized country, nor of a 200-mile dry stage to a well of bad water at that time making only a hundred gallons a day, could keep them back. The Granites was on the map as a new Coolgardie, and, life or death, they would be among the first.

The mallee and gibbers of that desolate patch were pegged for forty miles in every direction; 375 miles of fire-ploughed track that had never known traffic before became a high road. On it you could meet mining agents and mineralogists and miners under engagement, clerks and cashiers and motor-drivers, overlanders from Kimberley and Darwin and Queensland and Melbourne and Perth, a woman to set up a boarding-house, a storekeeper, a mining warden, a policeman, a surveyor, even a dentist, and a motley little crowd of unemployed from the cities who would scarcely know gold if they saw it ounces deep in the reef, yet had staked their last pound on a railway fare, a tin dish, the chance of a lift and a fortune.

Whittling their spearheads with a stone, and chewing the leaves for moisture on that waterless trail, the Warramunga and the Warramulla, stark naked philosophers who knew not the lure of gold, watched the headlights flashing through the night, and wondered what the white man was up to now.

Four days, and I could resist it no longer. With a miner's right and a waterbag, most kindly offered a lift by the members of a geological expedition, I, too, was off on the trail of gold. We met the original prospectors coming in. A few thousands had been placed to their credit, and typical gold miners, they were in to spend them on a spree.

In two days of helter-skelter travelling, two nights' camping on the plain, half-expecting a spear through the swag pillow any moment, we passed the outpost station of Conistan, where Mr. Randal Stafford had now been rudely disturbed after twenty years' seclusion, and made out across a light bush country of acacia and banksia, ti-tree and ironwood, native quince and native peach, and wild oranges with fragrant tasselled blossoms. The graces and the grasses were deceptive. Through all the smiling sweep of the country, there was no surface water, nothing but a few blackfellow soaks long since dry. A leaking radiator or a missing engine, and not a cupful to drink for 100 miles each way.

The bush thinned out to a silver belt of mulga scrub, the weird kingdom of the white ants. Here are the 'adobe dwellings in the savannah' that Dampier imagined to be 'the abode of Hottentots.' Here are inspirations for an Epstein in their millions; an unfinished Laocoon striving with his serpents; a Rodin Psyche; gryphons and gallants and monks and monkeys; children playing, bent together; a leering Madonna with an imbecile child in her arms; angels and devils; Victoria, to the life, cast in red desert sand, the little silk handkerchief folded upon her placid brow, a sceptre in her hand, noble and majestic as in the parks of cities, and just behind her a gorilla, 20 feet high, with a mighty maw and a black face—the groupings of a madman's gallery for a hundred insane moving miles.

At last we reached the Granites, a desolate patch of rock and low scrub, not a shrub above the height of three feet within fifty miles of it, no water save for a miserable trickle of sweetish grey from a crude well where a few blacks were camping, helping them to haul up the bucket. With a gummy mouth and a dry throat, I knew what thirst was on that trip, and the place was a living hell of flies—in a word, gold country. Men pay the price for gold.

I was the only woman on the field that night, with nearly a hundred men, all kindly. Some of them even offered me a drink of water, and that meant a good deal. Other women went out later, but none of them stayed very long. I watched the miners washing gold with that precious water of which they had not enough to drink, and heard their stories, and sent away my copy in an electric storm, the operator in a bough shade wirelessing it through for me to the cities on a portable set, its generator attached to the jacked-up wheels of a car.

Next day I returned to the Alice on a non-stop day and night journey of 400 miles. The old prospectors were showing powdered gold in little bags and bottles, and baby nuggets, and shouting for the whole town. Next night the fortnightly train came in with a multitude of company promotors and metallurgists and men with picks and shovels. They taxed accommodation to its utmost, and camped, scores together, on the creeks. A few women were with them. Five other newspaper representatives were there, working at top speed, and all of us sending streamer specials. We translated gold fever into headlines, and some of their copy was much more feverish than mine. Australia's welkin rang. In spite of the warning of our perhaps too picturesque description of dangers and privations —because of it, maybe—men still came from 3000 miles away, to disappointment. By the time they arrived, the adverse report of an independent and impartial geologist, Dr. C. T. Madigan, of the University of Adelaide, had pricked the company promotors' bubble. A day after the publication of that report, the shares and the golden hopes hit rock bottom, and the gold rush turned sadly homeward, mining 'experts' to search for another Eldorado, destitute men dependent upon the Commonwealth Government for their railway passages.

The old prospectors bought motor cars, and houses, and five £100 race-bets in a day, and heaps of friends in a crowded hour of glorious life, and oceans of beer, and even an aeroplane to go prospecting in. They were back on the quartpot trail within three months. Such is the way of the gold-seeker.

A few short months, and Tennant's Creek was the cry. For fifty years it was a lonely telegraph station in the ironstone hills, where a few old bushmen were contentedly finding a few ounces now and again. One of them was Bill Garnett, who had already made three fortunes and spent them. Bill's best story is of the time he found the Anakie sapphire-fields and made £27,000 out of them. He 'got through that' in three years. He hired a band in Sydney to follow him from pub to pub. It was before the days of wireless, and he liked music with his grog. Another was a young man, Udall, who opened an old shaft, erected a crude and ingenious stamper mainly out of an old motor car, and put through a crushing of six ounces to the ton.

Since then, Tennant's Creek has become the Mecca of hundreds of gold-seekers, and in the past two years a mushroom town with a permanent population of 700 has sprung up there. Tin houses and spinifex shacks mark the site of the mines, scattered over 35 miles of rough country, with shafts, open cuts, and pegged areas sold for as much as £15,000 apiece. With stores, a hotel, a police station, post office, hospital and school, Tennant's Creek, as a gold town has certainly come to stay for—well, the old hands give it ten years. Big fortunes have already been made by men who a year ago were wanderers, and among them, strangely enough, is a blind man.

A station-owner of Kimberley, Bill Weaber came south to look for new cattle country. He had never suffered from gold-fever—few of the cattlemen do, even when there is a lucky find in their own horse-paddock—but they gave him a stone to handle while he was camped at Tennant's, guided his finger along the 'yellow streak,' and took him out and 'showed' him where it was found. He thought there might be something in the idea, and pegged that claim with two others, his son to help him. He brought his family to live in a little bush house there, and paid £7 a week for the cartage of water from the telegraph well 20 miles away. His claims are now among the wealthiest of the field, valued at many thousands.

Tennant's Creek sent down £70,000 worth of gold in ounces last year to Adelaide banks. Thirty-seven pounds weight of it was stolen from the ' 'Ghan' in one shining lump on a trip not long ago. Nobody found out who the thieves were, and nobody seemed to mind much. 'Plenty more where that came from,' they said. Hope springs eternal.

The Granites was a fiasco, but it served its purpose in focusing the eyes of Australia upon the far-away, unknown Centre. The old fields and the new are fully of 'gully-scratchers' and mining agents. Year by year the bush tracks are becoming roads, and the roads crowded thoroughfares. Conditions of living are no longer grim. The isolation, deprivation and problems of life and death of the early days are a thing of the past. The motor car, the wireless and the telephone are a network of companionship and safety, and the old hardships unknown.

The presence of increasing numbers of white women has done much to redeem the country. Even far away from the comfort of the homesteads and settlements, there is many a happy family in a bough shade, sharing daddy's tucker and luck, travelling with him in all his wanderings, a goat and a few fowls on the truck for milk and meat supply, the home a tent in the brush, and the babies playing beside it. It is a clean life, and a free life, infinitely to be preferred to the squalid idleness of the back-streets of cities.

For in Australia's colonization, gold is the Great First Cause. It was gold that made a Commonwealth out of a convict station, that has raised cities in the sand, and carried the railway to them. The prospector is always the path-finder. 'Out of the cradles, endlessly rocking,' to misapply Walt Whitman, a colony at the world's end has grown to nationhood.

Gold changes the face of nature as well as the lives of men. The pick paves the way for the plough. Costeens become creeks, and the towering dumps, overgrown with grass and flowers, hills in the landscape. Ballarat and Bendigo and Gympie and Charters Towers, once barren as Tennant's Creek and the Granites, are agricultural centres to-day. Kalgoorlie that knew the untold horrors of thirst, is the centre of a wheat-belt, its railways radiating another golden future for the West.

Once again gold is in the air. It has caught the imagination of the Australian people. By aeroplane and motor-truck and camel, I have met prospectors scouring the Territory, from the wilds of Arnhem Land out to the West Australian and South Australian borders. They are opening up old shafts and scraping the virgin quartzite rock for 'colour,' patiently carting their ores for miles to wash them in the rockholes, dollying in the bough shades and dry-blowing in the sands. Any old miner could show me two or three ounces in a glass bottle for the month's 'gully-scratching,' and I have seen even the blacks winnowing the precious metal in the wind from dish to dish, blowing it and specking it out with a wet finger, to bring to the nearest white man for some flour and a billyful of tea.

The stage is set for a big discovery. Where will it be?

In immortal bronze, a typical old miner with his water-bag, Paddy Hannan looks out on the glamour of the Golden Mile, the forest of steel poppet-heads, the mountains of slag, the mighty mines and the twin cities of Boulder and Kalgoorlie that, even as the cities of the *Arabian Nights*, came out of a hole that he dug with his pick in the travail of '92. The spirit of Pat Hannan is not dead.

Old-timer or youngster, Don Quixote, with a shovel on his shoulder, out in the Central Australian wilds, still tilts at the windmills of Eldorado, led on from day to day, to death or fortune, across the mirage, to gold.

CHAPTER XXXVI

WONDERLAND OF THE ALICE

THERE is no small town in Australia that gives such promise of becoming a great city of the future as that little jewel of the Eastern MacDonnells, Alice Springs.

Ten years ago, 'the Alice' was a telegraph station, a few scattered homesteads and a store in the little-known heart of the Continent. To-day it is very much on the map, terminal of the great north railway and of all the Territory stock routes, and the centre of a mineral belt that extends for a thousand miles east, west and north of it, of which the great fortunes are yet to be found.

There is a school of thought, not only among the old faithfuls but in the cities themselves, which holds that Alice Springs must, in the march of nationhood, become the sixth great city of the Commonwealth, hub of its arteries of traffic by air and road and railway, capital of the Australian Middle-West. All that are needed are the discoveries of gold, the conservation of water, in which improvident Nature, now too generous and now too niggardly, is not a good manager, and the influx of colonists that these two will bring.

To look down from the hills that so closely gird it, with sunset smouldering into flame along the ranges, and the camels winding in to a well in the valley almost Biblical in its simplicity is to share a vista of the past, a dream of the future.

Through the gap to southward, where now the train comes in at dusk on alternate Saturdays, with the whole population of the Alice to greet it at journey's end, McDouall Stuart rode in at the head of his men seventy years ago, with eyes glazed from eternal contemplation of the seemingly eternal desert, to find himself in a paradise of green and smiling bushland, a glory of deep, still waterholes and little bubbling springs.

Not so long after him followed the first drovers, bringing up their flocks, men who rode undaunted for two years and more, to be rewarded in the end. I met a few of them in the streets of the Alice and on the stations beyond it. Old bearded bushmen, in for a yarn on the bench outside Wallis Fogarty's store, they are simple and gentle enough, little caring that their names will be written in history. The Alice has changed a good deal since they first saw it. They liked the old days best.

Blue smoke from a fire in the gully marks the last camp of the Arundta there, the first landlords. For a long time the title deeds of a thousand miles, glen and height and gully, were theirs alone. Never dreaming of a world and beings beyond the hills, they speared the euro by the water-holes where now the cattle come to drink, and gathered to corroboree where the house-lights shine and the wirelesses screech to the faraway timeless stars. Happy children of the sun, they have bartered their birthright for a stick of tobacco and a bag of flour, but they bear no malice. Flour and beef are 'plenty more better' than grass-seeds and goanna, and whites and blacks are all philosophers in this country.

Beneath lies the friendly little town, with its wide streets and deep-roofed bungalows a riot of dusky colour, with the camp of many a wanderer in its creek-beds, the tin shacks of a few Afghan teamsters, and goat-camps on the lower slopes, their grass-thatched roofs and roaming flocks, in that mellow light, a chapter of classic Greece. Alight with the fires of evening, to the east and west the surges of the hills break into rough seas of mountains, split by the Hammer of Thor into majestic chasms and gorges; the silver shadows of the billabongs at their feet reflecting their splendour—Emily Gap, Elsie Gap, Simpson's Gap, Standly's Chasm, but the blacks have more beautiful names for them.

With inexhaustible springs of clear crystal water 12 feet below the surface anywhere you like to dig, a heaven to come back to is Alice Springs, from east, west, north or south beyond its circling ranges.

A few years ago it was a baby capital in its own right, of the separate province of Central Australia, with V. G. Carrington as Administrator. But Darwin needed the whole 550,000 square miles, for some obscure reason, and now he is only deputy. Good fellowship is the keynote of his administration, and 'the Alice' is a home to all the motley and amusing people that happen along there.

I found a quaint trio bent over a grindstone in a bough shade polishing opals gummed to the ends of sticks. They were Mr. Tom Brady, one of the best-known authorities in opal to-day, Franz Kupeck, a Czechoslovak stone-cutter, and Black Alf, a negro from Demerara, who wanted to tell me all about the days when he spliced the main-brace and lived on weevily biscuits and hell-fire stew.

Brady is a man with opal eyes. Talking to him I was amazed to see that, from a life-time's constant reflection and appraisement of the remarkable stone, his eyes had become opalized. Colourless as crystal, with a ring of palest pink encircling a luminous blue-green, those eyes change in the light, showing extraordinary facets of many colours, even to an elusive flash of red. A humorous Irishman with a flair for high finance and a fund of comic anecdote, the opal-dealer is quite unconscious of the phenomenon. He has travelled the world with the stones in his pocket, from Lightning Ridge to Tiffany's, and Idar on the Nahr, and they never brought him bad luck.

They have a telescopic sense of distance in the far-away. Time and space count as little with the white people as the black.

'Just over the ridge' probably means 250 miles away, and 'up the road' a thousand miles up.

'How's Bob Buck doing out there?' I asked.

'He'll never do much,' they said. 'He hasn't enough country to swing a cat.'

'How much has he?'

'About 200 square miles.'

'Some cat!' I reflected.

Out east of the Alice lies a maze of mountains that blaze like opals themselves. I wanted to see what lay beyond those, and booked with the Winnecke mail.

The white-capped quartzite hills look down on Winnecke with the cool irony of the perpetual snows—Winnecke, sun-raddled in a Central Australian summer, ghost of a gold rush of long ago. Fifty miles out, by the rockiest of roads, it nestles like a Swiss village in a hollow of the range, a few ruined stone cottages, goats on the crags that are crested and capped with dazzling white in many a runnel and solid stone glacier in thaw. When you get closer, you see the bough wurlies, camels at the well, a few straggling blacks, and the typical Australian miner in a blue shirt boiling his billy. It seems wrong.

At the rusty old battery, in disuse for thirty years, I met Joe Webb of the noble white beard and twinkling eyes, all alone but full of gusto.

'Five hundred living in this very gully!' orated Mr. Joe Webb to me. 'Five hundred barrackin' a football match from this little hill, and betting in handfuls of alluvial! For three years men and women pushed their barrows and perambulators 340 miles up from Oodnadatta. They faded away like the bark of a tree. But they left the gold!

'Do I know where it is? What am I here for? Y'see that yaller hill? Y'see that blue hill? Well, the alluvial runs right down that gully and out along the creek for four miles. I got 479 ounces there in three months in 1902, and 385 ounces in 1904, but the last time I went up there with my packs and pannikins, a feller that was here sent a lubra to track me. I'm not telling. It's mine! Stickin' out like dogs' teeth all over the reef, but gold takes a man that knows where to find it!'

I rattled through those ranges for five days on a little prairie-schooner of a mail-truck, with the Danish driver, Mr. Johannsen, and I found them alight with stories. We made out across the plains of Claraville to the black shadow of Blackfellows' Bones, where the overhanging schist rocks are knife-edged and prickly like cactus, range of sinister memory where sixty years after you can still pick up bones and skulls of a terrible police raid that annihilated the tribes of the region after a white man's murder. There we met the mica miners, along cliffs and valleys ablaze with mica, and swept with the red brilliance of ruby dust. The mica is found in 'books' of multitudinous leaves, traversing gneiss or schist, and every book of mica has a caul of green beryl, diorite, little garnets, blue quartz, rock-crystal pebbles or tourmaline. A well-opened shaft, in its jewelled glitter, is more like the last act of a pantomime than a patch of Australian bush. These are the ranges where the blacks pick up precious stones in the porcupine grass, and winnow the gold with their breath.

We came to two or three beautiful homesteads, and farther out to many a pathetic little log shack where the bravest of all pioneers are fighting through, their sheep shepherded by the blacks each day, and brought to the fold at night. Some of them have dug thousands of feet before they have found water. There were at least two living tragedies among them. In one benighted gully I came upon a white man sitting in a thatched log hut cobbling his boots with raw-hide. He did not arise when we drew up, he seemed too broken in spirit. In front of him a ragged little hen, crazed with heat, turned over and over in vertigo.

'It won't die,' he assured me. 'I wish to God it would.'

In the very shadow of Mount Riddock, we came to the homestead of the Ben Webbs, and an epic little story of the royal road outback. I found the children at their correspondence lessons, sitting under a tree hung with the kitchen pots and pans beside an old horse-truck. It was only about a year since the road had run out to Mount Riddock.

Mother and father had come up in the Winnecke gold rush—a strange honeymoon, and settled in the ranges rearing cattle and sheep. Never in all those years had they left the valley. Under the auspices of Stella, their kind old lubra, five children had come into the world, and, until the eldest was nearly twenty-one, none of them knew the alphabet. They spoke four Allowera languages, it is true, and they were bright children. It often grieved the little mother, helping with the sheep, digging a new well for the cattle, looking after the garden and the family, that her children were utterly unable to write a letter or an order for stores, that in an age that had so much outdistanced the last, they knew nothing of figures and could not read a word. She was as innocent of learning herself, and could not help them.

One day an old mica-miner drifted in to the homestead, led by a blackfellow. He had been left without tucker, his boss having failed to send him stores. All he had was ten pounds of flour and a tin of treacle. Would they give

him stores and lend him a horse for the 160-mile journey
to Alice Springs? They would, and he stayed the night.
The children fled at his approach, like the wild bush
creatures they were, but at night, by the lamplight, they
came back—to hear tales of a world beyond the ranges, of
wars and cities and ships. They were open-mouthed, fascinated. That mica miner was destined to be the guiding
spirit of the long-lost family.

Next morning, he was approached by the mother with a
proposition. He was an old man, she said. There was
much unemployment in cities, and he may not be successful
when he returned. He possessed the magic knowledge that
she had missed. Would he stay and teach her children?
They could pay him nothing, but he might share all they
had.

The mica miner, a genial and gentle old man named
Walpole, stayed. He wrote for correspondence lessons to
the Adelaide Education Department, and once a month he
rode 40 miles to meet the mail and get them. He began at
the A B C and taught them the first rudiments of hand-
writing. In two years those children had reached the fifth
standard. They can now read the newspapers, work out the
possible price of the wool-clip, and have been complimented,
not once, but many times, by the Education Department on
their phenomenal progress.

'Wally,' as they affectionately call him, did more than
that. He induced the father to send mother and girls for
a trip to the city that they had never seen. He could see
that that mother was in dire need of medical attention,
though, in all her brave struggling, she would not admit it
herself. In Adelaide, the specialists looked grave. It was
too late. Twenty-five years of slavery in the loneliness had
written the death-warrant. She returned to her little home
at Mount Riddock just after I passed it—and they found
her dead under a tree.

I met many wonderful characters out east of Alice
Springs, on those far-flung holdings that stretch to the
Queensland border, modest little stations of about 800
sheep and 2000 cattle, scouring their own wool and shipping
it in by camel, tending their flocks and rearing their children,
children of resource and bushmanship, who will carry on

their epic work in a country that fights them every step of the way, but keeps their love and faith.

The farthest-out family, and one of the most outstanding, were the Chalmers. The father had been a school-teacher in western New South Wales, and, deciding to take up sheep country, just packed the wife and children into a spring-cart, and set out north-west across the border. When they arrived where the homestead is now, they found a tribe of uncivilized blacks in command of the dry creek. Chalmers sent the little people on to make friends—a gesture of peace —and the natives brought them offerings of honey-bag and wild currants. That was the beginning.

It was many years before they could afford to build a home there—all the family slept out beside the old lean-to.

Bush boys and girls, they were very keen and full of resource. They had made roads and built a dam that was a marvel of engineering in a small way. The girls were very well-read. It was their hobby to collect 'blacks' tucker' and send specimen-menus of the savage in drought down to the anthropologists in Adelaide.

It is a miracle how these blacks of the Centre can live where white men would starve in a week. From the sparse bush they had brought to those girls anaitcha, a sweet potato; nalal, the honey-blossoms; arandina, blackberries; no-goodya, the wild plum; eleven different kinds of edible grass-seeds; apareelya, the sugar from the gum-tree leaf; adnyimma, apples of mulga shrub; ichirriga, the wild fig; the wonderful langua shrub, of which they can eat blossom, leaf, fruit and root, and give the blossoms to the baby to suck—and a hundred other delicacies known to them alone.

Beyond the Chalmers, there was only old Tom Hanlon, scratching for silver lead in the Jervois Ranges, who comes in for his mail once in three months on packs.

CHAPTER XXXVII

KAI-UMEN'S SKULL

'ALL persons having business in this honourable court are commanded to draw near and they shall be heard. God Save the King!'

In February, 1935, in the little court-room of the administration offices at Alice Springs was held the first session of a Supreme Court in Central Australian history. From a 1,000-mile radius and 300,000 square miles of blankness they drew near, black men and white, gathered in at last by the long arm of the law, and not certain that they liked it For seventy-five years in a country where a goat or a pack-saddle or a nugget of gold would settle a debt, and white men, outnumbered by the blacks at ten to one, too far apart to quarrel, they had got along well without it.

Until the beginning of the nineteen-thirties, there were six petty sessions cases in a twelvemonth, and those a matter of form or a good jest. A dead blackfellow was nobody's business. A policeman on a pack-horse, appearing once in six months, was bushman first, friend second and policeman last, but quite enough to keep the spinifex wastes in order.

The railway brought civilization, and officialdom, and the agents of mining companies, and gold-seekers, a foreign element from the cities that could not be trusted with freedom, and at last a special magistrate, a solicitor and a copy of the Statutes. Valueless cheques became a matter for consideration, a bottle of beer in camp sly grog, mulga wires criminal libel, and a black eye common assault. Where the best man had won in a fight before breakfast, in the delight of a new toy the miners put down their picks and dolly-pots, and travelled in 500 miles to the Alice where a 'daring young man on the flying trapeze' of the law settled the argument for them with 'whereases' and 'hereinbefores'. The young solicitor made a good start in life, and his name a bit of a bogey. He secured convictions and remands to a higher court.

Prisoners, both white and black, were travelled under police escort a thousand miles north to Darwin, by truck and packhorse and train, at tremendous government expense. A good few of the blacks escaped on the way, and all of the whites were acquitted. So lenient is the outlook of the far North that twice has trial by jury been abolished there, the judges finding it quite impossible, even in the face of damning evidence, to sheet home a verdict of guilty.

This year, Central Australia, with eighty cases tried in each of the lower courts, and with two murders and a gold-stealing to its credit or discredit, demanded a circuit court of its own, granted by the Federal authorities. The Judge of the Supreme Court of the Northern Territory, with his Crown Prosecutor and Clerk of Courts, was instructed to proceed south to Alice Springs to conduct it. Because it was the monsoon season, and the Territory mostly islands in a swamp, the only way to do it was to fly. An aeroplane was chartered from the West.

The journey had a fatal precedent. It was exactly sixty years since the first Supreme Court session ever held in the Territory, to which Judge Wearing and his officers travelled five thousand miles by sea from Adelaide to Darwin. On the return, all three were drowned in the wreck of the *Gothenburg* on the Barrier Reef.

Making history in their turn, Mr. Justice Wells, Crown Prosecutor Mr. Eric Asche, and Clerk of Courts Mr. W. J. Nicholls, set out from Darwin undaunted. On the way down Mr. Nicholls, a Pooh-bah of the North with twenty-two different administrative positions including Master in Lunacy, fulfilled them all in turn. At Pine Creek he was awakened and asked to perform the marriage ceremony in a railway carriage at one in the morning, there being a joss house but no church at Pine Creek.

After a flight unique in Australian legal annals, the party, in shirts, shorts and topees, landed safely in the valley of the MacDonnells, where the population *in toto* assembled to meet them. My little folding Ica-Zeiss was the only Press camera.

The Stuart Arms had arranged for their accommodation, as though for a camel-string, with eight new water-bags hung round the verandas and festive gum-tips in every

corner, and was busy lining the balconies with beds for
sixty or seventy witnesses and others in town for the court.
That night the 'Ghan was crowded, and the Alice buzzed
with excitement. A Supreme Court proved nearly as good
for business as a gold rush.

The young solicitor had borrowed a wig and gown from
his father in Adelaide, and bent to his briefs. The dance-
hall was prepared for the retirement of the jury—that is,
a shower-bath and thirteen beds were installed there, and a
case of beer and a case of carbolic soap sent up. In the
crude little two-roomed gaol at the back of the police station
a lone white man and two myall blacks were awaiting their
trial for murder.

Each day the prisoners worked in the freedom of the
prison yard, the blacks in a gang with seven or eight others,
harnessed to a cart and guarded by an armed warder; the
white man tinkering with his truck. At night they were
locked in adjoining cells, a barred window 15 feet high
between them.

The white man played his gramophone, and patience—
he knew that his life hung in the balance. The blacks
neither knew nor cared. They had faced death either way.
Sometimes the white man would call them up to the barred
window with a whistle, just for companionship.

I was introduced to him one night, through the little
window of his cell, nothing but eyes visible, and he, in turn,
introduced his friends.

'Hey! Nanji!' he called. Climbing up on the backs and
shoulders of three of the others, Nanji appeared, clinging
to the bars like a chimpanzee at the zoo, the whitened palms
of his hands stretched out, not for peanuts, but for a scrap
of white-fella tucker saved over from the gaol tea. It was
just another of my strange interviews, another of the
weirdly casual associations of a weirdly casual country.

The session opened on a blazing day in February, and all
Alice Springs made early to the court-house to see a Scotch-
man's cinema in a country that had never known a picture
show. About thirty jurymen had been tallied with difficulty
—a man is not keen to sit in judgment on his fellows in the
Centre. A few of them turned up in shirt-sleeves and
stockmen's leggings, and were sent back to borrow coats. At

last the twelve good men and true creaked into the new jury box, smelling highly of varnish, and the first case was called—a Bret Harte story of the gold-fields.

For a long time there had been trouble brewing at Tennant's Creek. In a new gold country where neither guns nor claims were registered, where water is scarce and flies are bad, good fellowship had raddled. The men had hundreds of tons at grass, and there was no battery to crush their ores. The only policeman was camped in a tent seven miles away, and scarcely seemed to matter. There was grog on the field, and quarrels about claims, comradeships, about nothing. Three or four hundred men took the law into their own hands. They brandished their guns, and they fired them—always deliberately wide of the mark.

Unreasoning enmities crept in with the strangers coming in all directions to Eldorado. Among them was Michael O'Brien. With a man who had driven a flock of goats a thousand miles from Cloncurry to give the field milk and fresh meat, O'Brien drifted in casually one evening—to a grim rendezvous. So little reason was there for the tragedy that followed, so little was he known on the field, that even when he was dead, to most of them he was 'the feller with the beard.'

A foolish quarrel with gun-play one idle Sunday morning, and the Irishman made it his own. He raised his rifle. Whether he actually fired it or not, nobody knows, for the other man was quicker, and the other man was now in the dock. He had had no intention of firing the six-chambered Colt he held. He was afraid of none of the men on the field that he knew. O'Brien he did not know. They had never seen each other till that moment. The tragedy was over in ten seconds, and the stranger lay dying in a bough shade. So little did the sound of revolver shots mean to the Tennant that some of the men went on reading in their camps. Called by overland telegraph, Dr. McCann at Alice Springs made a 320-mile motor-car journey through the night to watch O'Brien die, and he died like a man.

'I told him he had an hour to live,' said the doctor, 'and he asked for a cigarette. "Hard luck!' he said, "I wasn't in the brawl." He appeared cynical, and didn't seem to care much—quite clear in mind and capable of making a statement, but he didn't want to be bothered.'

They brought the prisoner to him in the end, and the two looked each other in the eyes. The red glare of anger was gone, there was only regret left. The doctor and the constable were witnesses.

'If it's any use to you,' said the dying man steadily, 'you didn't do it, and I don't know who did.'

The accused hung his head. 'I'm damned sorry it happened,' was all he said.

They carried Michael O'Brien out a couple of miles on Joe Kilgariff's truck to a typical bush burial. Joe read the prayer. It 'started the cemetery' at Tennant's Creek. Within the year there were five others beside him, a pioneer found dying under a tree, another who perished on a 50-mile tramp, and a woman—'natural causes.' 'When a man is concerned, natural causes means the D.T.'s,' a trooper of the North told me once. 'When it's a woman, its a baby.'

At the trial there was no technical evidence. O'Brien's rifle had been handled by almost every man on the field before and after the police had charge of it. Nobody could say whether he had fired it or not. The accused had remained quietly in custody in the trooper's tent for weeks, with firearms within reach. The judge summed up in a clear case of self-defence, and the jury joyously returned the verdict of Not Guilty with a clear conscience. There were twenty-five Crown witnesses, and they won the case for the defence, and then shouted for the acquitted. At least two of them have made big fortunes in Tennant's gold since, and there were some hard cases.

'Hello, Snowy! I didn't know you were there!' one of them hailed the man in the dock. When evidence was brought to light of a vigilance committee 'to lynch some of the boys,' it was stoutly denied, but 'they let me down on that lynching party,' remarked a hard-bitten prospector to the crowd on the hotel varanda later, 'and now they have the cheek to ask me to join the race club!'

All's well that ends well in Central Australia. That night I saw jurymen, policemen, witnesses and gunmen all enjoying an ice-cream together at the little tin booth, but when I took my story to the post, to telegraph it away to five

States, they told me that a scrub turkey had flown into the wires down near Oodnadatta, and the lines were down!

Judge Wells was a man among men, 'and a good judge too.' Fidgeting in the heat, mopping his brow and smiling encouragement, his wig tip-tilted and his eyes twinkling, there was a Gilbert and Sullivan gaiety about him that was deceptive. Many an uproarious burst of laughter he stifled with a scowl, but Alice Springs was enjoying its first comedy-drama, it knew all the characters only too well, and, forgetting this was a murder trial, was irrepressible.

The next case was very different, from the sandy wastes round Ayer's Rock, 300 miles west. Two wild natives of the Pitchentara stood in the dock, charged with the murder of Kai-umen.

Kai-umen had shown his lubra the secret corroboree mark on his arm that a woman must never see, the little snick in the artery from which blood is poured over the newly initiated in the sacred ceremonies. The old men condemned him to die. Nanji and Numberlin, two striplings of the tribe, were told off to kill him. They knew very little of the white man's law, but in their own the penalty of disobedience was death. They took the boy Kai-umen out into the bush to track a kangaroo, and soon the signal-smoke spiralled into the skies that told that their work was done.

It was Kai-umen's lubra, Urabianna, who tracked her husband across the rocks and stones, by soak and sand-hill, wept above him and buried his body. She knew that in the tribal law, she, too, must die, and told the story to a white dingo-trapper, Bob Hughes. A month or two, and Mounted-constable McKinnon, with his camels and trackers, unearthed the body and arrested most of the tribe at Anerie Soak, murderers and witnesses including the dead man's lubra. One of the natives, Yokanunna, hiding in a cave on the way in, was shot while resisting arrest.

Kai-umen's skull beamed at us all from the Bench. It was a merry skull, or rather a mummified head. One front tooth was missing, the tooth of the first initiation, and it looked exactly like one of those bizarre cigarette-boxes with an automatic spring and a space for the cigarette. I would have liked to adopt it as a souvenir, but I think the

Clerk of Courts did. As it was, it was elicited in evidence that a dog had got hold of it one day in the court-house, and was about to bury it for later attention when it was salvaged, just in time to be Exhibit A.

With no ill-feeling it faced its murderers. With no remorse nor squeamishness whatever, they handled it and pointed out the wounds they had made. It was with a little thrill of horror that I saw it handed over to its wife for identification. She cheerfully accepted it, with no apparent emotion. She knew it well, the interpreters told us. 'Kai-umen, boy belong her, this belong him!'—which was putting it mildly.

A visiting anthropologist and a protector were called for the defence, but they could not save the youthful and good-looking murderers from ten years' hard labour. Nanji and Numberlin went back to their cells and their cart-harness, unknowing. To-morrow would be another day. If not, well, they had been between the devil and the deep sea, the white man's law and the black. As it was, they were lucky. Urabianna stayed in the Arundta camp at Alice Springs, and changed her name to Judy. She will never dare to go home.

The next day there was the trial of two men, Crowther and Maurer, a young Australian and an old German, who had found a lucky leader in their employer's mine out in the ranges, unearthed five pounds of gold in it, kept it to themselves, and seized the opportunity of a free ride north with it on the truck of the Chief Resident Engineer. It was found in their luggage 600 miles north at Newcastle Waters.

Five pounds weight! Nobody knew there was so much gold in one heap in the Territory. Exhibits in this case ranged from tobacco tins and cold cream pots of pure gold to a rock weighing half a hundredweight, and a specimen stone that showed 150 ounces to the ton and provoked another little rush. The defence was that the gold allegedly stolen had come from a claim five miles away that Crowther had pegged in his off time. The Government Assayer and a Sydney metallurgist, who happened to fly in that morning, were both enlisted to prove that the chalcedony and clay mixed with the rough gold in the tobacco tin were identical with the ores of the employer's claim and not with those of the new one. The court now resolved itself into a geology lesson, with piles of textbooks. The next day it adjourned to the crude one-man mine at Winnecke, 53 miles east of the Alice out through the rocky gorges.

Eagerly bending over the open cuts, watching the miners washing a dishful of raw earth from a hole in the hill to a shining 'tail' of gold, I suspected that His Honour and the learned gentlemen of the Bar were far more keenly interested at the moment in the processes of the precious metal than they were in the legal complexities.

Young Crowther conducted his own case, a quick-witted boy, self-educated, who, by some abstruse reasoning, had come to the conclusion that the wealth he had won by the sweat of his brow should be his. He faced the barristers as he faced the metallurgists, on their own ground, and made such a good job of his defence that both His Honour and the Crown Solicitor congratulated him upon his lively intelligence, and pointed the obvious moral. He was convicted and sentenced to two years' imprisonment in the Fannie Bay Gaol at Darwin, where, in the irony of it, the cracking of a cubic yard of stone a day is the allotted 'hard labour' of the white man. It may even be that he will find another lucky leader there. The tobacco tins and cream pots of treasure were returned to their rightful owners—and the young solicitor got half that gold.

A few minor cases, and the first Central Australian Supreme Court was history. At its conclusion, there was a Returned Soldiers' reunion to welcome the legal visitors, all three of whom could claim a distinguished war service record. A surprising number of those who attended were original Anzacs, now seeking adventure out in 'the dead heart.' At the close of the revelry, a few plates of sandwiches and sweetmeats left over were handed through the gaol window to the prisoners. The Centre is a land of good fellowship.

The plane set out north in the morning, and the Alice fell flat again.

CHAPTER XXXVIII

LUBRA—A HEROINE IN CHARCOAL

EYES half-blind and claw-like fingers raking the ashes, she peers into the camp-fire and sees—the past of every woman.

Piccaninnies and dogs play about her in the dust. Young and old pass her by, mocking her sightlessness, stealing her tucker.

'Debil-debil makim that way allabout,' they tell her lightly, and perhaps one of the kindlier will throw her a bit of offal, or lead her a little way on the end of a stick.

Sometimes she cries, a long-drawn howl of self-pity. Sometimes she sings, a shrill wail to her beating tins, and when it is all over, and the fires are dying, she crawls into her wurlie of withered spinifex, wide-eyed and shivering, beset by all the devils of the darkness in the shadow of death.

No one has ever paused to hear the story she will never tell. She goes down into darkness inarticulate—lubra, the world's least.

Unmemoried are the days of her youth when she slipped, a little black shadow between the trees, with the happy chatter of childhood. Forgotten the awakening and the first shy wonder of early girlhood, and the desire in the eyes of the young men, and forgotten the anguish of one whose love, in the law of tribal selection, must be denied.

Australia's poets have laughed at her. Painters and story-tellers have passed her by for the conventional island belle with a palm-leaf skirt and hibiscus in her hair. Yet, dreamy sensuousness of eyes and lips, a white smile in a dusky face, and the silky shining texture of her skin, the lubra, in extreme youth, is quite frequently a beauty, for a little while.

Civilization has clothed her in shameful rags that accentuate the spindle shanks and hide her swift and slender grace. To 'a smockless Venus,' a nymph in ebony, civilization throws an old felt hat and a quid of tobacco.

The outstanding virtues of the Australian lubra—virtues,

some say, that are shared too seldom by her white sisters—
are beautiful and expressive hands, a voice ever caressing
and rippled with infectious laughter, gentleness, a dog-like
fidelity and an innate and surprising modesty.

To see her sit down on the ground is a lesson in deport-
ment. Not long ago the manager of an outback station, on
holiday in Sydney, for the more fashionable clothing of the
homestead staff, invested in a dozen bright morning frocks,
low-necked and sleeveless, as worn by the flappers in cities.
To squeals of delight he made the presentation, but three
weeks later, noticing that the girls were still in their galatea,
he instituted inquiries.

'Too much chame,' they told him gravely, as with down-
bent heads and evident reluctance, they handed the models
back. Murramurie will cheerfully rig herself out in a
white-anted flour-bag if necessary, but once she has
awakened to the realizations of Eve, she likes to leave no
part uncovered except head and feet. A ragged shirt is the
height of mode, but shorts are scandalous.

Woman of a primitive race, her lot is never a happy one.
From babyhood she is betrothed to a man old enough to
be her uncle—in all probability he is her uncle. From
babyhood she must learn to find the vegetable food and
small game, to grind the nardoo, to sit patiently for hours
by an ants' nest and yandy the ants' eggs from the dust, to
bring home, not the bacon, but the goanna.

Walking thirty and forty miles in the day, her feet
impervious to the scalding sand or the torture of the bindi-
eyes, she dare not come back empty-handed for fear of a
flogging. The first right of food and water after famine,
the most succulent joint of the wallaby, the rib of the
buffalo and the tail of the 'gator are always her master's.
I have seen many an old lubra, lean as a skeleton, take
the morsel from her own mouth and hold it, horribly
saliva-ed, in a clammy hand, waiting to share it with a
strapping son.

None of the tribal secrets, none of the symbolic corroborees are disclosed to her. Her hour of travail she faces
alone, deep in the heart of the bush, unclean and avoided
by the tribe. Out on the trail, while her lord strides ahead
with a handful of spears, she lags behind with a piccaninny
in the coolamon, another on her shoulders, a load of fire-

wood under her arm, and a yam-stick in her hand—and even on the hottest days she never spanks those piccaninnies. Not until she is elderly and vindictive, when the shrill voice wins the argument, can she hope for the slightest influence in the affairs of the camp.

The part that the lubra has played in colonizing Australia is never acknowledged, except by a few of the more honest old pioneers. In wild country, where the white man ventures alone, she is always the first to make friends. Her sex is her protection. Whereas the man, with a superstitious and ignorant fear or greed, would kill the intruder offhand, her peeping eyes and intuition discover that he is a creature of harmless codes if left alone, and a rifle if he is not—a goose that will lay some golden eggs for a long time. Averse to bloodshed, she temporizes.

First to guide him to the secret waterholes, with her quick intelligence she picks up a word or two of his language, and learns that he is ready to barter tasty white flour and the magic tobacco for whatever mad quest he is out on. Time and again her intervention with the tribe has saved his life. Time and again her whispered word of warning has put him on guard—'Badfella that one all right, him been lookout longa you!'

As time progresses, and the cattle are brought to the fenceless paddocks and the creeks, and the shack camp becomes a homestead, to the best of her poor ability she is called in as cook and laundress, and, later still, as trusted companion to many a lone white woman, a loving nursemaid to her children, gardener and goat-shepherd and handy man generally.

Much more active and intelligent than the boys, in Kimberley and the Territory lubras are even to-day recognized as the best 'stock-boys' and easily the best trackers, and throughout the courts of the North and Centre, in nine cases out of ten, they are the interpreters.

The history of the far North is filled with instances of their devotion and loyalty. Some years ago a myall lubra saved the life of Mounted-constable Lyall Walters, menaced by a 'bad nigger' while arresting cattle-stealers out from the Fitzroy Crossing. Knocking a stolen rifle from the boy's hand with her yam-stick, this lubra, who is now a member of the police camp at the Fitzroy, grappled with him hand to hand while the policeman fixed up his faulty revolver.

It was a myall lubra out across the Roper who kept Harry Sweeney, a drover, alive for ten days and ten nights as he tossed at death's door in malaria, with water and lily-root from a nearby billabong. It was old Polly, one of the house-lubras, that rode from Waterloo Station to Rose-wood, 100 miles there and back in twenty-eight hours, to bring medicine and help for a dying child.

But such tales in the Territory are commonplace. There is an epic among them. In the 'king's camp' at Katherine, I met and talked with Jane, heroine of one of the most colossal tragedies in the tragic annals of the North. It is an old story now, and few there are left who remember it, but Jane herself could tell me, Jane, who is totally blind and long past seventy, a rag of skin and bone come back to her own country to die—and I have in my possession the written history that bears her out.

It was in 1883, fifty years ago, that five white men made out with a small band of natives from Tennant's Creek on a police patrol. They went to bury and certify the death of John Martin, a teamster, speared by the blacks. Their names were Mounted-constables Jack Shirley, Arthur Phillips, George Phillips, John Russ and Alan Giles, who was the telegraph operator at Tennant's Creek. On Brunette Downs country, eighty miles east of Attack Creek, they found themselves lost on a mighty arid plain with the waterbags empty.

Within three days days four of the white men and most of the blacks were perishing in the horrible agonies of thirst. It was Jane, then little more than a child, who saved the life of the only one who survived, Alan Giles.

'I been savvy water! I been tellem *that way!*' she explained to me, pursing her lips to the distance in the way that all blacks point direction.

'Which way you savvy, Jane?' I asked gently. 'You been long that country first-time?'

'No *more*,' said Jane. 'Belong topside country. I *savvy* water that way.' Her instinct had spoken. She did not know why she knew, but she knew. Walking forty miles through blinding heat, she brought back water to the semi-conscious man—with terrible realism she mimicked for me his haggard eyes and his swollen tongue. She splashed his face with it, forced it through the cracked lips, and then, leaving him with full waterbags, returned another forty miles to fill the ones he carried. On the the way in, she carried the exhausted and delirious man for fifteen miles on her back, crawling on hands and knees—the only way it was possible—to the salvation of the great water-hole of Attack Creek, which Jane calls Itheri-mindi-mindi.

Arrived at the telegraph line Giles cut the wire with a stone, and with the two ends together signalled X—X—X —X—— any station listen in! He was first picked up at Kapunda, a thousand miles south, to tell them that of those five men that left Alice Springs, he was the only one alive, and that he had been saved from their fate by a lubra.

Alan Giles shot himself two years later at Renner Springs after a duel in a gambling row. His grave, with its fallen marble tombstone on the main north road, marks yet another tragedy of the Territory—and Jane, who has mustered for Nat Buchanan, the pioneer of Wave Hill, Jane who was once accredited the best black stockboy and horse-breaker on all the stations between Ord River and Cloncurry, is a derelict.

Each Saturday morning at Katherine she is led in to the township, a three-mile walk for an old blind woman, for the meagre police rations that are inevitably stolen or cajoled from her by the able-bodied boys before she reaches camp. But that is as it should be to her. All that she asked of me was a fish-hook and line, that, sitting motionless for hours at a time on the banks of the Katherine, she may one day hook a 'big-fella barramundi' that would reinstate her with the tribe as one of its breadwinners still.

No Albert Medal bedecks that withered breast, but as she told me the story that the old hands know is true, with no understanding of its heroism, but with her sightless eyes seeing over again the circling of those madmen, and the horror upon their dead faces, it seemed that the bright Territory sunlight crowned that old white head with a nobility that goes deeper than race or colour. And when the end comes, as it must in a year or two, up there her single name will not soon be forgotten.

For such as Jane are history.

CHAPTER XXXIX

LEGION OF THE LOST ONES

TWO thousand miles due west and north of civilization, where even the cricket news scarcely matters, and the mails are carried three times a year or so by a blackfellow on foot, out across the King Leopolds, and the rivers of the North, and the great wastes of the Centre, where the silence is implacable as death, white men are living in the Great Australian Loneliness, and greeting it each morning as a friend.

Far from the beat of the drovers, and the bagmen with their 'mulga wires,' managing outpost stations or camped in a bough shade by a waterhole, the world forgotten, by the world forgot, their only visitors are an occasional dingo-hunter or an intrepid old prospector, and these not always welcomed, in that their very presence bridges a gulf of years.

Some of them are wanderers, riding long hours with a packhorse and a native, to whom they will speak a couple of words in as many days, pilgrims who leave only a few grey ashes and a half-burnt stick to mark their passing.

Splendid men, as all the outback will tell you, they are playing a tremendous part in the colonization of their country, but the silence has taken them, the loneliness has won.

All of them are philosophers. A few are cynics, but ever kindly cynics. Many are well-educated men, with exalted degrees tucked away somewhere in the nap, if rumour be truth. Of themselves they never speak.

At Billiluna, 200 miles south of Hall's Creek on the rim of Sturt's Salt Sea, a young man who less than ten years ago was a prefect of a leading college in Melbourne, has lived for five of those years utterly alone. It appealed to him, in extreme youth, to be the manager of a North-west cattle station, and it still does, although the blacks are bad at Billiluna, and three of his predecessors have been murdered there.

At Udialla, on the desert side of the Fitzroy, an Englishman named Torrance has supported himself for seventeen years with a little garden on a billabong, and a couple of hundred goats. It is the monthly delight of West Kimberley to count the crested envelopes that still arrive for him with an English postmark, and the Fitzroy believes him a peer incognito, or at least an Honourable. But coronets are unwieldy things in the pack-bag, and Torrance is content to let them think.

Until recently, when he went South to die, Kimberley had its own authentic bush baronet, with a genealogy traceable back to the Bruce. He was Sir Alexander Cockburn Campbell, son of Sir Thomas Cockburn Campbell, at one time Chief Justice of Western Australia, and a nephew of the late Lady Forrest. Known to every North-west and Territory station, and all the tracks between them, a tall, quiet figure, genial and yet aloof, it amused Sir Alex, some years ago, to receive from the road-bag, a month or two late, the first invitation issued by his State to welcome Royalty—an honour to which his rank entitled him. He read it to the boys with a smile, and put it under the billy fire.

Among the wags of Kimberley, with their flair for nicknames, he was always referred to with a dignified 'Sir Alex,' even when, in the bushman's direst poverty, he travelled without a swag.

Yet another personality of East Kimberley is Mr. F. C. Booty, who in forty-five years has watched his holding grow from a tent in the bush to a big station homestead on a main road, with many a passing car and the aeroplane once a week. Direct from an English university, he was brought to Australia in the 'eighties by his uncle, Captain Frank Osmand, owner of the Ord River Station, at that time the largest and most isolated cattle-run in the world. It was a far cry from London to the Ord, but the life appealed, and when the immense holding was sold at his uncle's death, he travelled overland to Queensland with a party of black stock-boys, brought back a mob of cattle, and stocked up a run of his own not far away.

During forty-five years of blank wilderness, this man has lost nothing of his intellectual keenness, nor the attractive English drawl of his youth. A gifted conversationalist, his discourse lightened on occasion with many a classic tag, he can sit on a petrol-case under the paper-barks, and smoke a good cigar with the air of a clubman. Of late years, a trip to the Continent and an occasional holiday to the South have altered his life considerably, but the country still holds him, and Kimberley knows he will always come back.

Barristers, school-teachers, engineers, a chartered accountant growing peanuts by a lily-pool, an ex-metropolitan bank manager content to be a station book-keeper, and a master-mariner who is now a cook—sometimes a camp-fire quibble or a point of law or of navy discipline discloses an identity that they themselves have almost forgotten. It was on the borderland country of Argyll, when a horse had dragged a stockman, inflicting terrible cerebral injuries, that a bagman of the creek, with unerring medical skill, performed a delicate operation and gave the advice that saved the man's life, but the bagman had gone on before the man regained consciousness, and he himself died of malaria at Katherine a month later.

The Territory still remembers Ted Leng, a unique character of the Marranboy district. Snaring birds of paradise in New Guinea and smuggling them over to Thursday Island, Leng had once been captured by cannibals of the Fly River, and tied to a tree. Simulating madness, for three days he capered to their childish amusement, at last to be set free. He watched his opportunity, slipped away to the coast, signalled a trading lugger and sailed to North Australia.

Prospecting north of the Roper, a weird figure in a flour-bag 'Jimmie Howe,' with shoes of raw-hide laced with pandanus, Leng carried no luggage save a pound of nick-nick tobacco, and lived for three and four months at a time on geese eggs and lily-roots and yams. Then he would come into Marranboy, with sometimes £50 worth of little gold slugs in a chamois bag, to invest in a shirt and trousers, amaze the store-keeper's wife with a rare courtesy and the grace of cultured speech, and, sitting out under the stars at night, delighted the family by tracing the silver river of Eridanus and the 'sweet influences of the Pleiades.'

Leng was an astronomer. A direct question one night elicited the fact that he had been for years a student at a world-famous observatory, under one of the most noted of English scientists. When I last asked about him in the Territory, it was to learn that he had not been heard of for eighteen months.

'He only had three months' tucker,' they said, 'and he'd have to come back this way. In all probability the dingoes have got him long ago—thirst, or malaria, or a quarrel with the blacks.' Of none of these things was he afraid.

It was old Dick Pruen, pottering about nearly as naked as a blackfellow, under the coco-nuts that he had planted at Shoal Bay, out on the north coast, who regaled me for an afternoon with the tales of his travel on the Continent. It was Billy Miller, whose name, he carefully explained to me, was not Billy Miller, who, in a quibble about a quotation, as I sat talking to him in his tent-and-pandanus shelter by the Katherine River, turned over an old envelope that was the only writing material he could find, and wrote me the sentence in the original Greek. I treasure that old envelope still.

The legion of the lost ones—the outback knows them all, but nobody knows why they 'go bush' so thoroughly. Beer, or a girl, or both, or neither, the search for health, failure in business, a weariness of cities, a need for solitude? There are many reasons. Out there in the quietness, in those moments when the cigarette burns down unheeded to the fingers and a listless rider, lost in memories, scarcely notices that the horse has left the track, there is no one to ask the question.

Sometimes, after a period of years, they tear themselves away, and make the long journey south, to find a changed world; a mother and sisters married, old cherished friends who fail at first to recognize them. Of that world they can no longer speak the language. Aimless and disenchanted through all the gaiety, gladly they turn again north.

At the last, the loneliness that they have valued far above the comradeship of their fellows takes them to itself, leaving a few nameless post-and-rail graves in the rank grasses, to mark the onward path for the younger and more hopeful men who come to take their places.

To-day that loneliness is alleviated by air services, road train services, the telephone, the A.I.M. pedal set wireless, the passing of hundreds of cars in the year, motor-transport for stores, to say nothing of the chars-à-bancs of tourists, thrilled to see life in the raw, and more than contented with the half-baked.

For me—Australia still spins round like a roulette wheel, the splendid cattle country and the rich mines and the cane-fields of Queensland, the patchwork carpet of fertility and industry and jostling populations that is New South Wales, and Victoria, and South Australia, the big timber and the gold-fields and the golden wheat-fields of the West, the Australia of the six million, but my heart is back in the Loneliness.

I reflect upon how little Australia means to the mother-country—a golden fleece, cold storage butter, a koala bear and a zoo kangaroo, and a few home-coming parvenus that mutilate the language. I reflect how little it means to its own people, who, with a couple of million square miles to let, build themselves blocks of ten-storeyed flats and live in the basements; of the six, and now alarmingly seven, big cities of premature birth, holding two-thirds of the popula-tion: of smug, colour-conscious White Australia below the twentieth parallel, and black, white and brindle struggling together above it. After one hundred and fifty years of occupation, a third of the coastline is still unsurveyed in this outsize of islands, too lazy to rise from the sea.

Ten thousand people are holding the land that could—and will, some day—make room for fifty millions, an unknown land dreaming away its youth in melancholy, that cries with all its voices for the love and faith of men.

No colour in Australia, cry the artists, packing their port-folios for Spain. No history, moan the novelists, forever delving in the unhappy convict past. Australia is history from the Stone Age down, in one sea-bound volume.

I have used the word desert often enough in these pages, but mainly in the dictionary sense of desertion. There is water everywhere, could it but be conserved. The desert soils are rich. Already miracles of irrigation are redeeming the waste.

Even as I write, the contours of the map are coming clearer. The aeroplane, the radio, and the motor-car are changing the face of nature, and the king-tide of colonization is setting to the full.

The men who subdued the wilderness with turkey red and tobacco are swiftly slipping away. I should like to be back there before the last of the conquistadors is gone.

GLOSSARY

Swag. A roll of strapped canvas in which the bushman carries all his worldly possessions and his home.

Spinifex. Spinifex hirsutus, spike-grass.

Lubra. Aboriginal woman.

Willie-willie. Hurricane.

Wurlie, mia. Native dwelling.

Mulga. A small tree shrub, acacia family, plentiful throughout Australia.

'Mulga wires.' Bush telegraph, gossip of the outback.

'Piccaninny daylight.' Pidgin for false dawn.

Bing-hi. Broome and Thursday Island name for blacks.

Pindan. Light shrub of sand country.

Billabong. Waterhole.

Shin-plaster. Bush currency, credit chits issued by an outpost store-keeper.

Squareface. Gin.

Damper. Unleavened loaf cooked under the ashes, its ingredients flour, water and baking-powder.

Digger. Gold digger.

Dugong. Sea-pig.

Quartpot. A small handled billy-can in universal use.

Gina-ginas. Lubras' dresses (North-west).

Coolamon. Bark basket (North).

A.I.M. Australian Inland Medical Mission, the greatest boon in history to the white settler.

Peedong. Wild natives of north-west deserts.

Myall. Wild natives of northern jungles.

Pink-hi. Holiday, walkabout.

Stone. A pearl.

Snide. A pearl that its rightful owner never sees.

Corroboree. Native dance, a New South Wales word familiar throughout the Continent.

Cobba-cobba. Native dance (North-west).

Dingo. Australian wild dog.

The wet. Monsoon rains of summer.

Bagman. Swagman.

Ironclads. Tinned stores.

Pituri. Native tobacco, indigenous.

Nick-nick.
Nigger twist. } Trade tobacco.

Gil-gil. Music sticks (North-west).

Didgeree-du. Music pipe (North-west and North).

Bender. Spree.

'Skin.' A black relationship.

341

'*Sit down.*' Stay, camp.

Ringers. Drovers' men, wheeling round the cattle day and night on the road.

Horse-tailer. Boy who catches the horses, usually a native.

Camp-sheet. The canvas wrapping of a swag, used as shelter and waterproof bed in sun and rain.

Soak. Water beneath the surface of the sand.

Gibbers. Stones of the vast stony deserts, rounded as though wave washed.

Donga. Depression in sandy country.

Tucker. Food.

Nap. Swag.

INDEX

ION IDRIESS

A biography by
Beverley Eley

*Flynn of the Inland...Lasseter's Last Ride...Back O'
Cairns...The Desert Column...*
Ion Idriess wrote 56 books and was one of the most
popular writers ever to have been published in Australia.
Known as 'Jack' to his friends and his enthusiastic
reading public alike, Ion Idriess lived a life as full of
adventures, tall tales, courageous deeds and momen-
tous friendships as the stories he told.

Barbara Eley was entrusted with 'twenty-three butter
boxes' full of the personal records of Jack Idriess, dating
back to 1911 when he first set up as a prospector on the
Cape York Pensinsula. She has used these records as
the basis for her meticulous reconstruction of Idriess's
life, until now little known.

IMPRINT LIVES
ISBN 1 875892 08 7
$19.95

50 Years of Silence

A memoir by

Jan Ruff-O'Herne

The long idyllic summer of Jan Ruff-O'Herne's childhood in Dutch colonial Indonesia ended in 1942 with the Japanese invasion of Java. She was interned in Ambarawa Prison Camp along with her mother and two sisters.

In February 1944, when Jan was twenty-one, her life was torn apart. With nine other young women she was plucked from the camp and enslaved into prostitution by the Japanese Imperial Army.

'This is an important book...the weight of Ruff-O'Herne's testimony is her willingness to tell us her story. Do read it.'   Peg Job *Canberra Times*

IMPRINT LIVES
ISBN 1 875892 00 1
$14.95

I Was Only Sixteen

An autobiography

by Roland Griffiths-Marsh

'The young Australians did not lose their innocence in the brothels and blood houses of Africa and the Mediterranean, they lost their faith when confronted by the mendacity of their leaders, and the sordidness unashamedly rampant in their homeland.'

So writes Roland Griffiths-Marsh in his tough and honest account of an Australian frontline soldier in the Second World War. First published as *The Sixpenny Soldier*, his autobiography has been hailed as a triumph of angry, realistic writing.

Winner of the Foundation of Australian Literary Studies Best Book of the Year
Winner of the Victorian Premier's Literary Award

'The book should be compulsory reading...'
Ron Belbin *The Reporter*

IMPRINT LIVES
ISBN 1 875892 09 5
$17,95

Margaret Preston

A biography by
Elizabeth Butel

Margaret Preston, Australia's foremost woman painter between the wars, sent a series of shock-waves through Sydney art circles, with her vital art, her spirited journalism and her belligerent enthusiasm for living. In this beautifully illustrated edition of the biography, Elizabeth Butel traces the development of Preston's art and ideas, against the ever-changing backdrop of her travels.

A journey into the art of the 'red-headed little firebrand' who stamped her own signature so lastingly on the aesthetic of Australia.

IMPRINT LIVES
ISBN 1 875892 02 8
$19.95